NEWCASTLE/BLOODAXE POETRY SERIES: 1

ELIZABETH BISHOP:
POET OF THE PERIPHERY

NEWCASTLE/BLOODAXE POETRY SERIES: 1

Elizabeth Bishop:
Poet of the Periphery

edited by
LINDA ANDERSON & JO SHAPCOTT

UNIVERSITY OF
NEWCASTLE UPON TYNE

BLOODAXE BOOKS

ISBN: 1 85224 556 5

First published 2002 by
Department of English Literary & Linguistic Studies,
University of Newcastle,
Newcastle upon Tyne NE1 7RU,
in association with
Bloodaxe Books Ltd,
Highgreen,
Tarset,
Northumberland NE48 1RP.

www.bloodaxebooks.com
For further information about Bloodaxe titles
please visit our website or write to
the above address for a catalogue.

Bloodaxe Books Ltd acknowledges
the financial assistance of Northern Arts.

In memory of Kathleen May Robertson, 1924-2002

Cover printing by J. Thomson Colour Printers Ltd, Glasgow.

Printed in Great Britain by
Cromwell Press Ltd, Trowbridge, Wiltshire.

CONTENTS

7   LINDA ANDERSON: Introduction

12   BARBARA PAGE: Elizabeth Bishop:
Stops, Starts and Dreamy Divagations

31   ANNE STEVENSON: The Geographical Mirror

42   DERYN REES-JONES: Writing ELIZABETH

63   JONATHAN ELLIS: The Snow Queen:
Elizabeth Bishop and Nova Scotia

87   VICKI FEAVER: Elizabeth Bishop:
The Reclamation of Female Space

103   PETER ROBINSON: Pretended Acts: 'The Shampoo'

113   JO SHAPCOTT: Confounding Geography

119   MICHAEL DONAGHY: The Exile's Accent

123   JAMIE McKENDRICK: Bishop's Birds

143   NICHOLA DEANE: 'Everything a Poet Should Be':
Elizabeth Bishop in Her Letters

159   LINDA ANDERSON: The Story of the Eye:
Elizabeth Bishop and the Limits of the Visual

175   NEIL ASTLEY: Elizabeth Bishop: A Bibliography

193   NEIL ASTLEY: Elizabeth Bishop: Chronology

201   *Index*

207   *Notes on contributors*

ACKNOWLEDGEMENTS

Acknowledgements and thanks are due to Farrar, Straus and Giroux, Inc. and the Elizabeth Bishop Literary Estate for permission to quote from the published and unpublished writings of Elizabeth Bishop. Acknowledgement is also due to Special Collections, Vassar College Library, for permission to quote from unpublished materials. Unless otherwise cited, quotations are taken from *Complete Poems: 1927-1977* (New York: Farrar, Straus and Giroux; London: Chatto & Windus, 1983), which replaced *The Complete Poems* (1969/1970) and includes the later collection *Geography III* (New York: Farrar, Straus and Giroux; London: Chatto & Windus, 1976), and from *The Collected Prose*, edited by Robert Giroux (New York: Farrar, Straus and Giroux; London: Chatto & Windus, 1984): copyright © Alice Helen Methfessel 1983, 1984. Most of the letters quoted are from *One Art: Selected Letters*, edited by Robert Giroux (New York: Farrar, Straus and Giroux; London: Chatto & Windus, 1994): copyright © Alice Helen Methfessel 1994.

Jo Shapcott's essay 'Confounding Geography' was first published in *Contemporary Women's Poetry: Reading/Writing/Practice*, edited by Alison Mark and Deryn Rees-Jones (Macmillan Press & St Martin's Press, 2000). An earlier version of the essay by Michael Donaghy appeared in *Metre* 7/8 (2000).

Some of these essays were first given as papers at the Elizabeth Bishop conference held on 26-27 November 1999 at the University of Newcastle upon Tyne, and thanks are due to both the University of Newcastle upon Tyne and Northern Arts for their support for the conference. Thanks are also due to a number of individuals for their expertise and support: Sarah Ferris worked tirelessly behind the scenes at the conference; Jonathan Ellis has assisted with the preparation of this book for publication; and Barbara Page and Sandra Barry have supplied information which greatly aided the preparation of the Chronology and Bibliography.

Details of further events and publications sponsored by the School of English Literary and Linguistic Studies, University of Newcastle upon Tyne, can be found at www.ncl.ac.uk/english/

LINDA ANDERSON

Introduction

Many of the essays in this collection were first presented at a conference held at the University of Newcastle upon Tyne in 1999 to celebrate Elizabeth Bishop's poetry and to mark 20 years since her death. Though there have been important conferences in the States dedicated to Elizabeth Bishop in recent years, and in Canada and Brazil, countries which could claim a special connection to her, none had so far been held in Britain. In this, our conference was something of a milestone, and a tribute to Bishop's growing influence and importance within the canon of 20th-century poetry. However, the further inspiration for this conference was the unprecedented significance Bishop seemed to have acquired for a younger generation of British poets. In 1979, hearing Bishop read at Harvard and feeling too shy to approach her, Jo Shapcott felt very much like 'a lone fan' as she tells us in her essay in this collection. Some 15 years later, in 1994, when *Poetry Review* published its interviews with the 'New Generation Poets', it seemed that many of Shapcott's contemporaries had become equally appreciative. When each of 20 poets was asked to cite their most significant influences, Bishop was the poet named most frequently. Why had Bishop become such an important poetic mentor? [1] This collection, including essays by two of the poets arbitrarily assembled under that banner of 'New Generation' – as well as many more – goes some way towards answering that question. It also – as did the conference – provides a format, rare in itself, for poets to be heard alongside critics and academics, sharing their insights into the work of one particularly influential predecessor.

However, even before the 90s, there had been strong indications of Bishop's growing reputation on this side of the Atlantic. Andrew Motion had already made her the subject of his Chatterton Lecture for the British Academy in 1984 [2] and Seamus Heaney honoured her in a similar way in his T.S. Eliot Memorial Lecture at the University of Kent in 1986.[3] Heaney, more recently, has again picked Bishop out for discussion in his 'Oxford Poetry Lectures', fascinated, it seems, by the 'unspectacular' way her poetry effects

its transformations: 'One has a sense of justice being done to the
facts of a situation even as the situation is being re-imagined into
poetry'.[4] James Fenton followed suit in his Oxford Poetry Lectures,
devoting one of his lectures to Bishop's 'many arts' and ranging
across her letter writing, poems, prose and paintings.[5] The publi-
cation of a selection of Bishop's letters in 1994[6] and of her paintings
in 1997,[7] as well as the availability of new biographical material,
through formal[8] and informal biographies,[9] has also helped to prompt
a reassessment of her. Tom Paulin described *One Art*, Robert
Giroux's edition of her letters, as 'an immense cultural treasure
suddenly unveiled' and said that Bishop would be acknowledged
'as one of this century's epistolary geniuses before the millennium
was out'.[10] Lavinia Greenlaw praised both the composition and use
of colour in her pictures but also saw them as extending our under-
standing of Bishop's 'poetics'. For Greenlaw the idea to publish
them had been 'inspired'.[11]

Many of the essays in this volume either focus on, or make use of,
this wealth of newly published material. Nichola Deane, for instance,
in her essay 'Everything a Poet Should Be: Elizabeth Bishop in
Her Letters' provides both a historical and critical context for an
appreciation of Bishop's letters as art, arguing for their originality in
the genre of the 'familiar letter'. In 'The Story of the Eye: Elizabeth
Bishop and the Limits of the Visual' I draw connections between
Bishop's writing and painting and refer to the newly available pic-
tures. As well as the published material, there also exists a treasure
trove of still unpublished materials in the Vassar College archive:
drafts and unpublished poems, as well as notebooks and journals.
In her essay 'Elizabeth Bishop: Stops, Starts and Divagations',
Barbara Page, following Bishop's characteristic ellipses, digressions
and shifting perspectives in her published poems, links them to her
'revisionary' modes of composition in unpublished drafts. Jonathan
Ellis in 'The Snow Queen: Elizabeth Bishop and Nova Scotia'
also draws on Bishop's unpublished notebooks to trace the coded
significance of ice and snow in her writing. Bishop always wrote
indirectly about her experience and eschewed the more directly
autobiographical or confessional writing of her contemporaries. Ice
and snow, in a productive ambiguity, according to Ellis, both con-
jure up her Canadian childhood, and indicate the 'cool' aesthetic by
which traumatic materials are refigured and made bearable. Bishop
learns through poetry to control loss. Heaney suggests that this may
be her 'supreme gift', 'to ingest loss and to transmute it'.[12]

Returning for a moment to Bishop's reputation, it is impossible,
of course, to assess the current enthusiasm for Bishop without

drawing attention to the special role played by Anne Stevenson on both sides of the Atlantic. As a young graduate student at the University of Michigan, she wrote a book on Bishop – the first full-length critical study[13] – and elicited in the process a rich correspondence.[14] Stevenson believes that Bishop opened her eyes 'to possibilities and directions for poetry I might never have explored without her example'. Stevenson's own move to England has ensured that some of those 'possibilities' were resonating in the poetry she herself began to publish in the 60s, to be then picked up by other poets. Her recent return to Bishop as a critic has been very welcome and full of the insights derived from her long involvement with Bishop's writing.[15] Her essay in this collection explores how Bishop's poetry, from her early baroque style, to her later engagement with the 'indelible recollections' of her childhood, characteristically uses the discursive mode to 'mirror her mind performing her perceptions'. Bishop's acts of seeing, are, according to Stevenson, acts of 'interpretive seeing', where nothing is completely and finally seen. This has ensured that her poetry is also constantly available to new readings.

The notion of a 'mind performing her perceptions' is important and coupled with the complicated nuances contained in the word 'pretense' provides one of the most important themes of this collection. Michael Donaghy illustrates the importance of Auden to Bishop and quotes from an early unpublished essay she wrote about him where she talks about the 'pretense' that it is necessary if a poem is to bridge the 'disproportion' between language and things. Bishop uses a range of personae in her poems; as Donaghy suggests, this use of pretence becomes 'a mechanism by which a self is invented for every poem', an act of self-creation all the more necessary for someone who had no strong 'natural' sense of self to draw on. Another 'New Generation' poet, Jamie McKendrick, in his eloquent essay, 'Bishop's Birds', shows us how Bishop writes poems which convince us that 'they did happen more or less as she said they did' and that the real 'takes precedence over the literary'. McKendrick helps to highlight the complicated literary 'pretense' that this involved and the extensive literary heritage Bishop drew on. As a result he details what is, in effect, an aesthetic of 'what really happened', which is in fact considerably removed from 'reportage and straight description'. Peter Robinson in 'Pretended Acts: "The Shampoo"' turns to the more formalised ideas of 'speech-act' theory, as they have been developed by John Searle, to help us understand the 'performance' involved in her poems, in particular in her use of direct address at the end of 'The Shampoo'. This, like the jokey voice, elsewhere, becomes a way, Robinson suggests, of expressing emotion, without directly referring to it or dissipating it in description.

Many critics have remarked how difficult Bishop is to "place" as poet. Deryn Rees-Jones begins her essay, 'Writing ELIZABETH', by admitting how hard she is to write about. This is so, however, not because there is nothing to say, but because her value seems to elude definition. As Rees-Jones notes, Bishop herself seems to warn critics against the dangers of articulacy, claiming in a letter to Robert Lowell that 'I've always felt I've written poetry more by not writing it than writing it'. Bishop also disliked being assigned to certain spaces within literary culture, particularly in relation to her gender, and successfully resisted the binary system of inclusion and exclusion by being both triumphantly mainstream and obliquely subversive, carefully re-ordering the natural hierarchies through which we know the world and our place in it. Her friend James Merrill noted the 'wonderful way in which she impersonated an ordinary woman' whilst encountering in herself and the world all the time both complexity and strangeness. Vicki Feaver's essay, 'Elizabeth Bishop: The Reclamation of Female Space', describes the spaces that Bishop discovers or creates in her poems as feminine spaces which, however, are not so much places of retreat as of transformation. Significantly, they are not relegated to one side of a binary, confined, as one might expect, to domestic interiors, but are to be found 'in the traditionally male domains of a boat, a garage, and a bus'. Deryn Rees-Jones' essay takes an imaginative and 'circuitous' route to Bishop's writing through her own dreams – an indirect approach that Bishop herself would have approved of – in order to explore not only what it means to be a woman poet but also Bishop's resistance to explanation and any definitive 'placing' of her. Her poetry, Rees-Jones concludes, is both 'homely' and strange, achieving its own artistic transformations yet assembled from whatever is to hand. It works *across* the nature and culture divide, at the same time as subverting any notion of rigid classification. As Rees-Jones observes, respecting the ambiguity of Bishop's art, her poems are 'order tied up in a range of meanings'. They are 'artful' in the best and deepest sense of that word, but resist closing off meanings, offering their ordering as finality or resolution.

The title of this volume alludes to Bishop's own emphasis in her famous letter to Anne Stevenson on the importance of peripheral vision, as a way of capturing elusive or unexpected 'moments of empathy'. In the same letter she writes about Darwin as a 'lonely young man', 'his eyes fixed on facts and minute details, sinking or sliding giddily off into the unknown'.[16] This collection of essays tracks both the elusiveness of Bishop's vision, and its strange 'slides' into the unknown, at the same time as recognising the centrality of her art. She wrote scrupulously, but never conclusively. And whilst this rich and varied collection of essays will help to answer the question of why Bishop is such an important poet now, it also resists any definitive summing up. Bishop might have approved, one imagines, of this reluctance to treat any statement about her as the final word.

*

NOTES

1. *Poetry Review*, 84 no.1, New Generation Poets (Spring 1994). Elizabeth Bishop was also selected by many poets and critics in an earlier feature, 'The Best Poetry Books of Our Time': *Poetry Review*, 74 no.1 (April 1984).

2. *Proceedings of the British Academy*, 70 (1984), 299-325

3. Reprinted in *The Government of the Tongue* (London: Faber & Faber, London, 1988) and available now in *Finders Keepers: Selected Prose 1971-2001* (London: Faber & Faber, 2002).

4. 'Counting to a Hundred: On Elizabeth Bishop' in *The Redress of Poetry: Oxford Lectures* (London: Faber & Faber, 1995), p.168.

5. 'The Many Arts of Elizabeth Bishop' in *The Strength of Poetry* (Oxford: Oxford University Press, 2001).

6. *One Art*: see acknowledgements.

7. Elizabeth Bishop: *Exchanging Hats: Paintings*, edited by William Benton (New York: Farrar, Straus and Giroux, 1996; Manchester: Carcanet Press, 1997).

8. Brett C. Millier: *Elizabeth Bishop: Life and the Memory of It* (Berkeley, Los Angeles and Oxford: University of California Press, 1993).

9. *Remembering Elizabeth Bishop: An Oral Biography*, edited by Gary Fountain and Peter Brazeau (Amherst, MA: University of Massachussetts Press, 1994).

10. Tom Paulin: 'Writing to the Moment: Elizabeth Bishop' in *Writing to the Moment* (London: Faber & Faber, 1996).

11. Lavinia Greenlaw: 'Poems made in pen, ink and water', *Independent on Sunday*, 14 September 1997, p.34.

12. 'Counting to a Hundred: On Elizabeth Bishop', p.165.

13. Anne Stevenson: *Elizabeth Bishop*, Twayne's United States Authors Series (New York: Twayne, 1966).

14. The correspondence is in the Special Collections Library, University of Washington, St Louis.

15. Anne Stevenson: *Five Looks at Elizabeth Bishop*, Agenda/Bellew Poets on Poetry: 1 (London: Bellew/Agenda Editions, 1998).

16. Letter to Anne Stevenson in Anne Stevenson, *Elizabeth Bishop*, p.66.

BARBARA PAGE

Elizabeth Bishop: Stops, Starts and Dreamy Divagations

Among the earliest assessments of Elizabeth Bishop's work stands the review by Marianne Moore of *North & South*, entitled 'A Modest Expert'. When we concentrate on Moore's sometimes minatory presence in Bishop's life, we may recall too well the adjectival stress upon modesty and neglect the emphasis in that review upon Bishop's expertise, as a poet of knowledge and self-inquiry. Yet the first lines Moore chose to quote in this review, from Bishop's very abstract poem 'Paris, 7 A.M.', are:

> ...It is like introspection
> to stare inside, or retrospection,
> a star inside a rectangle, a recollection...

Examining Bishop's technique, Moore remarks upon 'an expert disposition of pauses', and notes her accurate objectifying of 'sensation, yet more difficult to capture than appearance'. Moore describes *North & South* as 'this small-large book of beautifully formulated aesthetic-moral mathematics.' 'With poetry,' she notes, 'tentativeness can be more positive than positiveness', concluding that in Bishop, 'At last we have someone who knows, who is not didactic.'[1]

In one of the most recent books on the poet, *Five Looks at Elizabeth Bishop*, Anne Stevenson reflects on her earlier Twayne book, the very first written about Bishop, when only *North & South* and *A Cold Spring* had been published. In the Twayne book, Stevenson had brought to bear some ideas of Wittgenstein, only to be brushed off by Bishop's remark that she had never read him. With severely self-critical retrospection, Stevenson notes in the introduction to *Five Looks* that she had been sent poems that had appeared in *The New Yorker*, but 'was too young or too blindly intent on pursuing abstract ideas, to see how distinctly they marked a change of direction in her work'.[2] At risk of replicating that error (without the excuse of youth), I want to revisit Wittgenstein – lightly – and an American philosopher named David Appelbaum, as a means to an enquiry into Bishop's way of knowing. Movements of mind in Bishop are signalled by elements of technique – they might be called manner-isms – those 'slides', 'skids and recoveries', so aptly described by poet Eavan Boland, in 'An Un-Romantic American'.[3] To Boland's list I would add as well, stoppages, self-correction, and even self-repudiation. These can appear to be failures of a mind to sustain its own rhetoric or narrative, but I think instead that in Bishop's completed work (an ominous note here) they embody acts of knowing; one might say knowledge of feeling, or even knowledge as feeling.

The elements I want to dwell on here are, (1) at the grammatical or syntactic level, pauses and ellipses – those broken-off sentences that prevent the onrolling of a settled mind; (2) exclamations mark-ing eruptions of feeling into consciousness and new discoveries, often arrived at through a shift in perspective; and, (3) digressions, or, as Bishop puts it in 'The Moose', 'dreamy divagations'. I want finally to consider these elements in light of the Bishop archive, which presents visitors both an exhilarating wealth of material aug-menting the published work and a dismaying display of unfinished writing, ranging from merest fragments to whole poems, typed and apparently ready to be mailed. Let me begin my examination of these elements by way of a divagation of my own, into David Appelbaum's book on Descartes' *Dioptrics*. Its title is *The Stop*.

Wanting to 'question the sharp line we draw between fancy and philosophy', Appelbaum focuses on that moment in Descartes' treatise on the eye and the sense of sight when logic is interrupted by anecdote, with the appearance of a blind man, aided by a cane, who 'stumbles across the page and is gone'. Like Appelbaum, I am interested here in that moment when the language of metaphor or embodiment erupts because logic or argumentation will not suffice. Within philosophical discourse, such disruptions are often 'unwanted, rejected, dismissed, and cast aside'. This element, breaking the momentum of magisterial logic, Appelbaum calls 'the stop'. The very figure of the blind man, he writes, 'in his halting movement across the stage…groping for a path, labouring to avoid obstacles, occasionally coming to rest only…to lurch again into movement… impersonates the stop'. In Descartes, the figure of the blind man is subversive, he argues, providing 'a subtly distorted rendition of sight', undermining the notion in scholastic philosophy that the mind's eye is the locus of knowledge, and that spiritual perfection can be equated with visual clarity. Descartes' shift, however, carries as cost a severance from the notion that knowledge originates in the body. Appelbaum argues that the stop throws onrolling philosophical discourse off-centre and enables 'a new radius of investigation'; the first 'must come to a stop before the second can begin'. At this level his notion of a stop resembles the familiar concept of *aporia* from classical philosophy. He goes on, though, to argue that the stop is no theoretical construct but 'an actual moment, the moment of poise ...the poise before movement'. Poise, 'a gathering of attention', or an 'active concentration of awareness', prepares one for movement in any number of possible directions. It lives, says Appelbaum, 'in the interstices of action, an ordinary recluse'.[4]

My concern is of course with poetic process in Elizabeth Bishop, not with Descartes' philosophical procedures, yet the terms of Appelbaum's argument seem suggestive of moves in work by Bishop, complete and published, that bears relation to work remaining unfinished, fragmentary, stopped. Just as medieval theories of perspective were called into question with the discovery of the vanishing point, prompting Descartes, among others, to doubt the eye's mastery of the field of vision, modern (that is, post-Renaissance) theories of the mind's mastery of a unified idea of reality were shaken by events leading into the 20th century, prompting what we may now think of as a rear-guard effort of the high modernist avantgarde to shore up the ruins of idealism by means of masterful discourses of allegory and myth. As a second-generation modernist, Bishop inherits the sense of that effort on its way to failure and helps to define an emerging scepticism toward all mastering discourses of vision or voice. Eavan Boland distinguishes Bishop from the belated Romantics among American poets of her generation by 'the wonderful quicksand' of her work, the 'feeling...she expresses of perceiving a world she cannot control'.[5] Refusing the 'script' (Boland's word) inherited from the Romantics, one risks silence, the logic of Samuel Beckett, which fortunately he did not follow, and *sometimes* Bishop did not. But what, then, of her rhetorical and expressive inheritance remains at her disposal? To answer that question, I turn now to Bishop's published work, together with drafts and fragments of unfinished work, which give evidence of her poetic practice and of movements of mind and feeling, some flourishing, others stillborn.

A weighing of the fragile, devalued currency of her inheritance, or 'our abidance', was among Bishop's major themes, as when in her poem called 'Poem', through eye and memory she accepts what her great-uncle, the painter George Hutchinson, had to impart. In an early draft, 'this small painting that never earned any money / has passed its sixty years / a gift freely'. In the final form of the first verse, this painting, or sketch, is 'Useless and free', a feckless family relic 'handed along collaterally to owners / who looked at it sometimes, or didn't bother to'. By the end of the poem, the little painting, in one respect remains emblematic of diminished inheritance ('the little that we get for free, / the little of our earthly trust. Not much.'), but because of its 'touching detail', it has acquired fresh worth by joining life with life, through 'a gathering of attention' in Appelbaum's words, and through memory. For the reader, the connection between eye and memory is made of Bishop's words, but, for the speaker within 'Poem', it is made by her scrutiny of the paint itself, applied at and gesturing toward the place it evokes:

Heavens, I recognize the place, I know it!
It's behind – I can almost remember the farmer's name.
His barn backed on that meadow. There it is,
titanium white, one dab. [emphasis mine]

This is not a theoretical construct, as Appelbaum puts it, but 'an actual moment', a touching, as it were, that moves the inheritor, who nonetheless goes on weighing her diminished fortunes.

Among Bishop's revisionary practices as she composed her poems, several recur so often as to indicate an ingrained habit of mind. One of these is the move from greater to lesser security, optimism, or openness of possibility, until the poem achieves a hairline balance between affirmation and denial.[6] In 'Poem' we can observe this tendency in Bishop's revision of one among the several touching details that form the muted celebration of 'our abidance' at the poem's end:

...the munching cows,
the iris, crisp and shivering, the water
still standing from spring freshets,
the yet-to-be-dismantled elms, the geese.

Persistently, in successive drafts, the still – that is, lasting – water stands in parallel to 'the elms never dismantled', or 'never-to-be-dismantled', but finally time and its losses intervene, and 'never' is replaced by 'yet'. The elms would never be dismantled, if they were kept in memory only, or in Uncle George's painting, but in life and time they will.

Returning to the question of perspective, I want to take up Appelbaum's remark that Descartes 'provides a subtly distorted rendition of sight' that undermines faith in spiritual perfection through visual mastery, and to augment it with Bonnie Costello's inspired quotation of the painter David Hockney, in her chapter on Bishop's 'Active Displacements in Perspective', in her book *Elizabeth Bishop: Questions of Mastery*. Paraphrasing Hockney, she writes, 'To chose a single perspective is to be dead'; then she quotes Hockney: 'For perspective to be fixed, time is stopped – and hence

space has become frozen, petrified. Perspective takes away the body
of the viewer. To have a fixed point, you have no movement; you
are not there, really.'[7] Recalling Marianne Moore for a moment,
with her assertion that in Bishop 'we have someone who knows,
who is not didactic', we can see that one who is didactic does have
a fixed perspective, and from this angle is the enemy of the artist,
or at any rate of a poet of Bishop's disposition.

Introducing a discussion of 'Love Lies Sleeping', a grimly urban
and surreal poem of shifting perspectives on the business of dining
on one's heart, Costello writes: 'One alternative of modernism was
to idealise the alienated. But Bishop's vision multiplies or shifts
perspectives, aware of life at the peripheries of our interpretations.'[8]
Aware, also, I would add, of death. 'Love Lies Sleeping', a hungover
aubade, ends with morning coming to the figure of 'one, or several',

> whose head has fallen over the edge of his bed,
> > whose face is turned
> > so that the image of
>
> the city grows down into his open eyes
> inverted and distorted. No. I mean
> > distorted and revealed,
> > if he sees it at all.

Anne Stevenson asked whether Bishop had been entertaining a
theory of optics when she wrote 'Love Lies Sleeping'. Bishop replied
that she had in fact been reading Newton's 'Optics' about then, but
added in a devastating parenthesis: 'I think the man at the end is
dead.'[9] So what is revealed, and to whom, at the end of 'Love Lies
Sleeping'? In Appelbaum's reading of Descartes, it is the blind man
who reveals the falsehood of transcendent vision, and so too perhaps
for Bishop, who engages her signal rhetorical mannerism here, the
self-correction, together with the trailing end that calls what has been
revealed back into question: 'inverted and distorted. No. I mean /
distorted and revealed, if he sees it at all.' Certainly, seeing and not
seeing, death and a life of self-devouring love, stand interlineated,
as do waking and sleeping in this poem from Bishop's period of
greatest interest in the surrealists' exploration of relations between
dream and daytime life. As visitors to her manuscripts know, Bishop
drew inspiration from her own dream life and wrote detailed accounts
of many of her dreams, some of which, like this one, she illustrated
with a sketch:

> Dreamed I was dead, or at least in some other form of existence, and
> arranged on a card, like buttons. It was a white card with a fine gilt line
> around it near the edge – black tatters of my clothes hung around it.[10]

Here we have fixed perspective with a vengeance, from the temporal suspension of a dream, flattened, fixed and frozen – back to Hockney – except that this dream bespeaks terrible anxiety about bodily integrity and the power of movement, with the dispersal of body parts bearing tatters of the clothing that had surrounded the lost form. Among the literary spurs to this dream, Eliot's Prufrock, 'formulated, sprawling on a pin', seems most obvious, and also perhaps *Peer Gynt*'s failed souls, returned to the button maker. In her life, this dream most probably responds to the ghastly automobile accident in which her friend Margaret Miller's arm was severed. Much of Bishop's rhetoric aims at saving herself from such nightmares of finality and fixity. Even in the dire vision of this dream, she takes a verbal step back from the brink, with the redirection of 'Dreamed I was dead, *or at least in some other form of existence*' (emphasis mine). Bishop's poem of this moment and sensibility is of course 'The Weed', which begins:

I dreamed that dead, and meditating,
I lay upon a grave, or bed,
(at least, some cold and close-built bower).
In the cold heart, its final thought
stood frozen, drawn immense and clear,
stiff and idle as I was there;
and we remained unchanged together
for a year, a minute, an hour.

Bishop lived daily with great uneasiness, once remarking, 'I think I was born guilty', and she had a persistent yearning for sequestration, articulated in her early story 'In Prison' (in which her hero remarks that 'Freedom is knowledge of necessity'), and also in her late poem 'The End of March'. Appelbaum, in his analysis of the blind man in Descartes, remarks that blindness – traditionally held to be punishment for faulty vision – is mimicked by acts of confinement that strive 'to limit the vision of a prisoner'.[11] But in the classical treatments of blindness he discusses – Oedipus, Samson, Gloucester – blinding puts a stop to illusory visions of self-transcendence, enabling a movement 'toward an embodied awareness'. As he puts it: 'To stop is to uncover what is in hiding, which is to say, to experience ourselves in hiding.'[12]

I am going to risk a leap of logic here to connect this line of thought to Bishop's own "Oedipal" crisis with her missing mother, one that never, or almost never, resolved itself in completed work.[13] The exception is her story 'In the Village', where the mother appears as cloth, not body, and of course as the awful scream. In this story, the scream 'came to live, forever', whereas the mother did not; it 'hangs' like a permanent darkening of the landscape, 'unheard, in memory – in the past, in the present, and those years between'. Fixed, aestheticised, or perhaps memorialised – like Keats's unheard melodies, in 'Ode on a Grecian Urn' – a reminder that there is no safety in art, where life and not-life cohabit. In any event, in the distillate instant when the mother is lost, the child is thrown into a perpetual condition of disappearance: 'The dress was all wrong. She screamed.' (Past tense.) 'The child vanishes.' (Present tense, forever happening, in this text.) The child erased, sight is soon transferred within the story to an 'I', the hidden self who watches and remembers: 'Before my older aunt had brought her back, I had watched my grandmother and younger aunt unpacking her clothes, her "things".'

One of the manuscripts Bishop carried with her for years, a fragment, about fragmentation, displacement and traumatic fixation, bears evidence of her losing struggle to recollect her mother, in lines such as these:

A mother made of dress-goods
...
A mother is a hat
black hat with black gauze rose
...
A voice heard still
...
coming out of blackness –
    the blackness all voices come from

Bishop's inability to resolve the figure of the mother here turns, I believe, on the vanishing child, whose tenuous bond to the mother was severed by the scream of encroaching madness. Among the lasting effects of that severance – besides generalised guilt – were both what Bonnie Costello has described as active displacements of perspective, which become an accomplished aesthetic effect in Bishop's poems – many of which are about loss and partial self-recovery – and, less happily, a broken body of poem fragments.[14] A question hangs unanswered at the penultimate moment of 'In the Village':

All those other things – clothes, crumbling postcards, broken china; things damaged and lost, sickened or destroyed; even the frail almost-lost scream – are they too frail for us to hear their voices long, too mortal?

The question is not answered, and so remains hanging, stopped from resolution. Yet the story is resolved in its final words, or rescued perhaps, by an address to the senses, rather than thought or memory, in the form of a startling 'Clang', emanating from the blacksmith's shop, that permits a double relief, by reconnecting the child to human relations, and by shifting the balance of emotion from loss to desire:

> Nate!
> Oh, beautiful sound, strike again![15]

I want next to explore how starts like these, among her many outbursts of exclamation, function in Bishop's work, by way of Wittgenstein's useful remarks in the *Philosophical Investigations* about the figure of the duck/rabbit.[16] Looking at an ambiguous figure, Wittgenstein draws a distinction between 'the "continuous seeing" of an aspect and the "dawning" of an aspect',[17] in a way that illuminates, I believe, a preoccupation of Bishop's at least from her undergraduate days, when she read Morris Croll's 'The Baroque Style in Prose', the desire, that is, 'to portray, not a thought, but a mind thinking'.[18] Wittgenstein, we recall, wants to undermine the claim that one can bypass the mediation of language to arrive at a definition of ' "what is really seen" '. 'One must, instead, note false accounts of the matter as false.'[19] 'The concept of the "inner picture",' he argues, 'is misleading, for this concept uses the "outer picture",' which is faulty, 'as a model'.[20] This explanation speaks to at least one motivation for Bishop's compositional habit of having her speaker correct what she has just stated, as in the lines, 'inverted and distorted. / No. I mean distorted and revealed...' It also speaks to her admission that the inner model proposed by memory may be faulty and requires correction through encounters with present reality, which will in turn be selectively stored in memory – and in poems. Thus in 'Questions of Travel' her tussle with Pascal over the question of direct experience: '...*could Pascal have been not entirely right / about just sitting quietly in one's room?*' And the admission that launches 'Santarém': 'Of course I may be remembering it all wrong/after, after – how many years?'

But for Wittgenstein a further distinction remains between reporting on what one is seeing and sudden acts of recognition:

> I look at an animal and am asked: "What do you see?" I answer: "A rabbit". – I see a landscape; suddenly a rabbit runs past. I exclaim "A rabbit!"

Both things, both the report and the exclamation, are expressions of perception and of visual experience. But the exclamation is so in a different sense from the report: it is forced from us – it is related to the experience as a cry is to pain.

...If you are looking at the object, you need not think of it; but if you are having the visual experience expressed by the exclamation, you are also thinking of what you see.

Hence the flashing of an aspect on us seems half visual experience, half thought.[21]

Like Descartes' blind man, Bishop's speaker again and again impersonates the process whereby observation, often preserved in memory and queried because it is memory, encounters thought, or – because the end product is poetry – feeling. And because memory for Bishop is so often of trauma, the reassembly of the imagined body and the healing that it implies is complicated, sometimes to the point of blockage. This forceful pressure, then, is as necessary as it is difficult, especially in her poems of childhood remembered: without the 'flashing' of what is recalled as a felt present in thought, what is recalled can only be experienced, or re-experienced, as loss, not as healing or even a comforting of the dismembered self, the vanishing child. Curiously, in 'Crusoe in England', Bishop's Crusoe reaches for solace using the very word and experience Wittgenstein is trying to locate, only to discover blanks where knowledge should have been:

"They flash upon that inward eye,
which is the bliss..." The bliss of what?

Ellipses abound in Bishop, as virtual graphics, not of emotion recollected in tranquillity, but its opposite: emotion disrupting composure – and composition. As we all know, the lines Crusoe is trying to recall from Wordsworth's 'I wandered lonely as a cloud' concern a restorative memory of plenitude, of the dancing daffodils that are 'the bliss of solitude'. But Crusoe's – and too often Bishop's – moment is rather that of loss and depletion. Like his archipelago, the language sometimes 'petered out', leaking away through the ellipsis, as it does in the passage about Crusoe's knife that once 'reeked of meaning':

I knew each nick and scratch by heart,
the bluish blade, the broken tip,
the lines of wood-grain on the handle...
Now it won't look at me at all.

In contrast to such moments, both within finished poems and among the drafts that break off or peter out, stands that other category of interruption, the exclamation, the moment of arrest when the work of composition succeeds in bringing the poet to recognition or affirmation: 'Heavens, I recognize the place, I know it!' As Wittgenstein remarks, an exclamation carries the conviction: 'This expression is justified!' [22] It is a moment critical to Bishop, that carries her poem over the stops that break it down; paradoxically, it is itself an arrest that, in Appelbaum's words, permits a 'new radius of investigation', and it is represented, as he says, as 'an actual moment' that 'lives in the interstices of action'.[23]

I turn now to two late poems, one that Bishop was unable to finish and one that she did. The first bears variable titles, 'Vague Poem' or 'Vaguely Love Poem', though its imagery is anything but vague.[24] The second is 'One Art'.

The situation of 'Vaguely Love Poem' is Bishop's trip to Oklahoma in 1973 for a reading [25] and her encounter with some students who wanted to show her a local crystal formation called the rose rock, which had put them in mind of Bishop's poem, 'Faustina, or Rock Roses'. It begins, 'The trip west was like a dream', or, 'I think I *dreamed* that trip.'

> They talked a lot of "Rose Rocks"
> or maybe they are "Rock Roses"
> I'm not sure now...
> ...
>
> "This is one just beginning – see
> you can see, here, it's beginning to look like a rose
> It's – well, a crystal, crystals form –
> I don't know any geology myself."

So many Bishop signatures here: dreamlike memory; casual, hesitating speech; an effort to clarify sight; the dawning (in Wittgenstein's terms) of an aspect; self-limiting doubt. Then, the tentative move toward affirmation: 'faint glitters – yes, perhaps there / was a crystal at work within – '. And at the end of this draft, suddenly something uncovered of the hidden self, caught in a moment of intimacy gazing at the lover's body, the words hypnotically miming transfixion: 'rose rock, rose quartz, roses roses', and, since this is a poem in the making, also a movement of mind, indicated in the hand-written additions at top and bottom: whether the subject is the rose rock or the rose of sex, someone or something is 'exacting' it. And then the words hand-written at the bottom of this draft, that never make it into the subsequent typescript:

> exacting its roses from your body – ...
> to give them to me

The second, more polished, of the extant drafts ends with the lines:

> Crystallography and its laws:
> something I once wanted badly to study,
> until I learned that it would involve a lot of arithmetic, that is,
>   mathematics

Just now, when I saw you naked again,
I thought the same words: rose-rock; rock-rose...
Rose, trying, working, to show itself,
forming, folding over,
unimaginable connections, unseen, shining edges,
Rose-rock, unformed, flesh beginning, crystal by crystal,
in clear pink breasts and darker, crystalline nipples,
rose-rock, rose-quartz, roses, roses, roses,
exacting roses from ~~your~~ the body,
and the even darker, accurate, rose of sex –

The language itself is working here, edging toward the celebratory 'roses, roses, roses' that points straight back to Bishop's early triumph of radiance and release in 'The Fish': '...rainbow, rainbow, rainbow! / And I let the fish go'. But finally she does not let go of this erotic poem, that is on its way toward a remarkable reversal of her vision in 'At the Fishhouses', of the harsh maternality of the natural world, from which we wrest ever fleeting knowledge, 'drawn from the cold hard mouth / of the world, derived from the rocky breasts'.

Interestingly, too, Bishop is working on a characteristic revision, from more direct personal address – 'roses from your body' – to more 'objective', categorical statement – 'roses from the body' – an impossible shift, perhaps, in a poem that begins in a drift of anecdotal chat, seems about to gain point in the precision of objective science – crystallography – then leaps into eros: 'Just now, when I saw you naked again...' It may be finally that Bishop's well-known reticence – matching her famous "eye" – is all that prevents her from finishing 'Vaguely Love Poem', but it may be as well that an unbridgeable gap lies between what is exacted and what can be given. The thought that enters as she looks at the rock roses is of a study she 'once wanted badly' to undertake, but did not because it was too exacting, requiring mathematics. An analogy unfolds between the crystal that begins to form a rose and the (usually hidden) breasts and sex 'trying, working, to show' themselves. A gap remains, however, between some natural principle, or élan vital, 'exacting roses from your body' and a lover making a demand. What remains unarticulated is the move from the gaze to the bestowal of the roses. After such exactions, what will allow 'you', a term that stands under erasure here, 'to give them to me' remains unresolved.

Bishop's villanelle, 'One Art', is the nearest thing to a naked poem that she ever published. It is 'the cry of its occasion', as Wallace Stevens would say, and it 'is related to the experience', in Wittgenstein's words, 'as a cry is to pain', mediated to be sure by the virtuosity of its form. It was, moreover, among Bishop's fastest compositions: its occasion was the possibility, arising in late 1975, that Alice Methfessel, Bishop's last great love, might leave her for marriage; the poem was written in mid-winter and published in *The New Yorker* in April 1976 (by which time the crisis was over, and Bishop was feeling uneasy about her own candour – not to the point, however, of withholding the poem). A good deal has been written about 'One Art', including close studies of its 17 successive drafts, by Brett Millier and Victoria Harrison.[26] I want here simply to look at the two most persistent sticking points of the poem, both of them in the final stanza, which in its published form is as follows:

> – Even losing you (the joking voice, a gesture
> I love) I shan't have lied. It's evident
> the art of losing's not too hard to master
> though it may look like (*Write* it!) like disaster.

The first sticking point concerns just how ironic 'One Art' is: in asserting again and again that 'The art of losing isn't hard to master', is she lying or not? As the drafts reveal, while she composes the poem, Bishop is measuring the fine line between yes and no. In Draft 10, for example, she writes:

> But, losing you...
> ...
>
> all that I write is ~~false~~...   lies, now. I'm writing lies now. It's
> the art of losing isn't hard to master   quite evident
> ~~oh say it~~ –
>   Above's all lies
>   ~~I've written lies above~~. It's evident
>   the art of losing isn't hard to master
>   with one exception...

Here Bishop is leaning toward peripeteia, toward the confession that this loss is hard to master. One hold-up, though, is that the crisis is still in progress, and she cannot yet fathom the loss. What the ironic restraint of 'One Art' has already brought forward, however, is that all her former losses have not inoculated her against the magnitude of this one.

The second sticking point concerns whether, in confessing disaster, she should say it or write it. In Draft 10 she is rapidly shifting between the two expressions, and among several degrees of vocal intensity: 'oh say it', 'Say it.' 'Write it!' 'Say it – yes, disaster.' Two drafts later, these oscillations have only intensified, as Bishop works through the same final stanza over and over. In Draft 15, with the poem virtually finished, the line now hovers between 'these were [or are] not lies' and 'I still do not [or won't] lie'. Ultimately, the solution to the first confusion, as we know, is a time shift, from I

have, or haven't lied, to 'I shan't have lied', which throws the sit-
uation itself into the conditional, removing her from the need to
declare her claim a present truth or falsehood. The irony in the
finished poem no longer turns on lying or telling the truth, but
rather on the difference between what is evident – that she has
survived a great many losses – and what is immediately experienced,
what it looks like, namely, disaster. This is, I think, Appelbaum's
embodied vision: what it looks like is what it feels like, distorted
perhaps owing to a lack of perspective, but revealed as an experi-
ence of unmitigated disaster.

Now, back to the other crux in 'One Art', whether to say it or
write it, which has been resolved by the later drafts in favour of
writing, though the degree of heat behind the utterance has not
yet been settled, and in fact was not to be settled until the poem
was collected in *Geography III*, when Bishop made a final change
from the version printed in *The New Yorker*. Both the italicised
'*Write* it!' and the exclamation point lend credence to the moment
Wittgenstein singles out as a collision of immediate experience with
thought which *forces* an exclamation from one. In Draft 12, the 'ohs'
persist, but we also see, first given then cancelled, a self-addressed
anger against the reticence that keeps one in hiding, in '(Stupid!
Write!)', and 'Oh, go on! (Write it!)'. Helen Vendler once remarked
that there 'was something very cold about' Bishop, and that 'One
Art' reminded her of that part of her, saying in effect, 'I've lost it.
I'm all by myself. Nobody's going to be able to take care of me. I'm
not going to be able to hold onto anything. I am an encapsulated,
isolated child.' [27] Apart from its uncharacteristic lack of charity, this
remark seems to neglect the direction of the struggle in 'One Art',
away from the hidden self, toward open declaration and frank appeal.
But by moving in this direction, Bishop risks the naked confession-
alism she deplored. The change from saying to writing critically
shifts the balance back, from its direct source as an utterance from
the body to the mediation of symbolic form, a move again in the
Keatsian direction, not in this case to an unheard melody, but to a
cry stilled into writing and wrought into the exquisite art of the
villanelle.

The dawning of one aspect of consciousness, the one telling her
that she was part of the common human lot, gave Bishop as a child
a dreadful shock, recorded both in her story 'A Country Mouse'
and of course in 'In the Waiting Room'. Kinship and self-awareness,
as I've tried to suggest, were dangerous territory for the poet, owing
to the trauma surrounding the loss of her mother. The particularity
of that experience, however, is worth pausing over. In 'A Country

Mouse', while waiting in the dentist's office for her aunt, the child is overwhelmed by a 'feeling of absolute and utter desolation'. 'I felt...*myself.*' Among strangers, 'I was *one* of them too'. The discovery points in two directions at the same time: she is one, stuck in this essence, and she is one of *them*, called into the common lot, yet locked into her self: 'How strange you are, inside looking out.' The very thought careers out of control; it 'smashed into a tree. *Why* was I a human being?'

Cast into the world, Bishop's several personae become travellers at best, or tourists, often brought to a standstill, then partially rescued from painful fixities of condition by moments of poise issuing in redirection, new discovery, fresh perspective. In 'Questions of Travel', through 'childishness' 'we are determined to rush to see the sun the other way around', but 'surely it would have been a pity / not to have seen', 'not to have heard', not to have experienced the sheer strangeness of 'this strangest of theatres', the world. One wonders how far to claim general truth for the traveller here, who records in a notebook a doubt about the universality of Pascal's claim that one can form a full imagining of life '*just sitting quietly in one's room*'. For this traveller, one's room – one's home base – offers no secure point of origin: '*Should we have stayed at home, / wherever that may be?*' I certainly do not wish to maintain that Bishop's intent was to restore the unity of mind and body whose severance was bequeathed to us by Descartes' rationalism. Nonetheless, her traveller, in suggesting defensively that you really have to be there, alive in your senses, in order truly to know the world, takes a step toward restoring the body as an agent of knowledge. But is it because Bishop's earliest formations of an idea of the self are wounded and dispossessed from home that the travellers in her poems seek compensatory connection with 'things' and 'views' that will be, they hope, 'always, always delightful' and 'still quite warm'?

This frank speculation leads me to one last poem, Bishop's 'The Moose'. One of the longest in gestation, 'The Moose' was inspired by a bus trip Bishop took in 1946, from Nova Scotia to Boston, and was completed under the duress in 1972 of an invitation to deliver the Phi Beta Kappa poem at a Harvard commencement. For years, from North to South and back again, she carried sheaves of drafts bearing floating island stanzas, while she searched for the sequence that would bring them to rest, end her compositional journey, and recover its revelatory eruption of joy. The visit to Nova Scotia, Bishop's first in nearly 15 years, had been momentous, as Brett Millier writes in her biography, though saturated in 'miseries'.[28] On the Atlantic coast, she had made a note, the germ of

'At the Fishhouses' (published in 1947): 'Description of the dark, icy, clear water – clear dark glass – slightly bitter (hard to define). My idea of knowledge. this cold stream, half drawn, half flowing from a great rocky breast.'[29] Millier believes that 'this trip home gave [Bishop] back her childhood as artistic material',[30] and Bishop herself remarked that a lot of 'The Moose' 'is about "childhood recollections"'.[31] It is also a mid-life poem whose narrative, a 'dreamy divagation', unfolds as sunset yields to darkness, moonlight and mist and the bus enters 'the impenetrable wood'. 'The passengers lie back', lulled by

> Grandparents' voices
>
> uninterruptedly
> talking, in Eternity:
> names being mentioned,
> things cleared up finally
> ...
>
> "Yes..." that peculiar
> affirmative. "Yes..."
> A sharp, indrawn breath,
> half groan, half acceptance,
> that means "Life's like that.
> We know it (also death)."

Nothing further expected; in Eternity nothing changes. 'Now, it's all right now / even to fall asleep', the repeated 'now' enclosing the scene in a timeless present. Hallucination or dream, peaceful – and perhaps ominous. In a note for 'The Moose', Bishop wrote: 'our nature consists in motion; complete rest is death'. Paradoxically, the poem is startled from stuporous motion by an arrest, a stop that shakes the passengers awake, breaking off the narrative that so inevitably leads to the indrawn breath and an affirmation that sounds so much like acquiescence to death:

> – Suddenly the bus driver
> stops with a jolt,
> turns off his lights.

And there the moose stands, or looms. The passengers, startled awake,

> exclaim in whispers,
> childishly, softly,
> "Sure are big creatures."
> "It's awful plain."
> "Look! It's a she!"

Now, this brings me to the passage Bishop continued to work at even after the poem was finished enough to be read in public.

Here, first, as published:

> Taking her time,
> she looks the bus over,
> grand, otherworldly.
> Why, why do we feel
> (we all feel) this sweet
> sensation of joy?

But on the typescript bearing notes Bishop jotted down as intro-
duction to a reading of 'The Moose', we see that she continues to
weigh the emphasis to be given this question at the climactic mom-
ent of the poem:

> (Why) How, why does she give

replaced by :

> Why, why, do we feel
> (we all feel it) this sweet

or by:

> (we all feel) this sweet
> sensation of joy?

And to the right, as instructions to herself for elocution:

> Why, <u>why</u>, [superscript: (pause)] // do we feel
> (we all <u>feel</u> it) this sweet...

On this journey, importantly, there is no '*I, I, I*'; the poet, lulled by
the voices of grandparents, re-enters the condition before the child's
discovery, in the words of 'In the Waiting Room', that 'I was my
foolish aunt', the moment of self-definition and self-alienation, the
sickening sensation of falling, and the protesting question: 'you are
one of *them.* / *Why* should you be one, too?'

The risk of curling up with grandparents in Eternity and the risk
of assuming that things have been 'cleared up finally' is of course
the risk of death, or at any rate, of recession into knowledge fixed
by past experience and hung between poles called life and death,
one of those polarities, we remember, that are dissolved 'in that
watery, dazzling dialectic' of 'Santarém'. The saving shock in 'The
Moose' – 'Suddenly the bus driver / stops with a jolt' – thrusts the
passengers not into light but into the dark, when the driver 'turns
off his lights', the better to encounter the animal emerging from
'the impenetrable wood'. Suddenly, life is not a matter of the indrawn
breath, but of childish whispers, exclamations, and 'this sweet /
sensation of joy'. The answer to the child's protesting question:
'*Why* was I a human being?' had seemed to be the knowledge that

'Life's like that'. Here, suddenly, such knowledge is banished by
an impossible figure from the impenetrable dark, both homely and
otherworldly. The answer to the question '*Why* was I a human
being?' is another question: 'Why, why do we feel / (we all feel)
this sweet / sensation of joy?' In one realm of knowledge, to be
human is to be 'in for it', to be a you, 'inside looking out', but
suddenly, by the fact of living in 'our nature', it is also to rediscover
kinship with nature – the she-moose – and with fellow travellers.
The question hangs unanswered, but points to fresh inquiry and a
mulling over of the little that remains, 'our abidance' – in this poem,
the sensory trace of its moment:

> ...a dim
> smell of moose, an acrid
> smell of gasoline.

*

NOTES

Unless otherwise cited, quotations of published works are from Bishop's
Complete Poems: 1927-1979 or *The Collected Prose*, and of letters from *One
Art*. Quotations of unpublished work are from the Elizabeth Bishop Papers in
the Vassar College Library. An early version of this essay appears in a volume
of conference papers: *Poetry and the Sense of Panic*, edited by Lionel Kelly
(Amsterdam: Rodopi B.V. Editions, 2000).

1. Marianne Moore: 'A Modest Expert: *North & South*', in *Elizabeth Bishop
and Her Art*, edited by Lloyd Schwartz and Sybil P. Estess (Ann Arbor: Uni-
versity of Michigan Press, 1983), pp.177-79.

2. Anne Stevenson: *Five Looks at Elizabeth Bishop* (London: Agenda/Bellew,
1998), p.12.

3. Eavan Boland: 'An Un-Romantic American', in *Parnassus: Poetry in Review*,
14 no.2 (1988), pp.73-92.

4. David Appelbaum: *The Stop* (State University of New York Press, 1995),
pp.vii-xi.

5. Boland, p.73.

6. I have written about this practice as illustrated by 'Questions of Travel'
in 'Shifting Islands: Elizabeth Bishop's Manuscripts', *Shenandoah*, 33 no.1 (1982),
pp.51-62.

7. Bonnie Costello: *Elizabeth Bishop: Questions of Mastery* (Cambridge, MA
and London: Harvard University Press, 1991), p.14-15.

8. Costello, p.15.

9. Victoria Harrison questions the finality of Bishop's remark: 'That he
does not see because he is dead is challenged by the vitality of inversion, in
the principles of optics and in life. The risks of being "wrong"...do not stop
Bishop from repeatedly engaging subjects whose difference is their modus
operandi'. See her book, *Elizabeth Bishop's Poetics of Intimacy* (Cambridge:
Cambridge University Press, 1993), p.61.

10. Vassar Archives, Box 75.4, p.38.

11. Applebaum, p.3.

12. Applebaum, p.24.

13. Joanne Feit Diehl offers a detailed psychoanalytic study of 'In the Village', drawing on insights from object-relations theorists Melanie Klein and Christopher Bollas. See her book, *Elizabeth Bishop and Marianne Moore: The Psychodynamics of Creativity* (Princeton: Princeton University Press, 1993), especially pp.95-105.

14. For a study of this and other related manuscripts that concentrates on Bishop's effort to reconstruct her problematic relation to her mother, and therefore the constitution of her own subjectivity in relation to a world of objects, see Harrison, pp.134-37.

15. Diehl argues that the child discovers an alternative to the absent mother in the natural world and in masculine craft: 'Against the instability of the first relationship, the recurrent maternal absences, and the perception of an insecure relationship with the wounded mother, the child discovers an alternative possibility, one marked by assurance and security, an alternative that is not simply the blacksmith's, a world identified with masculinity and craftsmanship, but the displacement of craft into the natural world which lends a mutability that changes but does not destroy'. (103)

16. When Anne Stevenson undertook her comparison between Wittgenstein and Bishop, she argued that for both 'the ultimate ambiguity of experience derives not from the non-existence of reality but from the utter impossibility of knowing it'. See *Elizabeth Bishop* (New York: Twayne, 1966), pp.116-17. Bishop irritably rejected this approach, saying that she had never even read Wittgenstein. See *Conversations with Elizabeth Bishop*, edited by George Monteiro (Jackson: University Press of Mississippi, 1996), p.43. For my purposes, no such connection need be drawn. Rather, I am concerned with Wittgenstein's way of describing two distinct acts of mind that find expression in her stylistics.

17. Ludwig Wittgenstein: *Philosophical Investigations*, The English Text of the Third Edition, translated by G.E.M. Anscombe (New York: Macmillan, 1958), p.194e.

18. Morris W. Croll: 'The Baroque Style in Prose', in *Studies in English Philology*, edited by Kemp Malone and Martin B. Ruud (Minneapolis: University of Minnesota Press, 1929), p.430.

19. Wittgenstein, p.200e.

20. Wittgenstein, p.196e.

21. Wittgenstein, p.197e.

22. Wittgenstein, p.201e.

23. Applebaum, p.xi.

24. Published as 'Vague Poem' in *The New Yorker*, 21 & 28 February 2000.

25. Bishop visited Oklahoma only twice. In April 1976, in her speech accepting the *Books Abroad*/Neustadt International Prize for Literature, in Norman, Oklahoma, she remarked: 'The first time I came to Norman, Oklahoma – in 1973 – it was the farthest I had ever been inland in my life.' See Bishop's biography: Brett Candlish Millier, *Elizabeth Bishop: Life and the Memory of It* (Berkeley, Los Angeles, Oxford: University of California Press, 1993), pp.517-18. Her travels inland were a bit more extensive than this, however; in a letter of 1968, she mentions a trip to Tucson and says that she has crossed the continent twice by train. See *One Art*, p.501.

26. Millier offers an extended study of 'One Art' in her biography, pp.506-14, and a somewhat different version in 'Elusive Mastery: The Drafts of Elizabeth Bishop's "One Art" ', in *Elizabeth Bishop: The Geography of Gender*, edited by Marilyn May Lombardi (Charlottesville and London: University Press of Virginia, 1993), pp.233-43. Harrison's study of the drafts of 'One Art' appears in her *Elizabeth Bishop's Poetics of Intimacy*, pp.193-97.

27. See *Remembering Elizabeth Bishop: An Oral Biography*, edited by Gary Fountain and Peter Brazeau (Amherst: University of Massachusetts Press, 1994), p.333.

28. Millier, *Life and the Memory of It*, p.180.

29. Millier, *Life and the Memory of It*, p.181.

30. Millier, *Life and the Memory of It*, p.183.

31. *One Art*, p.638.

The Geographical Mirror

For a poet who, in America, is revered and loved perhaps more than any of her contemporaries, Elizabeth Bishop wrote remarkably little. In four published collections I count just 77 poems. Add ten or twelve unpublished ones, a few prose poems and poems written in youth, and you can make the number up to nearly a hundred. But there are far fewer than a hundred poems that Bishop herself considered worthy or finished. As an artist she was fastidious in the extreme, and she worked slowly. Twenty-six years to write 'The Moose' may be a record, but it is not out of scale in the light of her obsessive self-criticism and her determination never to publish incomplete or unsatisfactory work.

Bishop's first collection, *North & South*, was at least ten years in the making. Published in 1946, it straddled the Second World War, even though, with a few exceptions (notably 'Roosters'), it ignored it. In 1945 it won its author the Houghton Mifflin Prize, making her comparatively famous, but its sequel, *A Cold Spring*, did not appear until 1955. Even then, 19 poems were judged to be too few to stand on their own. Houghton Mifflin reprinted *North & South* and published the two books together in a slim volume simply called *Poems*. By that time Bishop's New York and Key West days were over, and she was sharing a house with Lota de Macedo Soares in Brazil.

Another ten years' hiatus ensued before *Questions of Travel* appeared in 1965, plainly marking a change of emphasis and style. Gone were her early experiments with baroque conceits, dream language and surrealistic psychology – in fact, such preoccupations very nearly disappeared from her work in the years leading up to *A Cold Spring*. They were replaced in *Questions of Travel*, her third collection, partly by a sequence of life studies and partly by poems – geographical, zoological, historical – set in Brazil. Only after 1950, when she was established in Brazil and corresponding regularly with Robert Lowell, did she begin to tap those indelible recollections of her childhood in Nova Scotia. The short stories 'In the Village' (which fills the middle pages of *Questions of Travel*) and 'Gwendolyn' turned out to be keys that unlocked doors to almost all her later poetry based on personal reminiscence. Bishop's final collection, *Geography III*, in which she published only nine original poems, appeared in 1976 (notice the ten-year span again) after her Brazilian life had come to an end, when she was teaching at Harvard. Three years after its publication, in October 1979, the poet died in Boston.

Elizabeth Bishop, then, during forty-odd years of writing poems, produced only four slender volumes. Why have they been so popular? What is still the appeal – to professional academics as well as to hundreds of poets and faithful readers – of this small body of work by a shy, often lonely, sometimes abrasive lady-traveller, artistically gifted, certainly, but deliberately lacking a political or social agenda, whose writing was at its best finicky and scarce, most of it taking the form of witty, rather elitist letters to her friends? Of course, we can all think of reasons for making a literary heroine of Elizabeth Bishop, the chief one being, probably, that the very fastidiousness of her writing ensured that her poems, despite their apparent lucidity, have meant different things to different people. Which is to say that while the poems can be variously interpreted, they can never be perfectly explained. Work as we will at analysing them, something tantalisingly eludes us; loose ends refuse to be tied down to any set of ideas; ambivalence haunts even the clearest descriptive passages. Like the hanging balls of tiny mirrors that, before the invention of strobe lighting, used to radiate fleeting lozenges of colour over the dance floors of my youth, Bishop's poems are almost infinitely reflective.

Mirrors, reflections, speculations are in themselves ambiguous, unpindownable idealogues (idea-words). In some ways they suggest passivity: a mirror, like an eye, can only reflect what's in front of it. But in another, more important sense, the mind, the imagination of any artist, reflects on what it sees; the interpretive, creative faculty goes to work immediately perception takes place. It was in this area of interpretive seeing that Bishop found herself struggling in a state of constant agitation between mirror and mind. The geographical mirror was only one of many that yielded alternative, sometimes distorted, sometimes playfully corrective pictures of the world – and of course of herself. Look, for instance, at the mirror images that crowd into early poems such as 'The Gentleman of Shalott' with its mirror 'along the line / of what we call the spine'; or 'From the Country to the City' in which 'as we approach, wickedest clown [New York City], your heart and head, / we can see that / glittering arrangement of your brains consists, now, / of mermaid-like, / seated, ravishing sirens, each waving her hand mirror'. In 'Love Lies Sleeping' this same city grows down into the open eyes (mirrors) of a presumably dead observer: 'inverted and distorted. No. I mean / distorted and revealed, if he sees it at all.' 'The Weed', in which a river, like human memory, is seen to 'carry all / the scenes that it had once reflected / shut in its waters…' is the first of a number of poems to associate mirrors and water. 'Paris, 7 A.M.', 'Quai d'Orléans', 'Sleeping on the Ceiling' with its chandelier-fountain, all play with the notion of world corrected or at least changed in reflection. These poems were, of course, early, semi-metaphysical ones (they owe a lot to George Herbert and perhaps, too, to Baudelaire), written soon after Bishop left Vassar and was living in New York or travelling in Europe. The mirror imagery disappeared when she moved to Florida, the exception being the lyric 'Insomnia' from *A Cold Spring*, in which 'the moon in the bureau mirror' fosters a glimpse 'into that world inverted / where left is always right, / where the shadows are really the body, / where we stay awake all night, / where the heavens are shallow as the sea / is now deep, and you love me.'

Bishop hit upon the expression 'the geographical mirror' when she was visiting Nova Scotia, after a long absence, in the summer of 1946. Houghton Mifflin, after many delays, had at last sent her copies of her first book, *North & South*. Bishop, restless and full of memories, did not altogether feel at home among her Nova Scotian relatives, most of whom, as might be expected, did not understand her poems. In her notebook she described the 'clear dark glass' of the icy river that runs through Great Village into the Bay of Fundy, reaching instinctively for that familiar metaphysical trope: water = glass. But then she went on to elaborate, '[It's] my idea of knowledge, this cold stream, half drawn, half flowing from a great rocky breast.'[1] It is not unusual to find passages of abstract musing in Bishop's notebooks, but only rarely in her poetry did she allow such ideas thinking-room. Though she insisted that the last lines of 'At the Fishhouses' came to her in a dream, there they are, plainly articulated in her notes. 'At the Fishhouses' therefore, seems to be a particularly revealing example, not only of how Bishop seized upon the idea of nature's offering of a geographical (as opposed to a metaphorical or psychological) mirror, but also of how Bishop thought her way through the composition of a poem, putting it together image by image, memory by memory, testing all the time for what at college she had identified as a 'mind thinking within the poem'.

Writing to a young poet (Donald Stanford) at Princeton while she was at Vassar, Bishop had made a point of distinguishing between poetry (like her correspondent's) that lay at rest on the page (by implication, inert), and baroque poetry like her own 'which strove for action within the poem'.[2] By 1946 Bishop had abandoned the baroque, Hopkins-like style of her youth, but, throughout her life, she remained dedicated to this concept of the mind acting within the poem. Almost all her discursive poems, then, are built so as to mirror her mind *performing its perceptions*; and that mind, with its never-sleeping eye, does indeed remain live and timelessly present in the completed work. Look at the way 'At the Fishhouses' develops as a scene or film unfolding slowly before our eyes in language so plain that it verges on prose.

> Although it is a cold evening,
> down by one of the fishhouses
> an old man sits netting,
> his net, in the gloaming almost invisible,
> a dark purple-brown,
> and his shuttle worn and polished.
> The air smells so strong of codfish
> it makes one's nose run and one's eyes water.

The lines proceed with this amble of observation for nearly a page and a half, as if the writer (surely Bishop herself and not a persona) were there, pointing to one thing, then another. There is even a certain awkwardness in the description of the fishhouses' 'steeply peaked roofs' and 'narrow, cleated gangplanks…for the wheelbarrows to be pushed up and down on'. It's at this point she interrupts herself to draw attention to the pervasive colour: 'All is silver,' she says, 'the heavy surface of the sea swelling slowly as if considering spilling over, is opaque' (in other words, mercury-like, not reflective, not a mirror), while the shore itself, with its benches, masts, lobster pots, frail old buildings, rocks, fish tubs etc. are all of 'an apparent translucence', covered with herring scales, 'creamy iridescent coats of mail, / with small iridescent flies crawling on them'. The detail here is so naturalistic that a reader may miss the suggestion that this fishermen's shore, or workplace, is, in contrast to the opaque, indifferent ocean, glass-like, window-like (translucent) and that the observer-poet, who enters the scene with 'The old man accepts a Lucky Strike', is taking part in an human incident whose multiple ramifications are still unfolding in the frames of her memory. The entire poem, in fact, may be described as a reflection both of and on the subject of living and making livings, and on what it means to be alive, or part of life in this world. The old man in his vest sequinned with herring scales represents the last of his kind. The fishing industry is dying in Nova Scotia; the fishhouses will soon be deserted wrecks. This is what seems to be implied as the old man and the young poet discuss 'the decline in the population / and of codfish and herring'. He was a friend of her grandfather who (though she doesn't say so) may once have helped to build the long ramp she takes so much trouble to describe as descending into the water where 'thin silver/tree trunks are laid horizontally/across the grey stone down and down/at intervals of four or five feet.'

Now, I'm certain that mentioning such mundane matters as silver tree trunks set at intervals of four or five feet, as earlier, the fisherman's 'black old knife', were details Bishop deliberately set down to draw attention away from the ontological meditation that the poem at this point, shows signs of wanting to develop. We get a sense of where it would go (and will go) once the poet lets her musings off the leash of her observations: 'Cold dark deep and absolutely clear, / element bearable to no mortal, / to fish and to seals...' The word 'seals' suddenly reminds the poet of an encounter with a particular seal, and her mind veers off in a new direction. Seals, she seems to correct herself, are mortal like humans (and fish), so she humorously begins to show us how much (and how little) she and this mammal without language, but for whom "home" is the icy Nova Scotian sea, have in common. The passage is comic, perhaps gently ironical: 'He [the seal] was curious about me. He was interested in music; / like me a believer in total immersion, / so I used to sing him Baptist hymns; / I also sang "A Mighty Fortress Is Our God".' The point made, but not articulated, is that a hymn likening God to a mighty fortress, though it may make an interesting sound, is, to a seal, perfectly meaningless. As so often in Bishop's poems about animals, the species are divided by unbreachable barriers of time and evolution, yet they do, in a heart-warming way, communicate. Bishop and the seal (and by implication the old fisherman) cannot help but share the conditions of their 'cold dark deep and absolutely clear' surroundings. You could almost say that the poet and the seal, given the unconscious, opaque reality of the water, *reflect* each other. If anything, the seal – wordlessly adapted to his environment – passes a sort of judgement on the poet's ignorance, very much as the moose does in that other magnificent poem set so memorably in Nova Scotia and New Brunswick.

If the poet intended to hint at the limitations of organised religion in the scene with the seal, she confirms this impression after the line 'Cold dark deep and absolutely clear' for a second time interrupts the flow of observations. 'Back behind us,' she says, 'the dignified tall firs begin. / Bluish, associating with their shadows, / a million Christmas trees stand / waiting for Christmas.' Again, the implication is ironic: the trees, of course, have no conception of Christmas any more than the seal has of God. Nature, the poem seems to want to say, even against the will of its author, knows nothing about our defences

against the a- or un-humanness of the world as given. As human
beings, we look into it – look into the mirror of nature, we say – but
we find there nothing we can identify except as it relates to images
of ourselves. As for what it is, in itself – that is a mystery beyond us.

Now, it's clear (to me, at least) that while she was putting 'At the
Fishhouses' together in her painstaking way, Bishop had no very
clear idea of where the poem was taking her. She saw what she felt
and felt very strongly about what she saw, but she kept her mind free
of meanings as she approached a conclusion – that might not after
all be a conclusion but a step, as it were, on the way. Notice how
she continues to pile up empirical details in the final 19 or 20 lines:

> The water seems suspended
> above the rounded gray and blue-gray stones.
> I have seen it over and over, the same sea, the same,
> slightly, indifferently swinging above the stones,
> icily free above the stones,
> above the stones and then the world.
> If you should dip your hand in,
> your wrist would ache immediately,
> your bones would begin to ache and your hand would burn
> as if the water were a transmutation of fire
> that feeds on stones and burns with a dark gray flame.
> If you tasted it, it would first taste bitter,
> then briny, then surely burn your tongue.
> It is like what we imagine knowledge to be:
> dark, salt, clear, moving, utterly free,
> drawn from the cold hard mouth
> of the world, derived from the rocky breasts
> forever, flowing and drawn, and since
> our knowledge is historical, flowing, and flown.

Bishop said herself that the finale of 'At the Fishhouses' was a *donnée*.
I, for one, believe her. The trance-inducing incantatory beauty of
these lines – so utterly different in tone and pitch from the careful
description that opens the poem – is the kind of godsend poets long
for all their lives but rarely receive. It won't hurt the poem to point
out that the dreamy, hypnotic effect of these lines is achieved by
the repetition of 's' sounds: seems, suspended, stones, same, sea,
same, slightly, swinging, stones, icily, stones, stones. As the passage
progresses, the words slowly work themselves closer and closer to
the elements: water, stones, the sea icily swinging 'above the stones
and then above the world', as if anticipating the naked planet's
ultimate victory over (and probable destruction of) the life it sus-
tains: 'as if the water were a transmutation of fire / that feeds on
stones and burns with a dark gray flame'. Earth, air, fire, water: our
most basic elements; and also elements of what we *imagine* knowledge

to be. For in the end 'At the Fishhouses' throws the world back at the poet who, looking for herself and losing herself in its geography, is returned to the ever-passing mirror of her own mind.

It is like what we imagine knowledge to be:
dark, salt, clear, moving, utterly free,
drawn from the cold hard mouth
of the world,* derived from the rocky breasts
forever, flowing and drawn, and since
our knowledge is historical, flowing, and flown.

* *notice, how careful she is not to say 'universe'*

How many paragraphs could be (have been) written on this passage alone? The poet James Merrill was the first, I think, to point out that the word 'flown' at the end is the past participle not of 'flow' but of 'fly'. 'Flown', chiming with 'drawn' in the penultimate line, sounds, of course, much better than 'flowed', but it also changes the sense. To the idea that knowledge is historical (suggesting that knowledge is an accumulation of what we have learned through past experience) is grafted the perception that the reality of the past has flown away altogether, and all that remains are memories: names, images, reflections, flowing endlessly over the earth's geological, geographical foundations. These are the rocky breasts that feed the poet, the fisherman, the seal, the tall firs, indiscriminately with a dark, salt, clear moving stream of continuous life. The vision is evolutionary, Darwinian, but also curiously spiritual, for it's essentially a vision of many millions of lives, like drops of water, each ephemeral but each one somehow carrying, as in 'The Weed', 'the scenes that it had once reflected / shut in its waters, and not floating / on momentary surfaces.'

Elizabeth Bishop once wrote, rather casually, in a letter to me that she and Robert Lowell sometimes thought of themselves as descendants of the Transcendentalists.[3] What she meant, I think, was that she and Lowell shared a more or less pantheistic approach to nature, feeling that they belonged to the natural world as much or more than to civilisation, and it was perhaps for this reason that they both rejected the rigorous Protestantism of their forebears. In a poem Bishop wrote over a considerable period of time but finished shortly before she finished 'At the Fishhouses' she looks back over her travels abroad (travels in search of that 'something, something, something' invoked in 'Sandpiper') in the light of her Baptist upbringing. The poem called 'Over 2,000 Illustrations and a Complete Concordance' takes it title from the Bulmer family Bible that, as a child, she had pored over in her grandparents' farmhouse in Great Village. 'Thus should have been our travels' it begins, recalling the

Bible's 'serious' engravings: 'The Seven Wonders of the World, Arabs plotting, probably, / against our Christian Empire...the Tomb, the Pit, the Sepulcher, / The branches of the date-palms...like files, / The cobbled courtyard where the Well is dry, / is like a diagram...' and so forth, until we reach this extraordinary passage:

> The eye drops, weighted, through the lines
> the burin made, the lines that move apart
> like ripples above sand,
> dispersing storms, God's spreading fingerprint,
> and painfully, finally, that ignite
> in watery prismatic white-and-blue.

I'm not sure I understand the connection between God's spreading fingerprint (a marvellous image that unites the engraver's burin with ripples over the sand) and this painful ignition in white-and-blue, but the passage leads into a second long, discursive stanza in which the poet's travels are described as if they, too, were, illustrations in some book of life. Scenes from Nova Scotia, Rome, Mexico, Ireland, England and Morocco culminate in a visit ('It frightened me most of all') to a holy grave that does not look particularly holy, full of dust that was 'not even the dust / of the poor prophet paynim who once lay there'. A third, much shorter stanza then begins with an exclamation of disappointment: 'Everything only connected by "and" and "and"'. These travel scenes only connect, in Eliot's words, 'Nothing with nothing.' Neither faith nor art hold them together, as the poet turns once more, this time as an adult, to the illustrated Bible:

> Open the book. (The gilt rubs off the edges
> of the pages and pollinates the fingertips.)
> Open the heavy book. Why couldn't we have seen
> this old Nativity while we were at it?
> – the dark ajar, the rocks breaking with light,
> an undisturbed, unbreathing flame,
> colorless, sparkless, freely fed on straw,
> and, lulled within, a family with pets,
> – and looked and looked our infant sight away.

That final line raises all sorts of questions that in my short guide, *Five Looks at Elizabeth Bishop*,[4] I tried, perhaps wrongly, to enumerate. It seems fairly evident to me now that Bishop is saying something like 'Why can't we remain childlike in the way we look at and learn to reject the truth of this pictured Nativity, for when we grow up, no matter how far we travel, we never find anything to put in its place.' The line 'and looked and looked our infant sight away' asks the question, 'Since infant sight will disappear anyway, wouldn't it be better to *look* it away than intellectually search for a replacement?' Well, as I remarked earlier, it is impossible unambiguously

to explain Bishop's poems, but one can, I think, learn from com-
paring the final lines of this poem with those that complete 'At
the Fishhouses'. Both poems end with revelations that move, first
with a step and then with a giant stride, away from the fixed im-
pressions of childhood. The Bulmer's Bible's 'Old Nativity' opens to
a dark *ajar.* That 'dark [not door] ajar' reveals the rocks 'breaking
with light' with a flame undisturbed and unbreathing – flames of
faith, we must suppose, and not of life. The vision, though beaut-
iful, is static. The final lines of 'At the Fishhouses', on the other
hand, recreate the icy sea as 'a transmutation of fire', one 'that feeds
on stones and burns with a dark gray flame'. In those six last lines
it seems to me that the poet does *look* her infant sight away. Instead
of longing for the stasis of an eternal myth, she perceives that know-
ledge is never permanent, that the ever-moving flames of the sea are
'dark, salt, clear, moving, utterly free'. This is an adult view of
knowledge, informed by experience and recognised precisely because
no prettiness deflects it. The 'cold hard mouth of the world' suckles
from no mythic Virgin, only from the rocky breasts of eternally
flowing matter – or energy, or time. With time, flows too, that
precious childhood that the startling word 'flown' tells us has dis-
appeared forever. Bishop's triumph in 'At the Fishhouses' was to
achieve the hardness of scientific truth without having sacrificed
anything of the poem's spirituality. And that seems to me to be an
important and courageous achievement.

Bishop completed 'At the Fishhouses' and its companion poem,
'Cape Breton', years before she took flight from America and went
to live in Brazil, but when she did, she took her geographical-geo-
logical mirror with her. Charles Darwin had landed on the coast of
Brazil in 1832; one of the first books Elizabeth Bishop read when *she*
arrived was *The Voyage of the Beagle.* She wrote of her admiration
for Darwin in a letter of 8 January 1964:

> But reading Darwin, one admires the beautiful solid case being built
> up out of his endless heroic *observations,* almost unconscious or auto-
> matic – and then comes a sudden relaxation, a forgetful phrase, and
> one feels the strangeness of his undertaking, sees the lonely young man,
> his eyes fixed on facts and minute detail, sinking or sliding giddily off
> into the unknown.[5]

For Bishop, whatever might be the case with Darwin, the 'beau-
tiful solid case' of her observations led her repeatedly into unknown
territory, though for her the unknown contained a psychological,
personal component that warms and humanises the poems of *Questions
of Travel* and *Geography III.* In the latter work mirrors, as such,
pretty well disappear from her imagery, though the mind acting

within the poem never ceases, as it were, to look out the window.
I sometimes picture Bishop's geographical poems – 'Arrival at
Santos', say, or 'Questions of Travel' – as train windows in which
the poet is herself reflected as she looks out at the passing world: a
prime example of the phenomenon she once defined as 'the always-
more-successful surrealism of everyday life'.[6] The window-mirrors
of her best work are at the same time geographical and personal,
and characteristically they frame questions that never resolve an
intriguing conflict between them:

> "Is it lack of imagination that makes us come
> to imagined places, not just stay at home?
> Or could Pascal have been not entirely right
> about just sitting quietly in one's room?
>
> Continent, city, country, society:
> the choice is never wide and never free.
> And here, or there…No. Should we have stayed at home,
> wherever that may be?"

These stanzas at the end of the title poem 'Questions of Travel' ask
questions; they don't expect to be answered. They mainly lead to
other questions which have to do with what Bishop is, after all, up
to. Look at the implied oxymoron in her use of the word 'imagin-
ation': '*Is it lack of imagination that makes us come to imagined places*'?
Why not too much imagination? Does the phrasing suggest that
believing too much in the imagination makes us come to actual
places? The reader feels pressured to question the question. Again,
why does Bishop declare that the choice of where to go and how to
live '*is never wide and never free*'. Never free of cost, one supposes,
and not only of financial cost. Everything gained from travel costs
something in terms of what we leave behind. No experience ever
comes free. On the other hand, free implies freedom, liberty. So
the line '*the choice is never wide and never free*' suggests that we
never really are given freedom of choice; our characters, our back-
grounds, the culture we inherit, despite our wishes, determine the
course of our lives. Again, the question leads not to a yes or no, but
to a further question that can be understood as general or personal
or both: '*Should be have stayed at home, / wherever that may be?*'
The first person plural, 'we', is undetermined and the question is
addressed to us all. Yet the details and references in the poem depict
a personal geography: the face, or the mind, of the poet reflected
in the mirror she is looking through.
    As I mentioned at the beginning, one of the strengths of Elizabeth
Bishop's poetry is its multivalency. Almost every significant line is
ambivalent as to import. Whenever we attempt to tie her interrogations

of life to an ideology or set of social theorems we discover that, read
in certain other ways, these same lines might signify their reverse.
Their mirror images, in other words, their reflections, whether
distorted or revealed, ambiguously appear to haunt them. Her poems,
then, for all their lucidity as art, admit to confusions. They never lie
at rest on the page, they never fit neatly into an intellectual category
or generalisation. This means, of course, that they continue to
challenge readers and tantalise academics, who would love to enlist
Elizabeth Bishop in the ranks of one cause or another dear to their
hearts. But the poems always resist. They refuse, in George Eliot's
language, to participate in the dehumanising power of abstract
thought. 'There is no general doctrine,' Eliot wrote in *Middlemarch*,
'which is not capable of eating out our mortality if unchecked by
the deep-seated habit of direct fellow-feeling with individual men
and women.'

Elizabeth Bishop's deep-seated habit of fellow-feeling and empathy
expressed itself in relation to the places and people she describes in
her poems. And the geographical mirror of her imagination, cloudy
as it sometimes seems with questions and ambiguities, is still not
reducible to an ideology or a system. It remains the world of her
art – the intensely observed, always possible world that her poems
reach out to share with us, and which encourage us to believe that
human beings – for all their weaknesses, misery and barbarities –
are also unique among the species and capable, as individuals, of
creating and sustaining goodness and beauty.

*

NOTES

Unless otherwise cited, quotations of published works are from Bishop's
Complete Poems: 1927-1979 or *The Collected Prose*, and of letters from *One Art*.

1. Brett C. Millier, *Elizabeth Bishop: Life and the Memory of It* (Berkeley,
Los Angeles, Oxford: University of California Press, 1993), p.182.
2. *One Art*, pp.11-13.
3. Unpublished letter to Anne Stevenson, 20 March 1963. From Elizabeth
Bishop Collection, Washington University.
4. Anne Stevenson, *Five Looks at Elizabeth Bishop* (London: Agenda/Bellew,
1998), pp.39-42.
5. Unpublished letter to Anne Stevenson, 8 January 1964. From Elizabeth
Bishop Collection, Washington University.
6. Unpublished letter to Anne Stevenson, 8 January 1964. From Elizabeth
Bishop Collection, Washington University.

DERYN REES-JONES

Writing ELIZABETH

Entrée: right of access; a dish served between main courses; a formal entry; the first entry of an actor or actress during a performance; (*Mus*) an overture or prelude

Ligature: anything which binds; any material such as catgut, silver wire, silk thread used by a surgeon to tie the blood vessels, or stitch a wound

Imago: the final, fully developed adult stage of insect development, following the larval and pupal stages [L.= an image]

Zanje: an irrigation canal

Abature: trail of a beast of the chase

Billabong: a backwater, a branch for a stream ending in sand, weed, etc

Eprouvette: a form of ladle or spoon used in metallurgy for sampling an assay

Threpsology: the science of nutrition

Hyaline: glassy; transparent; the sea or atmosphere when clear or transparent

[*Collins English Dictionary* edited by Alexander H. Irvine]

E

What is an Elizabeth?
Of what is an Elizabeth composed?

I find it very hard to write about Elizabeth Bishop. It is not that I have nothing to say. On the contrary, there is so much to say, so much that is so important, that somehow in the telling I lose what it is about Bishop that I value most. In the ten years that I have been reading her, my response to her work has been a mixture of love and resistance. I came to her work reluctantly: as an undergraduate I was urged to write about her and chose instead to write about H.D. Later I chose Sylvia Plath as the central focus for my doctoral thesis, again side-stepping Bishop, whose work I knew but for which I had little but an obligatory respect, rather than an enthusiasm. I didn't know what to do with *Geography III*, for example, when I tried reading it in 1993. I was, however, getting a strong sense of Bishop's influence through poets like Jo Shapcott and Lavinia Greenlaw, whose work I admired, and my curiosity about Bishop's work as a whole gradually increased. I remember buying the *Complete Poems* in 1995, and then later borrowing the *Collected Prose*. I wrote a brief conference paper on Bishop and what seemed at the time unsatisfactory essay on her;[1] I began to teach her occasionally to undergraduates: 'The Monument' (which I also used as a model for one of my own poems, an exercise in reminding myself how difficult it is to write a Bishop-esque poem) and 'North Haven'. Slowly, however, I have learned to appreciate the poems properly, and for each poem I remember the time and place I first read it. But even now, I haven't read all of Bishop's work: there is a sense that I want to save them. I have to read the poem for a long time, I have to really get to know it. Then there's a sense that, once read and reread, one cannot ever shake off the gaze of a Bishop poem. One has to travel with the poem, to understand it at the speed by which is was composed. For this reason, Bishop represents to me the poet who is dedicated to her craft, memorialised in Lowell's poem as he asks her 'Do you still hang your words in air, ten years / unfinished, glued to your noticeboard, with gaps / or empties for the unimaginable phrase, / unerring Muse who makes the casual perfect.'[2]

So why choose to write about Elizabeth Bishop? Bishop herself, notoriously self-effacing and modest, supports silence and a place for the unexplained: 'I've always felt I've written poetry more by not writing it than writing it'[3] she has written; 'I'm sorry I can't seem to say all the right things I'd like to. I really should learn to be more articulate, I know...'[4] In many ways Bishop herself could have become my alibi. And yet writing about women's poetry is the central focus of my academic research, the bulk of it focused around a mapping of the relationships between 20th-century women poets and their male contemporaries. *Not* to write about one of the key figures would have been an almost unforgivable omission. In a strangely domestic struggle, Sylvia Plath kept butting in, suggesting herself as a way of reading Bishop. Plath herself was a poet wary of Bishop, initially because of the model of femininity she offered which did not accord with her own severely heterosexual and maternal model. I found two references to Bishop in Plath's journals. The first sees her as a rival, as she saw most other women poets: 'No reason,' Plath supposes, 'why I shouldn't surpass at least the facile Isabella Gardner and even the lesbian & fanciful & jeweled Elizabeth Bishop in America.'[5] Later, she came to talk about Bishop with admiration: 'Her fine originality, always surprising, never rigid, flowing, juicier than Marianne Moore who is her godmother.'[6] I also turned to a contemporary poet, Anne Stevenson, who has written at length about both Bishop and Plath. In a recent interview she explains her admiration for them both:

> When I first read Elizabeth Bishop's poems – in 1960 – I was impressed by their originality and by the way they achieved an affinity with Herbert and Hopkins and yet struck out on their own. It wasn't because Bishop was a woman that her work stunned me; it was because she so perfectly exemplified Eliot's idea that poets have to root themselves in a language tradition before they can change it. Elizabeth Bishop completely understood and approved of that, as did Sylvia Plath, whose reliance on Eliot and Dylan Thomas when she began to write poems trained her to develop her own, extraordinary voice. I admit that I was particularly drawn first to Bishop then to Plath because I felt they had shared my experience, writing as women in a tradition hitherto dominated by men. I am not unfeminist in that respect. Both were obvious models. Neither one, however, made life easy for herself by retreating to a women's ghetto. They were out there in the cold all their lives – and incidentally, tougher, writing better than most men among their contemporaries...their Americanness attracted me because I "identified" with it; I had grown up in their world. I still share their values, moral and aesthetic, as I do their contempt for pretenders and self-excusers.[7]

What Anne Stevenson has to say about her own reasons for admiring Bishop and Plath sharpened my own sense of what Bishop and Plath shared, and at the same time did differently: a need to make a defence around subjective expression through an engagement with surrealist practices – I use the term in the loosest of ways – and the use of the dream. But whereas Plath foregrounded the dramatic elements and emotions of the dream, Bishop had found a way of keeping the dream airtight and untouchable, handing the reader a highly-charged version of the real that all the time was elusive and almost unknowable.

Still unable to write or even think about Bishop coherently, I did, however, have three very intense dreams which I want to take the liberty of recounting, not simply because they give me a way of talking abut Bishop, but because the dreams raise important issues about my feelings about role models, muses, the gendering of the self in poetry. My dreams, and their surreal happenings, show a need to code the subjective in the objective dream language, perhaps even in a way that is similar to the process in which poems are themselves composed. As such, I hope they allow me a way into thinking, and writing about Bishop; to discover things about my relationship with Bishop's work of which ordinarily I would not have been aware.

L

'I use dream-material whenever I am lucky enough to have any' [8]

In the first of these dreams I was standing on the windy, gothic ramparts of an imaginary university where I was due to give a talk on Bishop. As I spoke about her, I was aware that I was exposing myself. I had become not simply a vulnerable image – the image of a person standing naked before an audience having forgotten their speech – but a gross image of femininity. The voice with which I spoke came from a huge mouth, the female genitals. Not only was I exposing myself by talking abut Bishop, but my "I" had been reduced to its biology. I realised that the mouth was exposing a part of myself which was essentially female, but that it was also imaging a pun around an early Bishop poem, 'The Man-Moth'. The dream-work had transformed the "man-moth" into the "woman-mouth", a cunning trick of the unconscious which turned my speaking into a female version of a figure at the centre of a surreal poem which rather than being about talking, is about looking. Bishop's poem is itself about a slip, a Freudian error, a newspaper misprint which should have read 'mammoth'.

The surreal creature who lies behind the rampart in the poem, making only occasional forays to the surface is what? a kind of alter ego for the poet? a trope for her own furtive muse as 'Each night he must / be carried through artificial tunnels and dream recurrent dreams' ? [9] Is this an angelic figure of the unconscious, both male and female, the masculine 'I' who has the feminine and the mother also within her? The typo, 'man-moth' has taken the *mam* and left the *man*, transformed the *mouth* into *moth*, itself a truncated but decidedly other in its insect form, mother. The end of the poem asks that we regard its huge pupil, the eye filled with a large tear. For me ("I", pupil with much to learn) the eye itself had become displaced onto my gender. Was such an exhibition of my femininity being admonished by Bishop? Was I being reminded not to read Bishop as a woman poet, that part of her importance to me was that she offered a role model which did not foreground the feminine, or write stereotypically "as a woman"?

The second dream, later the same week, was much more conventional. In it I could not speak at all. I was there, standing before my imaginary audience, fully clothed this time, and I could not think of anything to say. I mumbled and shuffled. The embarrassing silence was broken by someone telling us that we were to retire to watch a film. I was both disappointed and relieved. What I was trying to communicate had been a failure. I could not capture the interest of my audience. The film, however, was only an interval, after which we could return. But after the film, I was told, no, it was probably better that we stopped for the evening. I thanked my host, was grateful and disappointed. I could not tell and had had my exposition replaced by showing. If the first dream was a warning about seeing in a blinkered overdetermined female way, the second was, it seemed, about the power of showing over telling and explaining. But I could also interpret this as a reminder that Bishop is a person I want to read, not one I want to write about critically.

In the third and final dream I was having to act as host at a literary party. Seamus Heaney was arriving for dinner, and I was cooking him trout. A male friend, also arrived: an English poet who was keen that instead of the fish I was proposing to cook, we eat steak. Gradually lots of poets arrived at the table; Lowell was there, but still I was the only woman. And not only that, but as a vegetarian, I was not able to take part in this Parnassian meal. Instead, I was obsessed with finding a recipe for cooking trout. In the dream, I telephoned another male friend who I felt sure would have a suitable recipe for the Nobel Laureate and the ghostly, white-haired Lowell. The friend I phoned, however, was away, and instead I talked to his wife, who gave me the recipe. The gender divide was such that even over the telephone it couldn't be overcome. This dream less easy but seemed to be about a kind of exclusion or difference from these amenable but remote male figures with whom I felt unable to communicate.

I

'The conversations are simple: about food' [10]

In the end, I e-mailed the poet who I thought might have the trout recipe. 'You're thinking of the Yeats poem, "The Song of the Wandering of Aengus"' was his astute reply. And so I was. (I also got the trout recipe for future reference).[11] Uncannily, this dream, through my association with the poem, links with my first dream. The Yeats poem begins:

> I went out to the hazel wood
> Because a fire was in my head,
> And cut and peeled a hazel wand,
> And hooked a berry to a thread
> And when the white moths were on the wing
> And moth-like stars were flickering out,
> I dropped the berry in the stream
> And caught a little silver trout.

Yeats's poem is about – in its most reductive terms – a female muse who runs off: 'And someone called me by my names / it had become a glimmering girl / with apple blossom in her hair / Who called me by my name and ran / And faded through the brightening air.' John Unterecker suggests several ways of reading this poem. Certainly there's a sense that in recalling the poem, I'm identifying with a poet's search for a muse. But where Yeats is frantically looking for Maud Gonne, whom, Unterecker points out, Yeats had first seen standing by a bouquet of apple blossoms, and whose complexion he always associated with apple blossom, I was still in search of Elizabeth Bishop. Unterecker also suggests that we can read the poem as both 'a versification of the legends Yeats paraphrases in his notes about women of the Sidhe who, disguised as fishes, enchant living men'.[12] But why then was I thinking of Heaney and Yeats? Heaney I associate with Bishop in a rather comic way as his poem 'The Skunk' has always made me think of Elizabeth Bishop décolletage in the poet's bedroom. Thinking of Heaney and Bishop brings a range of associations. Heaney's poem is clearly making reference to Lowell's poem, 'Skunk Hour', a poem which itself was written for Elizabeth Bishop and which was directly influenced by Bishop's poem 'The Armadillo'. 'Skunk Hour' ends with an image of female nurturing and resilience:

> I stand on top
> of our back steps and breathe the rich air –
> a mother skunk with her column of kittens swills the garbage pail.

She jabs her wedge head in a cup
of sour cream, drops her ostrich tail,
and will not scare.

Likewise, Heaney's presence at my empty dinner table (and my search for trout) seems to offer me an ambivalent but not unpowerful model of femininity: Heaney's skunk is a woman with her tail upended, like 'The intent and glamorous, / Ordinary, mysterious skunk, / Mythologised, demythologised, / Snuffing the boards five feet beyond me.' She becomes the skunk itself, in her 'head-down, tail up hunt in a bottom drawer / For the black plunge-line nightdress.'[13]

But this final dream also recalls Bishop in another way. The search for a way to cook fish reminds me of Bishop's poem 'The Fish' which I had used as a prompt to my own poem of the same title which attempts a Bishop-esque geographic mapping of the body. My own poem is about the way poems are elusive to both reader and writer; at the end the poem itself escapes, just as Bishop's captured fish, wire hooks lodged firmly in his mouth 'his brown skin hung in strips / like ancient wallpaper' is let go.[14] Searching for ways of cooking Heaney's trout, I'm not only searching for Bishop but poetry itself.[15]

Z

'really one should write philosophy only as one writes a poem.' [16]

Primarily my three dreams seemed to make me want to focus on several aspects of Bishop. The first is to do with anxieties about how to construct my femininity as a poet. How as a woman does one write? Bishop answers many questions in that respect: her poems give me an authority as a poet to both see and remember. When I read Bishop's poems they become, over time, an important part of the place from which I write; like the dream, they are 'art "copying from life" and life itself, / life and the memory of it so compressed / they've turned into each other. Which is which?'[17] This famous quote from 'Poem' goes on to ask 'how to live'; and in a sense I think all Bishop's poems ask that same question of their reader. Certainly two of Bishop's poems – 'The Moose' and 'In the Waiting Room' – are especially charged in my thinking about writing. It's no coincidence that these two poems touch on writing and female identity. In 'The Moose', the female poem/muse lumbers out of the woods, 'towering, antlerless', 'high as a church, /

homely as a house / (or, safe as houses)'. In 'In the Waiting Room', the key moment is the point at which the child realises she is female:

> But I felt: you are an *I*,
> you are an *Elizabeth*,
> you are one of *them*.
> *Why* should you be one, too?
> I scarcely dared to look
> to see what it was I was.

The use of syntax in these six lines is exquisitely precise, the switch between subject and object becoming gradually worked through. The dreams were also asking me to think of myself in relation to male poets and asking me to question the nature of my exclusion from their tradition. They were offering Bishop as a model for negotiating my own sense of my place within a poetic tradition, however minor that position might be.

A

'She was domestic, loved cooking – that too is a good "thinking" occupation: rolling out the pastry, stirring the sauce.' [18]

I want now to return to cookery and to my search for Bishop through my search for the recipe for cooking trout. Throughout Bishop's letters there are references to recipes, and experiments at cooking, whether it's bread or pears and junket or madeleines.[19] Ilse Barker, in her essay 'The Search for Earthly Paradise' writes movingly of her time spent with Bishop in North Haven, how Elizabeth would send them out to

> pick berries while she made pastry in the dark kitchen...The fruit tart would be part of our evening meal which we ate in the old-fashioned dining room...It had a big mahogany table, & here Elizabeth worked sometimes. I remember at any rate she had the table covered with small pieces of paper, typed lines and scrawled lines...and clippings from newspapers...the bits of paper, all higgledy-piggledy, presumably in some order that only Elizabeth recognised.'[20]

This image of Bishop and the insight it gives into her working methods sees her as a creator of *bricolage*, a not unlikely assumption, given her interest in Ernst's *frottage*, *grattage*, and collage techniques; and later her own Cornell-inspired artworks. There's a pleasing connection too that she is busy working at the same table at which later the evening meal is served. Bishop's interest in cookery is in many ways a very simple urge on her part to make, and share, food. It is another nurturing version of creativity, albeit one which

has long been embroiled in the social positioning of women. Yet
Bishop is also ironically aware of using the idiom of cookery to talk
about her aesthetic. In an account of her memories of Robert Lowell,
and their meeting at Randall Jarrell's house in late '46 or early '47,
she writes:

> We talked about poetry a lot; about Marianne Moore, I remember, but
> I don't remember now what we said. In my taxi on the way home to
> Greenwich village my genuine GV garet [sic] I remember thinking that
> it was the first time I had ever actually talked with someone about how
> one writes poetry – and thinking that it was it could be strangely easy
> "Like exchanging recipes for making a cake" [21]

Bishop is clearly using the analogy of the recipe to show how
immediately at home she and Lowell were in each other's company
and makes an oblique reference to her poem 'Exchanging Hats'.
Poems are both ordinary and experimental, acts of science, of weigh-
ing and measuring. They are wholly ordinary in their dailiness, and
wholly essential. They are order tied up in a range of meanings; they
nourish or please. And as every cook knows, the balance between
science and art in the act of cooking is often a precarious one.

Cooking and writing poems are metaphorically and literally
connected for Bishop. In the *Complete Poems* is a poem which
served as an inscription on the front of a cookery book given to
Frank Bidart in 1971:

> You won't become a *gourmet** cook
> By studying our Fannie's book –
> Her thoughts on Food and Keeping House
> Are scarcely those of Lévi-Strauss.
> Nevertheless, you'll find, Frank dear,
> The *basic elements*** are here.
> And if a problem should arise:
> The Soufflé fall before your eyes
> Or strange things happen to the Rice
> You know I *love* to give advice
>
> * Forbidden word
> ** Forbidden phrase
>
> P.S. Fannie should not be underrated
> She has become sophisticated.
> She's picked up many *gourmet** tricks
> Since the edition of '96

Bishop is referring to *Fannie Farmer's Boston Cooking School Cook
Book* (pictured opposite). This is the reissued edition she is giving
to Bidart – the original edition having been published in 1896, with
a dedication to the President of the Boston Cooking-School 'in
appreciation of her helpful encouragement and untiring efforts in

promoting the work of scientific cookery, which means the elevation of the human race'. Although I have only been able to locate a replica version of that '96 edition, it is an interesting and bizarrely key text through which to think about Bishop's aesthetic. The book begins with an epigraph by John Ruskin, worth quoting in full:

> Cookery means the knowledge of Medea and of Circe and of Helen and of the Queen of Sheba. It means the knowledge of all herbs and fruits and balms and spices, and all that is healing and sweet in the fields and groves and savory meats. It means carefulness and inventiveness and willingness and readiness of appliances. It means the economy of your grandmothers and the science of the modern chemist; it means much testing and no wasting; it means English thoroughness and French art and Arabian hospitality; and in fine, it means that you are to be perfectly and always ladies – loaf-givers.[22]

As a diagnostic preface to Bishop's own poems this is extraordinarily apt. Every sort of female power is addressed: Medea whose sorcery allows her to bring forth from a pot of dismembered old sheep a frisky young lamb, maker of sleeping potions and poisons; Circe whose potions and spells allowed her to change men into animals; Helen the most beautiful woman in Greece and the "cause" of the Trojan War; the Queen of Sheba who arrives at Solomon's court with a camel train laden with precious metals and spices and who tests Solomon's wisdom. For Ruskin, the loaf-givers (the female equivalent of the lord, the 'maintainer of laws'), the lady, has a responsibility not only to 'feed and clothe' her dominion but also to 'direct and teach'.[23]

Fannie Farmer's cook book is hardly Lévi-Strauss, jokes Bishop, and yet the book, the first to standardise measurements in the kitchen ('Correct measurements are absolutely necessary to ensure the correct results!') attempts to classify food and the cooking of it in the most 'scientific' of ways. Chapter one, for example, begins:

> Food is anything which nourishes the body. Thirteen elements enter into the composition of the body: oxygen, $62 \frac{1}{2}$ %; carbon, $21 \frac{1}{2}$ %; hydrogen, 10%; nitrogen 3%; calcium, phosphorus, potassium, sulphur, chlorine, sodium, magnesium, iron and fluorine the remaining 3%. Others are found occasionally, but, as their uses are unknown, will not be considered.

Chapter two defines the three essentials for cooking as heat, air and moisture. It includes detailed instructions on how to make a fire, the various ways of cooking and preparing food, and of measuring it, all under tightly defined headings. Again, if we look at the beginning of chapter three we see immediately the appeal of this particular textbook to Bishop. Beverages are classified in the following way:

A Beverage is any drink. Water is the beverage provided for man by Nature. Water is an essential to life. All beverages contain a large percentage of water; therefore their uses should be considered: –

I. To quench thirst.
II. To introduce water into the circulatory system.
III. To regulate body temperature.
IV. To assist in carrying off waste.
V. To nourish.
VI. To stimulate the nervous system and various organs.
VII. For medical purposes.

Freshly boiled water should be used for making hot beverages; freshly drawn water for making cold beverages.

True enough, this is not Lévi-Strauss, but it is uncannily comparable to his own categorising of the modes of cooking which form the basis of much of his thinking. There are similarities between Bishop's joke with the poetic inscription and her use of the geography text book *First Lessons in Geography*, 1884, the questions from lessons VI and X which frame *Geography III*. Bishop had almost certainly read Lévi-Strauss's study of Brazil, *Triste Tropiques* [24] (1955), a remarkable account of his journey from the Amazon basin to the jungles of Brazil and of the primitive tribes he found there. Aside from this particularly relevant connection – Bishop lived in Brazil for many years and wrote a travel book *Brazil* which was published in 1962 – Bishop must have also been more than aware of structuralism – a common method of approaching texts at the time when she was writing – and Lévi-Strauss's structural approach to social anthropology. In the briefest of terms, structuralism was a movement which drew on the work of the linguist Saussure who 'sought the underlying rules of language, the deep structures that must exist if language is to perform its function. These deep structures are independent of the human agents who use language... [the] displacement of the human subject from the focus of interest is one of the characteristics of structuralism'. [25] Lévi-Strauss uses structuralism as a way of understanding social relationships, perhaps most famously in his study *The Raw and the Cooked* (1964). Edmund Leach neatly summarises Lévi-Strauss' complex argument as follows:

It is the conventions of society which decree what is food and what is not food, and what kinds of food shall be eaten on what occasions. And since the occasions are social occasions there must be some kind of patterned homology between relationships between kinds of food on the one hand and relationships between social occasions on the other...
...Our survival as men depends on our ingestion of food (which is part of Nature); our survival as human beings depends upon our use of social categories which are derived from cultural classifications imposed on elements of Nature...food is an especially appropriate "mediator"

because, when we eat, we establish, in a literal sense, a direct identity between ourselves (Culture) and our food (Nature). Cooking is thus universally a means by which Nature is transformed into Culture, and categories of cooking are always peculiarly appropriate for use as symbols of social differentiation.[26]

Bishop's gift of the poem in the cookery book is a coded joke, one East coast poet to a West coast one, a textbook through which to transform the "raw" into the "cooked", experience into the poem (something especially charged for the new Boston school.) But what is the science of writing it espouses?

B

'things good for thinking not just good things to eat'[27]

Although structuralism has come in for much criticism, I'm interested in it in relation to Bishop's work because it works at the same time both for and against her aesthetic. In 'Faustina, or Rock Roses' Bishop questions the way in which interpretations are made:

The acuteness of the question
forks instantly and starts
a snake-tongue flickering;
blurs further, blunts, softens,
separates, falls, our problems
becoming helplessly
        proliferative.

There is no way of telling.
The eyes say only either.

Again, though much more cheerfully, we see this conflict over binary modes of thinking made much more explicit, in a late poem, 'Santarém', where Bishop talks in terms of, but also resists, structuralist criticism in her description of the 'conflux of two great rivers, Tapajos, Amazon':

                ...Even if one were tempted
to literary interpretations
such as: life/death, right/wrong, male/female
– such notions would have resolved, dissolved, straight off
in that watery, dazzling, dialectic.

The temptations of such literary interpretations, which were rapidly being criticised by the advent of poststructuralism which saw structuralism as rigidly authoritarian in its attempt to know the world through such a systematic mapping, are for the poet especially pleasing in their balance and resolution, but also inadequate. The associations Bishop seems to be making are acute. The gift of the cookery book, ironically to a poet who will later write a terrifying study of anorexia in his poem 'Ellen West',[28] is almost like the giving of a book of spells: spells which if they go wrong Bishop will be happy to advise about. And Bishop is very good, as she jokes in the poem, at giving poetic advice.[29] But the joke is also that about a Boston school of poets, a school which has become sophisticated. The impersonality of the poet so famously advocated by Eliot, born eight years before the publication of Fannie Farmer's book, has been replaced by the new Boston school which claimed Lowell as its centre.

E

'the first speech was all in poetry; reasoning was thought
of only long afterwards' [30]

In *The Savage Mind* Lévi-Strauss makes a distinction between two kinds of thought, the mythological 'science of the concrete' and 'modern science'. He defines mythological thought as 'a kind of intellectual *bricolage*, the *bricoleur* performs his tasks with materials and tools at hand, odds and ends.'[31] The modern scientist, however, thinks in terms of concepts. 'The scientist creating events (changing the world) by means of structures and the bricoleur creating structures by means of events.'[32] Art, for Lévi-Strauss falls between magic and science. Yet Bishop, who is often noted for her cool, objective, often scientific, voice, and who, it might be claimed, has spawned a whole poetic school (if not of poets then certainly of poems) I'd like to suggest is attempting in her work, her acute and detailed observations, to tap into universal mythological structures that Lévi-Strauss sees operating throughout the world, while at the same time always probing and doubting the way in which she negotiates the world in language. This becomes especially relevant if we remember the description of her worktable, and again compare this with an early comment on the writing process which she describes as 'an island feeling':

> On an island you live all the time in this Robinson Crusoe atmosphere;
> making this do for that, and contriving and inventing…A poem should
> be about making things in a pinch.[33]

At Bishop's best and most fluent the world becomes not simply, as she wrote to Lowell, material for poetry, but seems to 'be poetry'. 'If only,' she continues, 'one could see like that all the time! It seems to me *it's* the whole purpose of art, to the artist (not to the audience) – that rare feeling of control, illumination…'[34]

T

*'I've eaten armadillo at a game restaurant in Brazil, and boar,
and, long ago in Nova Scotia, bear'* [35]

Considering the number of occasions in which Bishop writes and
obviously takes great pleasure in writing about food in her letters,
it's interesting to note exactly when she does refer to food in her
poems.[36] Perhaps unsurprisingly in the light of her comments about
the connection between writing poems and the art of "making do",
a key occasion is in the late poem 'Crusoe in England'.[37] Defoe's
novel, *The Life and Adventures of Robinson Crusoe* (1719), influenced
strongly by the writings of Rousseau, is revisited by Bishop. The
relationship between Crusoe and Friday, between the tale of the 18th-
century man returned to a "primitive" condition on a desert island
is fascinating in its negotiation of opposition, and its explosion of
any simplistic idea of "Nature" and "Culture". Again, an engage-
ment with Lévi-Strauss looms large in the poem: Lévi-Strauss was
himself a great admirer of Rousseau, and his *Triste Tropiques* con-
tains a chapter called simply 'Robinson Crusoe'. The ambiguity that
the dramatic monologue brings to the poem (a female poet writing
in the voice of a man) and the refusal on the part of Crusoe to
engage in any same sex relations with Friday, in spite of his lone-
liness, dismantles a division of homosexual and heterosexual, estab-
lishing a gendered matrix of a non-binary kind. Here again we find
Bishop interrogating systems of classification while at the same time
being unable to resist the urge to classify. She addresses the anxiety
between nature and culture, the raw and the cooked, to use Lévi-
Strauss's term, and the place of writing in that divide.[38] There is no
literary culture on the island apart from misremembered poems: 'The
books / I'd read were full of blanks; / the poems – well I tried'. Like
so many of Bishop's poems it is aware of its own methods. It moves
between "raw" experience and the basic elements and the over-
prepared gourmet dish that has become far removed from its basic
function, to nourish. Dreams of food and love are "pleasurable" in
their most "raw" form, but become embroiled in the nightmare of
a seemingly endless classification and mistaken classification:

> Dreams were the worst. Of course I dreamed of food
> and love, but they were pleasant rather
> than otherwise. But then I'd dream of things
> like slitting a baby's throat, mistaking it
> for a baby goat. I'd have
> nightmares of other islands

stretching away from mine, infinities
of islands, islands spawning islands,
like frogs' eggs turning into polliwogs
of islands, knowing that I had to live
on each and every one, eventually
for ages, registering their flora,
their fauna, their geography.

The "proper" relationship between man and food becomes disrupted in the nightmares of cannibalism (the goat who becomes a baby) and the endless uncatalogued islands which multiply (unlike Crusoe or Friday who cannot procreate). Crusoe is culture returned to nature. When he returns to "culture" what had become his natural life becomes part of a system of fragments and classification in the museum. Even the knife which used to reek of meaning, says Crusoe, 'won't look at me at all'. The home-made wine which leaves Crusoe dizzy and dancing with the goats is, 'awful, fizzy, stinging stuff', yet it is much more satisfactory than the bored tea drinking of the return to culture. 'Home-made, home-made! But aren't we all?' exclaims Crusoe, thinking of his two pleasures, music, to which he dances, played on his home-made flute, and his home-brew. The resonance of the phrase home-made is vital in its recall of pleasure, cooking, the baby who in the nightmare transforms into the goat, and who is like all human beings, as Crusoe jokes, also 'home-made'. Following as it does 'In the Waiting Room', 'Crusoe in England' continues Bishop's exploration of memory and culture and gender identity. The young Elizabeth of 'In the Waiting Room' is forced to identify across the "nature"/"culture" binary with the 'black, naked women' of the *National Geographic*. Crusoe ends his life in a state of inescapable dissatisfaction with either his "primitive" or his "cultured" existence. His closest companion, who has left his "natural" state has been killed by the "culture" of the white man, having contracted measles.

Although Bishop is perhaps not assimilating Lévi-Strauss's terms directly, her work is clearly negotiating a divide between "nature" and "culture" while at the same expressing postmodern anxieties about the rigidity of placing and categorising the self within such a framework. Her sense of poetry as a special kind of cookery, her frequent references to food, are an interesting dimension not only of her poetry but of her working methods. It seems only appropriate that my own realisation of this dimension in her work followed a circuitous, but I hope not wholly inappropriate, route.

H

'it takes an infinite number of things coming together, forgotten,
or almost forgotten, books, last night's dream, experiences past
and present – to make a poem' [39]

Which returns me to my dream of cooking trout, and something
which I realise only at the end of this essay, that is the absolute of
Bishop's aesthetic. Much of what I've touched on in this essay has
skirted around the gender divide, the difference between men and
women, and Bishop's discomfort with the binary division through
which the world is often classified. The anthropology of Lévi-
Strauss is not a hundred miles away from the interpretations of
Freud and there's a sense that the heightened experience of the
Bishop poem comes from the charge of the told and remembered
dream. My poem 'The Fish' – indebted I realise not only to poems
of the same title by not only Bishop and Moore, but to my nego-
tiation with Yeats and Lowell and Heaney, is about not being able
to find the poem, the poem being centred in the body which it
explores. It is about the poem as dream which one can't remember.
Bishop's silence around poetry, her sense that it happens when she
is not doing it, her refusal to explain, place the poems as sacred,
personal, almost reach the status of the dream. For the poem has
to be 'home made' like the Moose who is homely as a house at the
same time as being strange and familiar and sacred. When I dreamed
of fish, and the cooking of fish it was important that it was Heaney
for whom I cooked, not just because of my own associations between
the two poets. My dream-logic had coded the trout again: spoken
with an overdetermined Irish accent it was less trout than truth.
What I learn from my dreams – themselves however much they
are subjected to the science of psychoanalysis – elusive and them-
selves subject to interpretation by others, and ultimately elusive –
is the importance of Bishop as a role model from whom I can learn.
Not because she is a woman poet, but because she demands of
herself the need to look into the self and transform the self and
the world in the process of writing. And surely that is what is at
the essence of Bishop's work – the "cooking of truth", the pain-
staking, creative nourishing vision of life she gives us, when, in
the words of her favourite poet, we sit down at her table and eat.

*

NOTES

Unless otherwise cited, quotations of published works are from Bishop's *Complete Poems: 1927-1979* or *The Collected Prose*, and of letters from *One Art.* Quotations of unpublished work are from the Elizabeth Bishop Papers in the Vassar College Library.

1. 'Objecting to the Subject: Science, Creativity and Poetic Process in the work of Lavinia Greenlaw and Elizabeth Bishop' in *Kicking Daffodils*, edited by Vicki Bertram (Edinburgh: Edinburgh University Press, 1997), pp.267-76.
2. Robert Lowell, 'For Elizabeth Bishop: 4' in *History* (London: Faber, 1973) p.198.
3. Letter to Robert Lowell, 1949, in *One Art*, p.180.
4. Letter to Robert Lowell, 1957, in *One Art*, p.351.
5. *The Journals of Sylvia Plath 1950-1962*, ed. Karen V. Kukil (London: Faber, 2000), p.322. Henceforth *Journals*.
6. *Journals*, p.516. In the journals Plath also relates one of her dreams, in which she places Marilyn Monroe as her own godmother: a perhaps not altogether useful model, though nevertheless fascinating when considered retrospectively in terms of the iconic status of both women. The figure of the mother was for Bishop always one of unrecovered loss. As a literary mother Bishop is an interesting and difficult case, largely because of her now infamous refusal to partake in anthologies that separated poets on the ground of gender.
7. Interview with Anne Stevenson by the author, 17 November 1999.
8. Elizabeth Bishop, describing 'Varick Street' to Anne Stevenson, cited in Bonnie Costello, *Questions of Mastery* (Cambridge, MA and London: Harvard University Press, 1991), p.27.
9. *Complete Poems*, p.14-15.
10. 'Under the Window: Ouro Prêto, *Complete Poems*, pp.153-54.
11. 'The Trout? Well, the best trout I ate was in July 1964! We caught them in the Leamlara river using jute bags as nets – which was a bit illegal and unfair. Basically, my cousins and myself jumped in the water and frightened the creatures into the bags. The Leamlara is completely overgrown, so you couldn't really fish it with rod and line anyway. The name means the Mare's Leap, so I suppose it's a put down for a river. I don't think its ever drowned anyone. We threaded the fish though the gills and brought them home hanging from our necks. My Auntie Peg cleaned them and cooked them for us. She dusted them with flour, salt and white pepper, and fried them much as she would slices of liver. These were brown trout, and they have a strong flavour. Salmon trout (remember Alisdair's?) are more delicate. And, in the supermarket, I usually go for the farmed salmon trout rather than rainbow trout or salmon. So this is what I do:

Salmon Trout with Sorrel Sauce
1 salmon trout, filleted. A 3lb fish will give 4 good sized fillets
1 big fistful of sorrel leaves
Small tub of Crème d'Isigny
Olive oil, butter, white wine, black pepper
Lemon wedges

If the fishmonger fillets the trout for you, it's a good idea to bring home the bones etc and simmer them in some white wine and herbs to make a stock. Tear up the sorrel leaves, removing all the fibrous stems. Young leaves are best. Gently melt a chunk of butter in a saucepan and add the sorrel. It'll melt into the butter. Use enough sorrel to make a rich green puree. Set aside. Dry the fish with paper towels and brush with a little olive oil. Heat up in the frying pan. It needs to be HOT. Place the fillets skin-side down in the pan. You want to sear the skin so it's crisp (and edible). But once this is happening you can lower the heat. You'll see the pink flesh turn pale as it cooks through, and when each fillet – they take different times – is just about cooked, flip it over for a few seconds and then set aside and keep warm. Splash some wine (or your fish stock) into the pan and swirl it about. Then pour this through a strainer into the sorrel puree. Pump in some black pepper. Then combine the crème d'Isigny a spoonful at a time, heating gently – but it won't curdle. You can judge the balance of the sauce for yourself. It should be tart, and it should be a smooth creamy green. To serve, spoon some of the sauce onto one side of a plate. Then add a fillet, skin down, so it's half on half off the sauce. It looks good, colourful, and goes well with buttered carrots and new potatoes, or saffron rice. And the lemon wedges will add to the effect, though you don't really need to squeeze them because of the lemony flavour of the sorrel...' (undated letter, 2000).

12. *A Reader's Guide to W.B. Yeats* (London: Thames and Hudson, 1959; reissued edition, 1988) p.91.

13. *Field Work*, p.48 (London: Faber, 1979). Published interestingly in the year of Bishop's death.

14. A poem which in turn also recalls Marianne Moore's poem, 'The Fish'.

15. It's a curiously pleasing synchronicity that Heaney turns up in one of EB's late letters at a birthday party for her, organised by Alice Methfessel.

16. Ludwig Wittgenstein, *Culture and Value*, revised 2nd edition, edited by G.H. von Wright, translated by P. Winch (Oxford: Blackwell, 1998) p.28.

17. 'Poem', *Complete Poems*, pp.176-77.

18. Ilse Barker, 'The Search for Earthly Paradise' at http://projects.vassar.edu/bishop/Barker.html

19. Bishop's recipe for chocolate brownies, found in her handwriting in one of her notebooks reads as follows:

4 squares bitter chocolate (or about a cup of cocoa)
4 eggs
$1/2$ cup of butter
$2 1/2$ cups of white sugar
1 cup of flour
2 tablespoons of vanilla
2 cups of chopped nuts

Melt the chocolate and butter together – or, if you use cocoa, melt along with half the sugar and a little water. Cool slightly and beat in eggs and rest of sugar. Sift in flour, add vanilla and nuts and beat. The butter is fairly stiff, doesn't run much. Bake in a <u>slow</u> oven – about 45 mins to an hour, depending on pan, thickness etc. They should be dry on top, just pulling away from the edges, but still rather damp in the middle. Cut in squares in pan and remove with spatula. This makes chewy brownies – for harder kind, use brown sugar and an extra egg – or half brown sugar. Can be made thicker and used hot with whipped cream on top for dessert.

20. See Ilse Barker, 'The Search for the Earthly Paradise'.

21. Box 54.6. Vassar archives 'Lowell reminiscences'.

22. I am so far unable to trace the origins of this quote, but see Ruskin's

Sesame and Lilies (London: Collins). This edition undated, but first published in 1865.

23. See *Sesame and Lilies* p.146-48.

24. *Triste Tropiques* (New York: Penguin, 1992). This fascinating study ends with a desire to give up the desire to account and analyse myths in terms of binary oppositions giving up on the systematic approach to culture in favour of what seems like a much more instinctual knowledge in a marvellously lyrical passage:

> Oh! Fond farewell to savages and explorations! – in grasping, during the brief intervals in which our species can bring itself to interrupt its hive-like activity, the essence of what it was and continues to be, below the threshold of thought and over and above society: in contemplation of a mineral more beautiful than all our creations; in the scent that can be smelt the heart of a lily and is more imbued with learning than all our books; or in the brief glance, heavy with patience, serenity and mutual forgiveness, that, through some involuntary understanding, one can some-times exchange with a cat. (*Tristes Tropiques*, pp.414-15).

25. *Postmodern Thought*, edited by Stuart Simm (Cambridge: Icon, 1998), p.365.

26. Edmund Leach, *Lévi-Strauss* (Glasgow: Collins/Fontana, 1979), pp.32-34. Henceforth, *Lévi-Strauss*.

27. Edmund Leach, summarising Lévi-Strauss, in *Lévi-Strauss* p.114.

28. The poem begins: ' I love sweets, – / heaven / would be dying on a bed of vanilla ice cream...' *Desire: Collected Poems* (Manchester: Carcanet, 1998). The poem compares interestingly, in its desire to establish a female identity, with Bishop's 'In the Waiting Room'.

29. Anne Stevenson has pointed out to me that the joke about words which are not allowed possibly refers to a policy of *The New Yorker*, which had a list of forbidden words.

30. Jean-Jacques Rousseau, 'Essai sur l'origine des langues' (1793) cited in *Lévi-Strauss*, p.38.

31. *The Savage Mind*, referenced by Janine Mileaf at http://www.english.upenn.edu/~jenglish/Courses/mileaf.html

32. *The Savage Mind*.

33. From a notebook written in 1934, cited by Bonnie Costello in *Questions of Mastery*, p.208.

34. *One Art*, p.350.

35. Letter to Frani Blough Muser, *One Art*, p.625.

36. Jonathan Ellis points out, in a letter to the author (3 December 1999), some of the variety of food references in Bishop's poems:

> the first lines of 'The Moose' where Nova Scotia is scooped up as a province 'of fish and bread and tea'; in the same poem the churches are described as 'ridged as clamshells'; also the early sestina, 'A Miracle for Breakfast' about crumbs of bread and coffee; 'the fried fish/spattered with burning scarlet sauce' in 'Jerónimo's House'; the 'mackerel sky' in 'Invitation to Miss Marianne Moore'; the cabbages, lettuces, carrots and pumpkins in 'Manuelzinho'; 'In the Village' is also full of cooking and eating, potato mash, bread porridge, humbugs...

37. *Complete Poems*, pp.162-66.

38. *The Raw and the Cooked* (London: Pimlico, 1994). First published in

French as *Le Crut et le Cuit* (1964). See pages 246-48 for a discussion of the way in which fish are connected with the origin of the rainbow, especially p.246: 'In South America the rainbow has a double meaning. On the one hand, as elsewhere, it announces the end of rain; on the other hand, it is considered to be responsible for diseases and various natural disasters'; and p.249: 'The heroine in the Bororo myth has two aspects. First, she is a bad mother since she abandons her child in order to be able to stuff herself with fish; next she exudes the fish from her body in the form of diseases which kill large numbers of human beings.'

39. Letter to Jerome Mazzaro, 1978, *One Art*, p.621.

JONATHAN ELLIS

The Snow Queen: Elizabeth Bishop and Nova Scotia

Although I think I have a prize "unhappy childhood," almost good
enough for the text-books – please don't think I dote on it.[1]

Elizabeth Bishop was always wrestling with the problem of how to
use biographical facts. A virtual orphan from the age of five, she
was continually haunted by her mother's madness and by her own
subsequent uprootings north and south of the American/Canadian
border. Yet this 'text-book' personal history was never converted
into the standard, confessional portrait. From the outset, Bishop
cast a cold eye on what she would later dismiss as 'Romantic and
self-pitying' poetry.[2] As a student at Vassar in the 1930s, she was
already on her guard against her contemporaries' 'awful emphasis
on personality'.[3] From Brazil 30 years later, she recoiled from the
direction Ginsberg and others were taking, preferring 'the exquisite
form of a tubercular Mozart' to the 'wild electronic wails' of the
Beats.[4] Bishop was not opposed to autobiographical writing per se.
What she objected to was the confessionals' sensationalising of
experience, particularly their celebration of subject over form, of
matter over music. Bishop sought instead for a balance between
reticence and self-exposure, favouring a poetic voice that shifted
its feet, moving in and out of focus, towards and far away from
the reader. As James Merrill states, her poetic 'life [is] both shaped
by and distinct from the lived one'.[5] There is more tension than
harmony between art and life.

In spite of being a prolific letter writer, Bishop was never a pro-
lific poet. While Sylvia Plath completed half of her *Ariel* poems in
a month, Bishop rarely finished more than a couple of poems a year,
resolving 'never to try to publish anything until I thought I'd done
my best with it, no matter how many years it took'.[6] The only trace
of this tortuous rewriting lies outside the published poetry, in drafts,
notebooks and incomplete typescripts. She used this work-in-progress
to write around awkward emotions, grounding and re-routing several
charged memories. The casual tone of her completed poetry hides

the presence of these difficult feelings, but it does not entirely erase them. While her Canadian childhood is referred to explicitly in only a few poems and stories, it can, I think, be felt elsewhere too. Images that preoccupy her in her unpublished reminiscences of Nova Scotia recur in a recognisable form in her published prose and verse, particularly those associated with ice and snow. These images of coldness can be seen both as metonyms for the poet's life in Nova Scotia and for her non-textbook use of these experiences in art.

Bishop took years translating her 'unhappy childhood' into writing. The process was a gradual one, quite different from the epiphanic breakthroughs of her contemporaries. Whereas Plath described childhood memory as a 'complex mosaic' that had to be 'yank[ed]' onto the 'black-and-white of the typewriter';[7] for Bishop, memory was 'always there, clear and complete'. She did not 'even have to try and remember, or reconstruct' it.[8] In 'Memories of Uncle Neddy', for example, the child's grandmother forgets nothing. Her total recall of her son's failings is evoked through the constant motion of her rocking chair which the narrator compares to 'a memory machine'.[9] Bishop seems to have possessed a similar memory machine all her life, continually looking for a clarity of expression to fit her similar clarity of recollection. At the same time she always avoided using biography in the confessional way. As April Bernard states, 'The intimacy that Bishop develops with the reader is best characterised as the sort that Rilke characterised as "true love", wherein two people gaze not at each other, but at a third, shared thing'.[10] The third thing is of course the poem, the 'shared' gift that embarrasses neither poet nor reader.

Bishop's fullest examination of her autobiographical impulses came in her correspondence with Robert Lowell. Her comments on *Life Studies* show her grappling with the problem of how to write about her own life:

> They all...have that sure feeling, as if you'd been in a stretch (I've felt that way for some very short stretches once in a while) where everything and anything seemed to be material for poetry – or not material, seemed to *be* poetry, and all the past was illuminated in long shafts here and there, like a long-waited-for sunrise. If only we could see everything that way all the time! It seems to me *it's* the whole purpose of art, to the artist (not to the audience) – that rare feeling of control, illumination – life *is* all right, for the time being. Anyway, when I read such an extended display of the imagination as this, I feel it *for* you.[11]

Bishop seems to appreciate Lowell's ability to illuminate past experiences through art, however her admiration for Lowell's "new" style of poetry is undercut by her tongue-in-cheek tone. To Lowell's illumination of the life, Bishop adds 'that rare feeling of control'.

This tone of hard-won equanimity – 'life *is* all right, for the time being' – is more characteristic of Bishop's writing than of Lowell's. It lies behind the 'mastery' of 'disaster' in the villanelle 'One Art' and is one of the few constant notes in her writing. In art (as in life), Bishop's 'whole purpose' is to stave off crisis. She does so not by ignoring feeling, but by placing formal 'control[s]' on it. Lowell's failure to practise similar restraint is implicitly criticised here. Her scruples about *Life Studies* relate not to Lowell's '[re]imagination' of biography, but rather to his failure to master emotion through form. Bishop's poetry draws on life too but, unlike Lowell, she never 'display[s]' the results.

This aspect of Bishop's poetics has been commented on by several critics. Penelope Laurens draws attention to the way in which Bishop's 'cool surfaces' reveal 'emotional depth[s]',[12] while Lorrie Goldensohn has also noted the extent to which 'volcanic emotions' are 'cooled into rhyme, and wired into rhetorical figure'.[13] Bishop uses form as a kind of icepack in which to shield and control difficult feelings. Some wounds are obviously more serious than others, which is presumably why she chooses so many intricate structures to bind and protect them. The most awkward feelings tend to be found in the most difficult forms, almost as if the mastery of structure mastered the memory of life at the same time.

Bishop's incomplete work can be seen as a kind of store-room in which to hold memories and sensations too awkward to publish immediately. She raids them for material, retiring there to begin writing:

> Sometimes I wish I had a junk-room, store-room, or attic, where I could keep and had kept, all my life the odds and ends that took my fancy...Everything and Anything: If one had such a place to throw things into, like a sort of extra brain, and a chair in the middle of it to go and sit on once in a while, it might be a great help – particularly as it all decayed and fell together and took on a general odor.[14]

The imaginary 'junk-room' is the place where unpublished material is kept. It is 'a sort of extra brain,' an antechamber connected to the main corridors of composing. Bishop filters biography through several sorting rooms before it can become poetry. Emotion escapes from the waiting room of the notebook only when it has 'decayed' enough to change shape. Metaphors and tropes linked too directly to her childhood never escape the 'store-room'. Most stay in the poet's attic, locked shut, their presence felt in the published poetry only in the 'general odor' of loss.

Metaphors of ice and snow tend always to evoke Bishop's memories of childhood, even if the connections are hidden. In a notebook entry from 1935, she compares her anxiety about writing to the experience of being buried alive underneath an avalanche of snow, akin presumably to memory:

> Somewhat the railroad-snowplow feeling – all the time that has drifted in to be pushed ahead. Trying to hold up your head in the air when all the pressure from below is gone (= the non-importance of the last 2 weeks) and the weight (the future, the arrival) is all on top.[15]

At the time of this entry, Bishop was considering giving up writing to pursue a career as a doctor. These doubts about the future may have been prompted by a delayed reaction to her mother's death the previous year. Marianne Moore certainly thought this to be the case when she commented upon the extent to which Bishop's mother 'must hover over' her 'health and writing' [Moore's underlining].[16] As Moore points out, Bishop's mother is a kind of ghost presence continually hovering over her life and art. Her inability to write is connected to her inability to forget a traumatic past. It is even given a name: the 'snowplow feeling.'

The pressure of these emotions is particularly apparent in a letter to Moore from 1940 in which Bishop compares composing poetry to the experience of having an aneurysm or stroke:

> I have that uncomfortable feeling of "things" in the head, like icebergs or rocks or awkwardly placed pieces of furniture. It's as if the nouns were there but the verbs were lacking...I can't help having the theory that if they are joggled around hard enough and long enough some kind of electricity will arrange everything.[17]

The 'things' in the head, like 'icebergs or rocks or awkwardly placed pieces of furniture', hint at childhood feelings again. Bishop's problem in her poetry is how to dissolve certain emotions into language whilst at the same time freezing others. As she says in 'Memories of Uncle Neddy', 'there are all the memories I want to keep on remembering – I couldn't forget them if I tried'.[18] It is of course impossible to melt one half of an iceberg without threatening the rest at the same time. The 'electricity' that transforms feeling into language runs the risk of charging the wrong emotions. Whilst it may be risky to keep these emotions inside the head, it seems just as hazardous to release them in a poem.

Bishop's desire to control awkward emotion can certainly be heard in a letter to Moore from 1937:

> "Mother-love" – isn't it awful. I long for an Arctic climate where no emotions of any sort can possibly grow, – always excepting disinterested "friendship" of course.[19]

Bishop is actually referring to the cloying love of a friend's mother, but it is difficult not to imagine the phrase also alluding to the poet's own mother. Whereas here she seems overwhelmed by too much 'mother-love', Bishop had in fact complained of receiving too little during her childhood. By placing 'mother-love' within an 'Arctic climate' of cool containment, the poet attempts to prevent its being exposed. The 'Arctic climate' can be seen in its literal sense as a geographical space in which Bishop sets poems and in its figurative sense as a formal technique for enclosing emotional secrets. She is a cold poet in both senses of the term, as a writer fascinated by literal chilly geographies and by their formal equivalents.

Bishop's memories of Nova Scotia are often linked to its literal coldness. In a letter to her Aunt Grace in 1960, Bishop thanks her for a gift of maple syrup and for the memory it awakens: 'Every time I taste it again I remember the time when I was little (about six) and in bed with bronchitis, and Pa put the dishpan filled with snow on the bed and poured maple syrup over it to make taffy'.[20] The taffy's bittersweet taste is a wonderful metaphor for Bishop's entire aesthetic. The cold snow causes the child's bronchitis but the maple syrup acts on it to form a home-made antidote to disease. Playful and sticky like treacle, it runs through the child's hands, distracting her from illness. Bishop's poetry is made out of a similar convergence of two elements to form something restorative. Her sense of humour is poured over a poignant sense of loss creating a language characterised by shifts in tone and voice, as the taffy is characterised by its runny consistency. Her writing plays with the life but is still made from it, just as the taffy obscures the taste of snow but cannot exist without it.

'For C.W.B.' (1929) is a playful version of this process of turning life into art. Bishop wrote the poem at Walnut Hill, a girls' boarding school in Massachusetts. In a letter to her friend Frani Blough Muser in 1928, she copied out the Christmas card note her English teacher, a Miss Prentiss, had given to her. It contained an invitation for Elizabeth to visit her in 'her little cottage by the sea' where 'there is a Christmas moon of clear silver beauty'. There, the teacher promises to share with her 'things that can only be told' in secret. Bishop mercilessly makes fun of the teacher's obvious affection for her: 'Auntie read it and said our friend had an "aching void." All she needed was a little snow.'[21] The proximity of the poem's composition to Bishop's reception of the card suggests some correspondence between the two events. It irreverently mimics the teacher's tone, exaggerating the setting of her 'little cottage by the sea' and her promises of intimacy there. Bishop even adds the 'little snow' recommended in the letter:

Let us live in a lull of the long winter-winds
    Where the shy, silver-antlered reindeer go
On dainty hoofs with their white rabbit friends
    Amidst the delicate flowering snow.

All of our thoughts will be fairer than doves.
    We will live upon wedding-cake frosted with sleet.
We will build us a house from two red tablecloths,
    And wear scarlet mittens on both hands and feet.

In the Christmas card, the teacher promised 'nothing...save friend-
liness & poems & contentment'.[22] By setting the poem within an
Arctic climate, Bishop implies that her teacher's meaning of friend-
ship is more interested than it first seemed and perhaps requires a
little cooling. The 'long winter-winds' and the 'wedding-cake frost-
ed with sleet' are her ludicrous answers to Miss Prentiss' fireside
dreams. The *abab* rhyme imitates the parodic theme of the poem,
particularly its ridiculous half-rhymes (doves/tablecloths, dark/stork,
home/gnome). Bishop takes her teacher's sentimental fantasies for
a walk in the cold. The excessive alliteration ('let us live in a lull
of the long winter-winds') begins the impersonation. The incon-
gruent companionship of 'shy, silver-antlered reindeer' with 'white
rabbit friends' continues it, as does the house built from 'two red
tablecloths' that seems to be taken from the fairy-tales she read as
a child. Even the snow is 'flowering' in this idyllic never-never
land of Bishop's nonsense-inspired imagination as she transforms
the teacher's possibly sexual narrative into a surreal pastiche of
Andersen or Grimm. Her first ice poem follows her later works'
cooling of emotion into literal 'Arctic climate[s]' and figurative
cold forms. She is an expert in adding 'a little snow' to feeling,
both in her comic and serious moments.

The dilemma about how to live with and control feeling is ex-
plored in a more baroque idiom in 'The Imaginary Iceberg' (1935).
Readings of the poem tend to turn on its opening proposition:

We'd rather have the iceberg than the ship,
    although it meant the end of travel.

Lorrie Goldensohn suggests that we might look at the poem 'as
an ironic counterpoint to Kafka's image of the frozen sea, and our
need to plumb our emotional depths'.[23] She sees the poem's apparent
preference for the iceberg as an early rebuke to Bishop's own con-
fessional impulses. Anne Colwell reads the poem in similar terms
as a desire to 'annihilate the self, a way to stop looking, to escape
the body'.[24] Colwell phrases the debate employing a different anal-
ogy to Goldensohn, though it is easy to see how both are using
the same interpretative axis. Goldensohn allegorises the poem into

an emotion/mind opposition just as Colwell speaks of the body
and soul in tension. My misgivings about these interpretations
relate not to a baroque frame being used – Crashaw and Traherne
are clear influences in the poem – but rather to the argument that
the iceberg and ship stay still as symbolic figures. Bishop mis-
chievously unravels the proposition she sets up in the opening
lines of the poem, disrupting the kind of readings Goldensohn
and Colwell bring to it. 'The Imaginary Iceberg' is a baroque
poem as spoken by an unbeliever in absolutes. Bishop is troubled
not by the conflict between body and soul, but by the insistence
that such distinctions exist.

Her use of the ambiguous 'we' through which to voice the poem
is a good indicator of her irreverent intentions. Hiding an 'I' within
its shifting perceptions, Bishop refuses to take a consistent position
herself:

> We'd rather have the iceberg than the ship;
> we'd rather own this breathing plain of snow
> though the ship's sails were laid upon the sea
> as the snow lies undissolved upon the water.
> O, solemn, floating field,
> are you aware an iceberg takes repose
> with you, and when it wakes may pasture on your snows?

The iceberg that for Goldensohn and Colwell represents the mind
or soul takes on the characteristics of an emotional body here. It
is a 'breathing' form that 'takes repose' with the ship, more like a
sleeping companion than a philosophical concept. The ship that
allegedly embodies corporeal desires and feelings in fact becomes a
'solemn, floating field'. Bishop upsets notions of the iceberg and
ship being confrontational figures, warning us not to mistake the
iceberg's cold exterior for a lack of emotional warmth within. She
is by analogy making the same point about her poetry. Bishop's
art may seem cold and distant like the iceberg, but it too hides a
'breathing' life-force within that may wake to disturb the reader.
She encourages us to equate imagination with life, deconstructing
the dualism between art and biography which many of her readers
believe she is protecting.

The poem's theme must be seen in aesthetic rather than in meta-
physical terms, being more about the construction of art out of
the emotional icebergs in the head than any debate between body
and soul. It is possible that Bishop is alluding to her own prose
writings here, particularly to a student essay on Gerard Manley
Hopkins. There, she criticises Hopkins' occasional failure to bring
thought to life:

At times the obscurity of his thought, the bulk of his poetic idea seems
too heavy to be lifted and dispersed into flying members by his words;
the words and the sense quarrel with each other and the stanzas seem
to push against the reader, like coiled springs in the hand.[25]

Bishop's sense of poetry as an exercise in lifting ideas into language
lies behind her description of the iceberg in the second stanza:

> ...The iceberg rises
> and sinks again; its glassy pinnacles
> correct elliptics in the sky.
> This is a scene where he who treads the boards
> is artlessly rhetorical. The curtain
> is light enough to rise on finest ropes
> that airy twists of snow provide.
> The wits of these white peaks
> spar with the sun. Its weight the iceberg dares
> upon a shifting stage and stands and stares.

Bishop takes us metaphorically backstage to see how a poem is
composed, rehearsed and released into being. The iceberg's shift-
ing movements are akin to the 'flying' motion of ideas and words
described in the essay on Hopkins. The iceberg is a figure for the
staging of art, particularly for the staging of poetry. It 'rises / and
sinks again' following the reader's intonation of the poem's metre.
The iceberg's shape also resembles 'correct elliptics in the sky',
perfect geometrical figures akin to the poem's perfect twelve-line
stanza structure. 'Elliptics' suggest ellipsis, hinting at omissions in
the poem which the poet has perhaps covered up or 'correct[ed]'.
Bishop is certainly a 'correct' writer in both senses of the word, as
an artist who adheres to a strict code of emotional reticence and as
a poet who obsessively 'correct[s]' her own work. The 'glassy pin-
nacles' of the iceberg which rise and sink seem to imitate the scored
typescripts of the drafts, corrected and reworked in Bishop's famous
illegible handwriting. The white 'scene' which the iceberg 'treads'
across further suggests the poet's pen cautiously moving over the
page as language warily side-steps emotion.

The iceberg's final appearance in the poem suggests further links
to the drafts. Bishop subtly calls our attention to the poem's pos-
sible relationship to her own life with the sly insertion of the deter-
miner 'this':

> This iceberg cuts its facets from within.
> Like jewelry from a grave
> it saves itself perpetually and adorns
> only itself, perhaps the snows
> which so surprise us lying on the sea.

The iceberg's smooth surface hides 'facets' of detail within, just as Bishop's frigid surfaces conceal similar layers of meaning within them too. The iceberg is cut by division like the poem, the former by crystals, the latter by emotions. Bishop covers up this split through a tight control of form but its existence can still be felt. 'This' iceberg's protection of the poet 'within' anticipates the monument's similar status as a 'shelter' for 'what is within'. The iceberg is compared to 'jewelry from a grave', but it is not a literal coffin for the poet. Rather it is what remains of loss, 'perpetually' saving itself as Bishop saves herself through writing. The final poem is akin to a jewel, hewed out of the 'snows' of childhood and transformed into something as precious and valuable as art:

> Icebergs behoove the soul
> (both being self-made from elements least visible)
> to see them so: fleshed, fair, erected indivisible.

Bishop reflects on the ways in which poetry is constructed and perceived. She is conscious of the poem as an artefact 'self-made from elements least visible', as an object made out of the 'facets' of a chaotic life. The 'elliptics in the sky' hint at the biographical secrets she wants to 'correct' but can never entirely cancel out. Yet at the same time, she acknowledges the human need to see poetry as 'fleshed, fair, erected indivisible', as an organic object connected to the body, to life and to feeling. 'We'd rather have the iceberg than the ship' because it means 'the end' of uncertainty signified by 'travel.' This idea of art hides the self's divisions from view, erecting an ideal of 'indivisible' selfhood in its place, however fragile.

The association of coldness with feeling is particularly explicit in the notebooks written after her mother's death in May 1934. In an entry from 1935, Bishop records a dream in which a ride on a sled downhill leads back to her grandparents' house in Great Village:

> Last night I had a very strange, pretty dream. I was seeing what I told myself was an allegory taking place. A tiny little boy on a little yellow sled was sliding rapidly down through great cloudy-looking snow-hills …Then I realized that the little boy was the moon, going through its various phases out in the sky. I said to myself, wrongly (but the attempt towards the right vocabulary is rather interesting), "Oh, there is the solstice." As I watched, I became the person seated on the sled, wrapped up in blue, I became the moon. I bumped over one cloud and became a snowfall, rolling longer and longer, and the moon was growing full; the cloud reeled off again, and the moon was waning. Then the common falling sensation of dreams began; I shut my eyes and fell, and when I opened them the sled had landed in front of the house in Great Village, and I was sitting on it, still the moon. My grandmother was standing near me, not paying any attention, not having even noticed that the moon had fallen from the sky.[26]

The 'allegorical' meaning of the dream relates to Bishop's remembered sense of loss as a child, particularly to the figurative experience of 'falling' without being noticed. In the dream, the speaker attempts to stabilise herself through language, grasping for the 'right vocabulary' to describe her bewildering metamorphosis. 'Oh, there is the solstice' she remarks as the moon whirls rapidly through its cycle. Bishop's choice of words is 'rather interesting' as she typically understates. The solstice refers to the shortest and longest days of the year. It also describes the apparent standing still of the sun at the tropics of Cancer and Capricorn during these days. Bishop tries to fix the twisted images of the dreamscape into a kind of frieze. The dream refuses to settle though and she is thrown into events more fully, becoming the person in the sled rolling down the hill.[27] Talking to herself about the solstice in the middle of a dream is an incredibly rational thing to do. Bishop tries to control her imagination through a very particular type of language. She pegs back her surrealist tendencies, reading the unconscious through the eyes of a rather pragmatic geographer. This geographical gaze is replaced by the dizzying insistence of the dream's own narrative. Bishop may want to analyse and petrify this story but she does not have the time to do so. The sensation of being continually moved on may in some way relate to her early memories of childhood, shuttled north and south between Nova Scotia and New England. In 'The Country Mouse', she writes of the sensation of 'being kidnapped' by her paternal grandparents.[28] In 'In the Village', the child's mother comes and goes with bewildering regularity. The geography of snow falling, freezing and melting replicates this feeling of dislocation and seems always to connect Bishop to her life. Holding on to the 'right vocabulary' is often one of her best defences.

What Bishop corrects and erases in draft form often underlies the written work. In an early version of 'The Country Mouse', she remembers her first winter away from Nova Scotia with her paternal grandparents in Boston:

> One night after this I was taken to the window in the upstairs front hall to see the ice on the trees...All the maple trees were bent by the weight of the ice; branches had cracked off – the telephone wires were covered too and the thin elms that grew all along the street. It was a great pale blaze of ice-writing filling the vision completely, seeming to circle and circle if one squinted a bit it circled and circled. Two aesthetic experiences – [29]

Boston's snow-covered trees remind the child of her former home in Nova Scotia. The New England maples and elms are similar to the 'sugar maples' of 'The Moose' and 'the yet-to-be-dismantled elms' of 'Poem'. The child's longing to be elsewhere is written on the landscape outside. The features she notices from the window poignantly recall her sense of distance from Nova Scotia. The maple trees are bent double by the weight of the ice and the branches of the elms are cracking. Bishop's coinage of the term 'ice-writing' hints at the way in which she uses geography to expose and conceal biographical secrets. The trees cracking underneath the weight of snow suggest a poet similarly cracking underneath the pressures of memory. The reference to 'aesthetic experiences' shows the extent to which life is always being transformed into art in Bishop's writing. In the published version of the story Bishop corrects this passage, cancelling out any reference to 'ice-writing' or to 'aesthetic experience'. This makes the 'vision' of ice seen from the window a less obvious message in the snow. The child's homesickness is still present in the final draft, but the scene becomes more literal than figurative. Bishop rubs out 'writing' from her written work, creating a seamless, indivisible story which has nonetheless come out of a divided self. 'Writing' is the elliptic biography taken out of the story as much as what is literally left behind.

The phrase 'ice-writing' recalls not only the landscape of Nova Scotia, but also the books and poems Bishop read and encountered there. In drafts for an autobiographical novel about Great Village (late 1930s),[30] she remembers her grandfather's reading of Burns each night:

> We seldom talked much in the evenings. Now and then my grandfather would read out loud, a little from Burns or the Bible…It pleased my grandfather to be able to give us that particular feeling of foreignness – a drop of red wine into the clear yellow of the lamp-lit evenings… Easter never joined in with our feeling for Grandfather's reading. She liked Burns, too – once she had asked grandfather to read "Oh, wert thou in the cauld blast", but almost always she lay on the sofa with an arm across her eyes, her other hand open hanging down so that the white hand lay on the floor.[31]

Lucius' mother, Easter, is detached from the other family members in the room. She is a listless nonparticipant in the grandfather's colourful impersonations. The only poem the child remembers her requesting is Burns' 'O, wert thou in the Cauld Blast'.[32] The poem was Burns' last, written for his friend Jessie Lewars who was nursing him during his final illness. Bishop does not specify why Easter asked for this poem in particular. Spoken by a dying man to his female nurse, its theme of grateful devotion and promise of shelter may relate to the recent death of Easter's own husband. Whatever her reasons for choosing the poem, it is clearly linked in the child's mind with her mother's withdrawal. The 'cauld blast' and 'bitter storms' of Burns' verse are connected to Lucius' and Bishop's loss of mother-love. Bishop alludes to this loss whenever she writes in ice.

A more comical example of ice-writing occurs a little later in the story during the child's memory of attending mass with his grandfather. While the collection is being passed around, the grandfather surreptitiously slips Lucius a peppermint:

> Grandfather then got out a small wad of blue paper, unfolded it and discovered two old fashioned peppermints – the kind that taste like large pills and have CANADA written across them. "Suck it," he whispered gravely, and handed me one. I did, although they always burned and made me terribly thirsty. When I breathed in sharply after eating one of Grandfather's peppermints it was like an icy blast whistling through a belfry.[33]

Lucius' experience is similar to the taffy Bishop remembers her Pa making out of snow. Here the grandfather distracts the child with a peppermint, but Lucius' memory of the poem and by implication, his mother's desperation, still comes through his choice of language. The cold mint has 'CANADA' written across it and resembles a large pill. References to ice and snow in the published work also seem to come from the poet's experiences in Canada, even if they never say so directly. Writing about her Canadian childhood was always an ambivalent task for Bishop. Like swallowing pills, it was both necessary for her health whilst at the same time underlining that something was wrong.

The 'icy blast' of memory penetrates the published poetry too. 'Paris, 7 A.M.' (1935) is typical of Bishop's understated, perhaps even unconscious, use of the Lucius' drafts and fragments which she was writing at the same time. Critics tend to balk at the poem's location of Paris and its date of composition in the midst of the Surrealist movement. Thomas Travisano represents this tendency to read the 'Paris' poetry as 'difficult' when he describes 'Paris, 7 A.M.' as an 'experiment with surreal disjunctions, set in the surrealists' favorite city'.[34] Travisano's reading of the poem's style stops short of a full analysis of Bishop's surrealist use of memory. He takes the Paris of the title literally, instead of realising that the city may actually be a dislocation of her childhood memories of Nova Scotia. 'Paris' is for Bishop what 'New York' is for Lorca, a landscape that encourages recollections of first homes, trampolining both poets back across time and space. This movement away from the literal moment of composition is implicit in the poem's opening lines:

I make a trip to each clock in the apartment:
some hands point histrionically one way
and some point others, from the ignorant faces.
Time is an Etoile; the hours diverge
so much that days are journeys round the suburbs,
circles surrounding stars, overlapping circles.

Bishop began the poem at a friend's apartment in Paris, surrounded
by its owners' collection of antique clocks. It had originally been
titled 'Two Mornings and Two Evenings' in a further nod to the
important theme of time. To Moore's recommendation to cancel
the word 'apartment', Bishop countered that for her, the word
suggested 'a "cut-off" mode of existence' which she wanted to
preserve. Separation from the self and the world she is nominally
a part of, is central to Bishop's sense of the poem's meaning. The
'trip' she makes out of reading the time emphasises this detach-
ment from everyday life. Her perception of the clocks' faces as
'histrionic' and 'ignorant' adds an element of panic to the scene.
The speaker seems to be looking at the world sideways-on, either
literally from bed or figuratively from the perspective of a dream
or a hallucination.[35] Time in the poem is seen as a bewildering
'Etoile', suggesting a constellation of stars and also the star-like
convergence of streets in Paris ('étoile' has both meanings in French).
To imagine time both as a series of marks like stars and as a series
of lines like maps is somehow to transform the way we see and
experience it. The nightmare of clocks all telling different times
relates to Bishop's idea that loss is felt retrospectively long after it
has literally happened, upsetting a person's sense of chronological
order. The speaker in the poem is not so much remembering loss,
then, as re-experiencing it, hence the alteration of time, symbol-
ised by the clocks' transformation into stars. The étoile's second
meaning of a star-like map also invokes geography. The clocks'
'overlapping circles' suggest compasses, the needles of which 'point'
first 'one way', then the 'other'. The poem's sense of place is as
disrupted as that of time. Bishop's 'trip' back in time through
memory parallels the 'journeys round the suburbs' of her mind.
    This is made even more apparent in the second stanza where the
speaker's observations of the courtyard *outside* trigger 'recollection[s]'
of that which lies *inside*:

Look down into the courtyard. All the houses
are built that way, with ornamental urns
set on their mansard roof-tops where the pigeons
take their walks. It is like introspection
to stare inside, or retrospection,
a star inside a rectangle, a recollection:

this hollow square could easily have been there.
– The childish snow-forts, built in flashier winters,
could have reached these proportions and been houses;
the mighty snow-forts, four, five, stories high,
withstanding spring as sand-forts do the tide,
their walls, their shape, could not dissolve and die,
only be overlapping in a strong chain, turned to stone,
and grayed and yellowed now like these.

The speaker attempts to hold on to the world outside by describing
its 'ornamental urns' and 'mansard roof-tops', almost as if she were
a portrait painter or surveyor. Bonnie Costello has written percep-
tively of Bishop's observations 'free[ing] her from herself as much
as they reflect back',[36] though in this instance the reverse seems to
be the case. The exterior, however banal, cannot help but remind
the speaker of her own feelings. Moore recognised Bishop's habit
of doing exactly this in a perceptive letter: 'This exteriorizing of
the interior, and the aliveness all through, it seems to me are the
essential sincerity that unsuccessful surrealism struggles toward. Yet
the sobriety and weight and impact of the past are also there.'[37]
This past begins to assert itself when the poet goes looking for
similes to describe the urban landscape. She compares looking at
the courtyard to 'introspection'. Staring inside the quadrangle
suggests further 'inside[s]': that of 'retrospection' and 'recollection'.
By the time she has reached this point, the 'hollow square' has
been replaced by thoughts of 'there', displacing the here and now.
The hyphen breaking up the stanza has the impact of an intake of
breath before carrying on. Bishop frequently uses it for moments
of emotional drama or change of perspective. In 'The Moose', it
is employed before the bus driver 'suddenly...stops with a jolt'. In
'One Art', it occurs directly before the speaker faces the hardest loss,
that of 'losing you'. In 'Five Flights Up', it prefaces the speaker's
own difficult memories of 'yesterday'. Here, it seems to signify the
emergence of the 'there' of childhood memories over the 'here' of
present day observations. The 'proportions' of memory take over
those of reality, indeed they seem to become heightened reflections
of it, fulfilling Apollinaire's definition of surrealism as 'super-reality'.
Memory's snow-forts are 'four, five, stories high'. Unlike the static
houses, they change shape through time. At first 'childish', they
later become 'might', then 'strong', before finally being turned to
'stone'. Bishop emphasises the permanence of memory over the
impermanence of temporal structures. She significantly associates
recollection with snow again, as if owning up to her favourite meto-
nymy for representing life. The 'walls' and 'shape' of recollection are
defined by the contours and defences of an iceberg-like structure,

surely one of the figures connoted by a snow-fortress, five stories
high. Transformed into stone, 'grayed and yellow', memory can
also be seen as a monument for the poet to read and study. In her
notebook at the time, Bishop commented on the reappearance of
incidents out of the past, comparing them to 'family monuments',[38]
their meanings gradually visible through time. The 'snow-fort' is a
similar monument to memory, whose relationship to Bishop's bio-
graphy is only visible through comparison with the unpublished
material. The 'strong chain' of connections to childhood is an 'over-
lapping' one which takes in all of the genres and structures Bishop
tried.

The final verse turns back to the world of clocks, pigeons and
urns:

> Where is the ammunition, the piled-up balls
> with the star-splintered hearts of ice?
> This sky is no carrier-warrior-pigeon
> escaping endless intersecting circles.
> It is a dead one, or the sky from which a dead one fell.
> The urns have caught his ashes or his feathers.
> When did the star dissolve, or was it captured
> by the sequence of squares and squares, and circles, circles?
> Can the clocks say; is it there below,
> about to tumble into snow?

The 'piled-up balls' of ice are the emotions and feelings yet to be
melted and exploited in the published work, but already being
deployed in drafts, dreams and fragments. 'Star-splintered hearts
of ice', they reveal the poet to be divided again. The language of
assault and war underlines the violent nature of Bishop's auto-
biography. As Goldensohn states, 'dangerous feeling is held at bay'
here.[39] The poem's perspective returns to 'this sky' of Paris, with-
out the 'endless intersecting circles' of memory, an image of intro-
spection and recollection. The clocks cannot say what is 'there
below' in memory any more than the reader can, but at least we
can recognise its shape. 'About to tumble into snow', Bishop places
memory on the threshold of taking off its disguise and revealing its
heart more clearly. It is of course an uncertain unveiling, grounded
in the poem's equivocal final question mark.

'Cirque d'Hiver' (1938) is perhaps a more successful exercise in
controlling loss. Coldness here refers not so much to the pressure of
individual memory, but rather to that of collective memory, espe-
cially as it relates to gender construction. The poem's mechanical
toy is a divided creature. It comes in two distinct parts: the male
circus horse with his 'formal, melancholy soul' and implied supe-
rior intelligence, and the female dancer whose body and soul lack

any defining characteristics. Such at least is the view of the speaker, the 'me' indicated in the fourth stanza. The poem can be seen as an ironic commentary on the rhetoric of sexual politics at the time Bishop was writing (the 1930s), explicitly criticising the ideological bias that favours men over women. In a letter to Moore in 1939, Bishop complained about her token inclusion as the only woman in an anthology of poets James Laughlin was preparing: 'I somehow feel one should refuse to act as Sex Appeal, don't you?' [40] Forty years later, she felt similarly, thinking it was 'a lot of nonsense, separating the sexes'.[41] She always resented reviews referring to her gender, thinking it better to 'be called 'the 16th best poet' with no reference to my sex, than one of 4 women – even if the other three are pretty good'.[42]

Bishop's comic impudence to conform, either to literary trends or to literary criticism, shines through the poem, particularly in its heavily ironic last three stanzas:

> His mane and tail are straight from Chirico.
> He has a formal, melancholy soul.
> He feels her pink toes dangle toward his back
> along the little pole
> that pierces her body and her soul
>
> and goes through his, and reappears below,
> under his belly, as a big tin key.
> He canters three steps, then he makes a bow,
> canters again, bows on one knee,
> canters, then clicks and stops, and looks at me.
>
> The dancer, by this time, has turned her back.
> He is the more intelligent by far.
> Facing each other rather desperately –
> his eye is like a star –
> we stare and say, "Well, we have come this far."

Bishop pokes fun at the performance of masculinity and femininity. The circus horse's formal gestures – his deferent steps forward and his finely-judged bows – mirror the formality of his 'melancholy soul'. He behaves like P.G. Wodehouse's Jeeves, endlessly helpful and awfully well-mannered. The female dancer is similarly bound by the expectations of her sex. 'She stands upon her toes and turns and turns', accomplished in circling the action of the male before taking her position side-stage, a kind of toy version of Salome's dance. Bishop shows the ridiculous nature of such performances. The two face 'each other rather desperately' because the game they are playing is 'desperately' outdated, 'fit for a king of several centuries back' as the narrator remarks rather angrily. The final line of the poem typically employs the ambiguous 'we' to confuse perspective.

The 'we' that 'stare and say' may be the mechanical figures, but perhaps they are also the human speakers of the poem whose relationship is cruelly reflected in the bleak turns of the horse and dancer. The distance either couple has travelled in reimagining gender is perhaps not very 'far' at all. The wintry circus of the poem's title refers to Bishop's realistic perspective on the childish games adult men and women continue to play.

The conflation of personal and collective histories also lies behind the subject of 'In the Waiting Room' (1971). The moment of crisis the poem recalls can be seen in a different form in 'The Country Mouse', written a decade earlier. In the story, Bishop compares her sudden awareness of selfhood to 'coasting downhill...into a tree'. This in its turn refers back to the early dream of tumbling through a snowy Nova Scotian sky. Alice Ostriker has suggested that 'In the Waiting Room' might be a poem Bishop 'waited a lifetime to write'.[43] This seems literally true if we associate images in the early notebooks with images in poems written forty years later. Bishop is using the 'junk-room' of unpublished material again.

Although the poem describes an ordinary experience – the act of sitting in a waiting room on a wintry afternoon – Bishop somehow fills it with the 'general odor' of her life. This is particularly apparent after the ambiguous cry of pain that seems to come both from the Aunt and from the child:

> Suddenly, from inside,
> came an *oh!* of pain
> – Aunt Consuelo's voice –
> not very long or loud.
> I wasn't at all surprised;
> even then I knew she was
> a foolish, timid woman.
> I might have been embarrassed,
> but wasn't. What took me
> completely by surprise
> was that it was *me*:
> my voice, in my mouth.
> Without thinking at all
> I was my foolish aunt,
> I – we – were falling, falling,
> our eyes glued to the cover
> of the *National Geographic*,
> February, 1918.

As soon as the cry comes from inside, Bishop's poetic disguises and mannerisms fall away from the poem. The experience of 'falling' is linked to the 'falling sensation of dreams' in the notebook. The slippage from 'I' to 'we' occurs everywhere in Bishop's poetry and is emblematic of her transformation of personal loss into emotion commonly felt. Trying to 'keep her eyes glued to the cover' is what the poet is always doing. She uses language to give order to experience and to stop herself from 'falling' back through time into memory. Announcing the date 'February, 1918', as she announces the time and location in 'Paris, 7 A.M.', is a way of shoring up the imagination, of grounding it in literal facts and history. And yet the cry still finds a way through.

The 'falling' sensation gathers pace in the poem as Bishop fails to halt the rare exposure of selfhood in writing:

> I said to myself: three days
> and you'll be seven years old.
> I was saying it to stop
> the sensation of falling off
> the round, turning world
> into cold, blue-black space.

The 'round, turning world' is the space of clocks and compasses marking out time and place in a way that reassures us. The 'cold, blue-black space' is the home of Bishop's memories, the Arctic climate without mother-love. Compressed into a metaphor of an icy black hole are all those other images of ice and snow connected to childhood loss. It is perhaps possible to interpret this space as the place within writing, linked to literal and figurative ellipses, where Bishop allows silence or suggestion room on the page. The 'space' can further be seen as a figure or metaphor that seems impenetrable or as the hyphen or parenthesis that prepares the way for releasing emotion. Occasionally it is a secret the poet protects, such as the identity of the speaker or the relationship between art and life. Written in the last decade of Bishop's life, the 'cold, blue-black space' is also the place of death, both of those close to her, such as her lover Lota de Macedo Soares, as well as that of her own, imagined one.

The association of ice with death is everywhere in Bishop's poetry, from the narrator's dream of death in 'The Weed' to the frozen cousin in 'First Death in Nova Scotia'. The Lucius-novel contains a further instance of this trope as the narrator watches the snow melting to reveal something that seems to have the appearance of a frozen body:

> As I walked I noticed that the whole surface of the snow seemed to be separating from the underneath parts, like a semi-clear rind of fruit. There were large pale yellow patches and where the underneath snow had been gullied by the trickle of water it had the appearance of bluish veins running a loose – unhealthy network.[44]

The imagery of 'bluish veins' exposed is a haunting one. It suggests death, perhaps even suicide. In one of Bishop's few recorded memories of her mother, she recalls taking a swan-boat ride with her during which a swan bit her mother's gloved finger, drawing 'a drop of blood'.[45] The snow's transformation into the appearance of veins running loose, like blood, taps into these recollections. Bishop fails to complete the passage, presumably because of the 'unhealthy network' of associations linked to the snow's melting.

In Bishop's published poems and stories, there are a number of similar iced-up bodies. In the early poem, 'Dead' (1920s), winter is the male lover of a dead girl leaving her 'estranged and white and cold',[46] a retelling of the fairy-story of the Snow Queen into Bishop's Snow King. In 'The Baptism', Lucy dies of fever after being immersed in a river still full of melting ice. In 'The Farmer's Children', Cato and Emerson freeze to death hugging each other tightly. Bishop also left drafts of poems about her mother's and grandfather's death, both of which are set in a similar 'Arctic climate'. Each of the poems depicts a child separated from a relative, unable to go back for or keep up with the other person. In the poem based on her relationship with her mother, the fragile ice holds up the child but lets the mother slip through. The mother has to return home for snow-shoes while the child 'slide[s] in shine and glare' on the melting crust.[47] In the poem dedicated to her grandfather, the child is too far behind to reach him and kiss his cheek. 'Please, Grandpa, stop!' she screams: 'I haven't been this cold in years'.[48]

'First Death in Nova Scotia' (1962) is the companion piece to these more private elegies. The title's implied promise of there being more poems to write – this being the poet's 'first death in Nova Scotia,' not her last or only one – is unfortunately unfulfilled. Bishop compresses her published experiments in prose and her unpublished accounts in verse into a poem that uses the narrator's first experience of death to stand in for her many subsequent experiences of it. Bishop's 'little cousin Arthur' was actually her cousin Frank, a two-month-old baby who died when she was four years old. Much has been written on the poem's displacement of emotion onto the objects in the parlour surrounding the dead cousin's body. Anne Stevenson comments on the ways in which 'language circles round the fact of death itself',[49] while David Kalstone perceptively notices the deflection of loss onto the figure of the loon: 'Objects hold radiant interest for her precisely because they help her absorb numbing or threatening experiences.'[50] The loon is another dead body, stuffed and domesticated by Uncle Arthur to accompany the chromographs of the English royal family. Bishop envies the loon's perspective on loss, particularly its reassuring detachment:

> Since Uncle Arthur fired
> a bullet into him,
> he hadn't said a word.
> He kept his own counsel
> on his white, frozen lake,
> the marble-topped table.
> His breast was deep and white,
> cold and caressable;
> his eyes were red glass,
> much to be desired.

The loon's silence can be seen as a figure for the poet's own reticence. Bishop also fills her work with eloquent pauses and spaces. In 'The Gentleman of Shalott', 'half is enough' for the poem's Chaplinesque tramp, fooling about in front of the mirror. In 'O Breath', the figurative space between intimacy and strangeness, between the body and language, is given a literal blank space on the page separating each line. In 'Questions of Travel', Bishop encourages us to listen to the 'sudden golden silence' that gives the traveller time to write and the reader time to reflect. Some form of the ellipsis is used in almost every poem, a feature of Bishop's writing as identifiable as Emily Dickinson's famous dashes. The loon that keeps 'his own counsel' is in many ways the poet's first aesthetic advisor. He replaces the mother's advice to 'come and say goodbye' by offering her an alternative method of speaking: that of art. The loon the child caresses is an aesthetic object more real for her than the dead human body or the distant images of royalty. 'Cold and caressable', the loon is another metonymy for the Arctic climate of the poem where emotions exist, but the growth of which can be monitored and controlled. The 'red glass' eye is the eye of the poet, coveted and desired. In drafts for a piece on the problem of writing poetry, Bishop compared the situation of her grandmother's glass eye to the situation of the artist: 'the difficulty of combining the real with the decidedly un-real; the natural with the unnatural; the curious effect a poem produces of being as normal as <u>sight</u> and yet as synthetic, as artificial, as a <u>glass eye</u>'.[51] The loon's glass eye is the symbol for Bishop's poetic synthesis of the 'natural with the unnatural'. Like the faceted jewel in 'The Imaginary Iceberg', it also keeps the poet's secrets within a cold stare. At the same time, the red eye also suggests the aftermath of grief and the physical effect of crying on a person's eye. It is a kind of semi-opaque mirror, absorbing and reflecting loss.

The transformation of the coffin into 'a little frosted cake' is one
of Bishop's favourite defence strategies. She changes the apprehen-
sion of loss into an icy sweet similar to 'the wedding-cake frosted
with sleet' in 'For C.W.B.' and the grandfather's Canadian pepper-
mints and taffy. The 'frosted cake' cannot of course be eaten by the
child, though in seeing death as 'cake' she seems to imagine it as
something to look forward to, perhaps even to taste. The red-eyed
loon the child relates to also eyes it with desire, perhaps seeing it
as an end to his frozen state, in between life and death, nature
and artifice. James Fenton has recently written about the trope of
suicide running through many of Bishop's poems.[52] The represen-
tation of a coffin as a 'frosted cake' obviously supports this reading.
     Bishop compares Arthur to a doll that has yet to be painted fully:

Arthur was very small.
He was all white, like a doll
that hadn't been painted yet.
Jack Frost had started to paint him
the way he always painted
the Maple Leaf (Forever).
He had just begun on his hair,
a few red strokes, and then
Jack Frost had dropped the brush
and left him white, forever.

The figure of Jack Frost painting the boy red can be seen as a
representation of the poet trying to transform death into art. The
'cold, cold, parlor' of the Aunt and Uncle's sitting-room becomes
a funeral parlor in which the child's dead body can be repainted
and re-adjusted. The poem is also a place of reimagination, an
artist's studio in which loss can be disguised and covered up.[53]
Bishop draws attention to her similarity to Jack Frost who adds 'a
few red strokes' to disguise events as she adds a few metaphors to
disguise emotion. Jack's inability to continue painting the boy red
is perhaps a sign of the child's lack of connection to his homeland.
The red 'Maple Leaf (Forever)' is the emblem of Canada. He is
left 'white, forever', without "home" or roots. Bishop's own dis-
placement from Nova Scotia as a child is re-enacted in the Maple
Leaf's erasure, as if the boy's whiteness in some way reflected her
own blank sense of nationality.
     The poem ends with the chromographs on the wall seeming to
invite Arthur to join them:

The gracious royal couples
were warm in red and ermine;
their feet were well wrapped up
in the ladies' ermine trains.

They invited Arthur to be
the smallest page at court.
But how could Arthur go,
clutching his tiny lily,
with his eyes shut up so tight
and the roads deep in snow?

Bishop balances the royal couples' warmth against Arthur's cold-
ness, contrasting their companionship with his isolation. Their
'red and ermine' offers a further visual counterpoint to his white
figure, 'clutching' a 'tiny lily'. The chromograph is another art
object like the silent loon. Its textured surfaces block out coldness,
keeping the figures perpetually warm. 'Well wrapped up', art is
like a secure parcel protecting fragile material within. In inviting
Arthur 'to be the smallest page at court', Bishop seems to be
employing a page in the sense of a sheet of paper in a book. She
recognises the difficulty of transferring emotion into language which
is why the poem ends on another unanswered question. The exper-
ience of death, both the boy's and the narrator's, is represented in
an image of blindness and suffocation. Bishop uses art to see loss
differently, dipping emotion in cold form and metaphor and warm
humour and sensitivity. The red-eyed poet keeps her 'own counsel',
crying with joy and sorrow.

Although Bishop runs away from biography, she is always being
brought back to the self, like Keats in 'Ode to a Nightingale'. He
is tolled back to the self through the single word 'forlorn'. Bishop
recollects the self – particularly the childhood self – whenever she
mentions ice or snow. In 'The Imaginary Iceberg', nature's 'shift-
ing stage' corresponds to the poet's 'shifting' childhood travels. In
'Cape Breton', images of 'rotting snow-ice' and 'ghosts of glaciers'
hint at biographical secrets. In 'Varick Street', loss of love is con-
nected to the image of a 'captured iceberg / being prevented from
melting'; whilst in 'Electrical Storm' the opposite is the case as
sexual intimacy is expressed through the ecstatic tumbling of huge
'wax-white' hailstones. In 'The End of March', the landscape is as
'withdrawn' and 'indrawn' as the poet's emotions. Its 'lone flight
of Canada geese' takes her back to Nova Scotia again. In her pub-
lished poetry, Bishop uses 'ice-writing' to control the growth and
expression of biographical loss. Yet in a sense the mention of ice and
snow cannot help but remind the reader of the 'snowplow feeling',
of 'icebergs' in the head, and of the 'unhealthy network' of associ-
ations that bind geography and biography in Bishop's mind.

*

NOTES

Unless otherwise cited, quotations of published works are from Bishop's *Complete Poems: 1927-1979* or *The Collected Prose*, and of letters from *One Art*. Quotations of unpublished work are from the Elizabeth Bishop Papers in the Vassar College Library.

1. Unpublished letter to Anne Stevenson, 23 March 1964. From Elizabeth Bishop Collection, Washington University.

2. Elizabeth Bishop: *Conversations with Elizabeth Bishop*, edited by George Monteiro (Jackson: University Press of Mississippi, 1996), p.35.

3. *One Art*, p.13.

4. Unpublished letter to Anne Stevenson, 23 March 1964

5. Cited by David Kalstone in *Becoming a Poet: Elizabeth Bishop with Marianne Moore and Robert Lowell* (New York: Farrar, Straus and Giroux, 1989), p.207.

6. From 'Efforts of Affection', *Collected Prose*, p.137.

7. *The Journals of Sylvia Plath 1950-1962*, ed. Karen V. Kukil (London: Faber, 2000), p.168.

8. From 'Primer Class', *Collected Prose*, p.4.

9. *Collected Prose*, p.243.

10. April Bernard: 'Exile's Return', in *The New York Review of Books*, 13 January 1994, p.16.

11. *One Art*, p.350.

12. From *Modern Critical Views: Elizabeth Bishop*, edited by Harold Bloom (New York: Chelsea House Publishers, 1985), p.136.

13. Lorrie Goldensohn: *Elizabeth Bishop: The Biography of a Poetry* (New York: University of Columbia Press, 1992), p.59.

14. Vassar Archives, Box 72 A3, p.36.

15. Vassar Archives, Box 72 A3, p.38.

16. Cited by Brett C. Millier in *Elizabeth Bishop: Life and the Memory of It* (Berkeley, Los Angeles, London: University of California Press, 1993), p.173.

17. *One Art*, p.94.

18. *Collected Prose*, p.249.

19. Cited by Millier, p.125.

20. Vassar Archives, Box 28.3. 'Taffy' has the consistency of nougat or toffee. It is still eaten in and around Great Village, made by pouring maple syrup over snow as Bishop describes. In Nova Scotia nowadays, it also refers to a type of sweet eaten at Halloween. This version of 'taffy' is made by boiling various types of molasses together which children mould and shape into figures as the mixture cools. (Grateful thanks to Sandra Barry, Ann Marie Duggan and Brian Robinson for "local knowledge" of this and many other Great Village goings-on. And of course for maple syrup supplies...)

21. *One Art*, p.3.

22. *One Art*, p.3.

23. Goldensohn, p.108.

24. Anne Colwell: *Inscrutable Houses: Metaphors of the Body in the Poems of Elizabeth Bishop* (Tuscaloosa and London: University of Alabama Press, 1997), p.41.

25. Vassar Archives, Box 70.10, p.11.

26. Vassar Archives, Box 72 A3, p.25.

27. This shift in perspective from detachment to immersion marks many of Bishop's most memorable poems. It features in the movement of 'At the Fishhouses' from cautious description to quasi-religious affirmation and of course in 'The Moose', in the poem's several gear changes from a literal sense of place to a figurative sense of home.

28. *Collected Prose*, p.14.
29. Vassar Archives, Box 52.2.
30. Bishop uses a male narrator here as often in her published work. The young Elizabeth becomes Lucius de Brisay. Bishop took the name from her childhood Des Brisay friends who summered in Great Village on their grandparents' farm.
31. Vassar Archives, Box 54.13.
32. Robbie Burns: *A Choice of Burns' Poems and Songs*, edited by Sydney Goodsir Smith (London: Faber & Faber, 1966), p.137.
33. Vassar Archives, Box 54.13.
34. Thomas Travisano: *Elizabeth Bishop: Her Artistic Development* (Charlottesville: University Press of Virginia, 1988), p.44.
35. Bishop's Paris painting, 'Sleeping Figure', offers a visual counterpart to this reading.
36. Bonnie Costello: *Elizabeth Bishop: Questions of Mastery* (Cambridge, MA and London: Harvard University Press, 1991), p.3.
37. Cited by Kalstone, p.45.
38. Vassar Archives, Box 72 A3, p.31.
39. Goldensohn, p.105.
40. *One Art*, p.86.
41. *Conversations with Elizabeth Bishop*, p.90.
42. Victoria Harrison: *Elizabeth Bishop's Poetics of Intimacy* (Cambridge and New York: Cambridge University Press), p.33.
43. Cited in *The Geography of Gender*, edited by Marilyn May Lombardi (Charlottesville and London: University Press of Virginia), p.53.
44. Vassar Archives, Box 54.13.
45. Vassar Archives, Box 54.13.
46. Vassar Archives, Box 87.3.
47. Vassar Archives, Box 68.3.
48. Vassar Archives, Box 65.19.
49. Anne Stevenson: *Five Looks at Elizabeth Bishop* (London: Agenda/Bellew, 1998), p.30.
50. Kalstone, p.220.
51. Vassar Archives, Box 68.2.
52. James Fenton: 'The Many Arts of Elizabeth Bishop' in *The New York Review of Books*, 15 May 1997, p.14; later reprinted in *The Strength of Poetry* (Oxford: Oxford University Press, 2001).
53. Bishop's 'Key West' paintings, 'Tombstones for Sale' and 'Graveyards with Fenced Graves', also use the figure of red to signify life against the tombstones' grey representing death. See *Exchanging Hats*, edited by William Benton (New York: Farrar, Straus and Giroux, 1996; Manchester: Carcanet Press, 1997).

VICKI FEAVER

Elizabeth Bishop: The Reclamation of Female Space

If and when I reach the rock, I shall go into a certain crack there for the night. The waterfall below will vibrate through my shell and body all night long. In that steady pulsing I can rest. All night I shall be like a sleeping ear.

('Giant Snail')

Like 'The Sandpiper' whose habit of 'running along the edges of different countries and continents, "looking for something"' Elizabeth Bishop admitted resembled her own life and behaviour,[1] the 'Giant Snail' seems to be another version of a self-portrait. Like Bishop it is a poet/artist who leaves 'a lovely opalescent ribbon' as a mark of its progress and discoveries. Like Bishop it is an explorer who paradoxically longs for a home: who more specifically has a fantasy of going back to the womb, of finding a space that is confined and dark and secure where it will be lulled by a sound like the 'steady pulsing' of a heartbeat. In the prose-poem this remains a dream in the future. However, there are three poems – 'The Fish', 'Filling Station' and 'The Moose' – in which, I want to argue, Bishop creates versions of wombscapes not just as imagined retreats, or resting places from the difficulties of her life as woman and poet, but as actual spaces that becomes spaces of transformation and/or revelation. They are spaces that like the crack in the rock also bear a physical resemblance to a womb. They are spaces that are also characterised by rhythmical patterns that echo the 'steady pulsing' of the heart-beat, or the introduction of non-verbal sounds, or the kind of slippages of language and meaning that – like the chora of Kristeva's semiotic – erupt within and disrupt symbolic language. They are spaces where, I would suggest, Bishop reclaims not just the female space from which she was ejected at birth, but the psychic female space lost to her in early childhood through her mother's severe mental illness and subsequent incarceration in an asylum. Paradoxically, they all are spaces created not, as one would expect, in the female interiors of the home but in the traditionally male domains of a boat, a garage, and a bus.

The traditionally female space of the home is almost always in Bishop's work a place of pain and loss, of psychic and actual chill. The 'cold cold parlour' of 'First Death in Nova Scotia', for example, is the place where Jack Frost has visited the corpse of cousin Arthur, painted a 'few red strokes on his hair' and 'dropped the brush / and left him white for ever'. The house in 'Sestina' is cold despite its Little Marvel Stove. There are attempts at normality. The grandmother cuts bread and says 'It's time for tea now', and the child, like a normal child, 'draws a rigid house / and a winding pathway'. But the man she puts in the house has 'buttons like tears'. The grandmother's teacup is 'full of dark brown tears'. The child's obsession with seeing tears in everything – 'tears' is one of the repeating end words of the form – overwhelms all efforts to pretend there is nothing wrong, to conceal, what is never stated but is nevertheless understood, that her actual father and mother are missing. The only house that can be called a "a home" – a house with hot food ('one fried fish / spattered with burning / scarlet sauce') and children's clutter, and battered beloved objects ('an old French Horn repainted with aluminum paint') – is a man's house, 'Jerónimo's House'. Even that is fragile, 'perishable', a 'grey wasps' nest / of chewed up paper / glued with spit', a 'shelter from the hurricane'.

This split between the anxiety associated with the conventionally female space of a home and the relative security of a male domain is most obvious in Bishop's autobiographical story 'In the Village'. Here the grandparents' house is a place of broken off conversations, of ominous and 'awful' words. It echoes with the scream of a mad and unpredictable mother who comes and goes and finally never returns. Nate's forge, in contrast, although potentially a dangerous place with its coals that 'blow red and wild' and 'tub of night-black water' where the horseshoes 'drown...hissing, protesting', appears to the child to exude security and comfort. It's smelly and filthy. Nate is 'sweating hard' and has 'a sooty black face' and there are 'black and glistening piles of dust in every corner'. But everyone feels 'at home'; even the horse – manure piling up behind him – is 'very much at home'. It is a place associated with sounds rather than with language: 'the creak of bellows', the horse stamping its foot. From a distance the clang of the hammer on the anvil sounds 'pure and angelic': a sound that 'turns everything else to silence', even the mother's 'frail almost-lost scream'. It radiates from a space that in its blackness and warmth seems to have implanted itself in Bishop's imagination as a kind of home/womb, a substitute space of maternal nurture; a space in which substances like tar and horse shit and dust and soot become sanctified. It's a version of this space,

I will argue, that Bishop constructs in the three poems I want to consider.

The location of 'The Fish' – a boat on the open sea – couldn't apparently be less homely or feminine. Bishop sent the poem to Marianne Moore with the deprecatory warning: 'I am sending you a real "trifle". I'm afraid it is very bad and, if not like Robert Frost, perhaps like Ernest Hemingway! I left the last line on so it wouldn't be, but I don't know...' [2] It shows Bishop not just "taking on a man's subject" – the capture of a huge fish – but also the already legendary writer who dominated the big game genre.[3] The poem's opening boast, with its emphasis on size, seems to deliberately mimic the beginning of a fishing yarn:

> I caught a tremendous fish
> and held him beside the boat
> half out of water, with my hook
> fast in a corner of his mouth.

It's rather like the cock's crow of 'Roosters', a poem Bishop wrote at the same time – just after the outbreak of World War Two – that relates even more directly to the desire for domination and possession.

Hemingway's *The Old Man and the Sea* wasn't published until 1951, eleven years after Bishop's poem. But its story of an old man whose open boat was dragged out to sea for two days and two nights behind a huge marlin was contained in an essay Hemingway published in *Esquire* in 1936 and may well have provided inspiration for the poem.[4] The five hooks embedded in Bishop's fish's jaw reveal the history of a fish equally determined to evade capture. But while Hemingway's emphasis in the essay is on the heroic battle between man and fish, particularly on the endurance of the fisherman, the emphatic denials of Bishop's poem deny her narrator any possibility of heroic action:

> He didn't fight.
> He hadn't fought at all.
> He hung a grunting weight,
> battered and venerable
> and homely. Here and there
> his brown skin hung in strips
> like ancient wallpaper,
> and its pattern of darker brown
> was like wallpaper:
> shapes like full-blown roses
> stained and lost through age.
> He was speckled with barnacles,
> fine rosettes of lime,

and infested
with tiny white sea-lice,
and underneath two or three
rags of green weed hung down.
While his gills were breathing in
the terrible oxygen
– the frightening gills,
fresh and crisp with blood,
that can cut so badly –
I thought of the coarse white flesh
packed in like feathers,
the big bones and the little bones,
the dramatic reds and blacks
of his shiny entrails,
and the pink swim-bladder
like a big peony.
I looked into his eyes
which were far larger than mine
but shallower, and yellowed,
the irises backed and packed
with tarnished tinfoil
seen through the lenses
of old scratched isinglass.
They shifted a little, but not
to return my stare.
– It was more like the tipping
of an object toward the light.

Bishop had first-hand experience of fishing – she'd just been on a
canoe trip with a harpoon through the 10,000 Islands. But her
narrator is far less concerned with describing the capture of the
fish than with describing its appearance and the response to it. After
the initial active verb 'I caught', all the verbs attached to the 'I' of
the poem are concerned with seeing and meditation: 'I thought', 'I
looked', 'I stared and stared'. The poem's main source seems to be
Bishop's habit of precise observation and note-taking. In a letter,
written to Marianne Moore, just before writing it, she described a
parrot fish she caught as 'all iridescent, with a silver edge to each
scale, and a real bill-like mouth just like turquoise; the eye is very big
and wild, and the eyeball is turquoise too – they are very humorous-
looking fish'.[5] The letter went on: 'Mrs A. is confronting a huge
fish in the kitchen right now – Red Snapper, but it is gilt-rose.'
The poem focuses not just on the exterior of the fish but on the
painterly yet unsqueamishly accurate details of its interior anatomy.
The 'dramatic reds and blacks / of his shiny entrails, / and the pink
swim-bladder / like a big peony', for instance, could only have been
described by someone who had given close attention to gutting a
dead fish.

The poem also owes something to Marianne Moore's animal poems. It is both a homage to Moore's fish that 'wade / through black jade' and a kind of dare, an assertion of difference, a challenge from a rebellious literary daughter to her literary mentor/ mother. Whereas Moore's fish are generic, and held at a distance by the decorative language, Bishop's fish is confronted in the flesh, a 'grunting weight'. He is infested with lice (Moore had objected to the plainer, more direct word 'lousy' in an earlier draft).[6] Bishop's narrator literally holds his life in her hands as she hauls him out of the sea, 'element bearable to no mortal', and into her element that is death to him, where he can only suffer – 'breathing in the terrible oxygen'.

In a sense the poem is about capture. Bishop tries to hold the fish within the framework of her poetic psyche, to contain his alien being within imagery borrowed from house and home that, as Helen Vendler has shown, is her way of domesticating the strange.[7] She begins almost sentimentally by describing him as 'battered and venerable / and homely'. But the pursuit of noting precise visual detail reveals his body as a palimpsest where she cannot avoid reading ruin ('his brown skin hung in strips / like ancient wallpaper'), and nature's attack on the weak ('infested / with tiny white sea-lice'), and the vulnerability of flesh ('the frightening gills, / fresh and crisp with blood, / that can cut so badly'). There is a witty surrealism in a fish skin that resembles a pattern of full-blown roses on wallpaper, or fish flesh packed in like feathers in pillows, but the effect is far more to emphasise the otherness of the fish than to render it familiar. He is in fact not 'homely' at all. When she looks into his eyes –'irises backed and packed / with tarnished tinfoil / seen through the lenses / of old scratched isinglass' – she confronts doubly insuperable barriers to the return of her gaze. 'The most satisfaction,' Hemingway argued in his essay, 'is to dominate and convince the fish and bring him intact in everything but spirit to the boat as rapidly as possible.' But though physically Bishop's fish doesn't put up a fight, his spirit remains intact.

He is utterly resistant to her gaze. His 'eyes shifted a little, but not / to return my stare'. The fish refuses to be contained in a domestic feminine world, so Bishop shifts the metaphorical frame to the masculine world of war:

I admired his sullen face,
the mechanism of his jaw,
And then I saw
that from his lower lip
– if you could call it a lip –

grim, wet, and weaponlike,
hung five old pieces of fish-line,
or four and a wire leader
with the swivel still attached,
with all their five big hooks
grown firmly in his mouth.
A green line, frayed at the end
where he broke it, two heavier lines,
and a fine black thread
still crimped from the strain and snap
when it broke and he got away.
Like medals with their ribbons
frayed and wavering,
a five-haired beard of wisdom
trailing from his aching jaw.

The body of the fish now becomes the site where she can read his history as soldier. In recording the evidence of his survival instinct and courage – the 'weaponlike...five big hooks' and their trailing pieces of fish-line and wire leader and swivel that have 'grown firmly in his mouth' – she combines the metaphoric skills of the poet with forensic eye of the pathologist. Ironically, the fish is finally "captured" in language that discovers a human equivalent for his record of breaking free from capture. The hooks and broken lines are 'like medals with their ribbons / frayed and wavering, / a five-haired beard of wisdom'. The fish's victory is also the poet's victory.

What Bishop admired reading Darwin, she wrote to Anne Stevenson, 'was the beautiful solid case being built up out of his endless, heroic *observations*, almost unconscious or automatic – and then comes a sudden relaxation, a forgetful phrase, and one feels that strangeness of his undertaking, sees the lonely young man, his eye fixed on facts and minute details, sinking or sliding giddily off into the unknown'.[8] It couldn't be a better description of what happens at the end of the 'The Fish' when Bishop's eye suddenly slides away from the recording details of the fish to the interior of the boat:

I stared and stared
and victory filled up
the little rented boat,
from the pool of bilge
where oil had spread a rainbow
around the rusted engine
to the bailer rusted orange,
the sun-cracked thwarts,
the oarlocks on their strings,
the gunnels – until everything
was rainbow, rainbow, rainbow!
And I let the fish go.

There is no doubt that the passage draws on a conscious, allusive and sophisticated, verbal wit. The rainbow, appearing as a sign of God's covenant with Noah when the waters of the Flood receded, is a symbol of peace and reconciliation, of a bridge between this world and heaven. It is also visually witty: an oily film literally creates an all-over rainbow sheen. But in the sudden linguistic slippage by which 'victory' becomes identified with the oil there is also a sense of it operating on a level that is half unconscious, of Bishop 'sliding giddily off into the unknown'. The hollow interior of the boat – one of Freud's dream symbols of for the uterus,[9] literally a "vessel" – becomes a fluid "wombscape" where the oil from the bilge, normally in the context of boats, a substance with negative associations, is sanctified by its association with rainbow. It becomes holy oil, spreading its rainbow on each object, named in turn, to each appended a description of the damage of age and use, like a kind of blessing. 'Nothing mundane is divine', Marianne Moore asserted.[10] As if Bishop was proving the opposite, the list of mundane objects in the interior of the boat becomes charged like the language of prayer. The litany of words that touch each other with assonance and strings of repeated 'l's and 'r's – 'filled', 'oil', 'bilge', 'pool'; rented', 'rainbow', 'around', 'rusted', 'orange', 'cracked', 'thwarts', 'oarlocks', 'strings', 'everything', 'rainbow' – slows the rhythm almost to a standstill. The final repetition of 'rainbow, rainbow, rainbow' breaks into the poem as a radiance of both colour and "pure sound", a repeated rhythmic pulse like the clang of the forge, spreading out into space and time.[11] The passage moves the reader, it could be argued, because it has a *jouissance* that is in excess of logical meaning; because it is taken over by a beat that is more primitive and instinctual than the artificial metres of poetry that resembles the rhythmic flow of sounds heard by the baby in the womb.[12]

The final line of the poem, 'And I let the fish go', deliberately reverses the expectations of the first line. Bishop transforms a narrative about possession and domination and death into one about sympathy and survival and the triumph of love. It is interesting to set the poem alongside the work of two other women writers who tackle the subject of masculine aggression. For instance, in her poem 'Fishing Off Nova Scotia' Sharon Olds also employs domestic imagery ('hooks jerking / like upholstery needles through the gills') and implies feminine values opposed to the 'blood culture' of the male.[13] But unlike Bishop's boat that is transformed into a womb/shrine where the only possibility is to let the fish go, Olds' womb/boat remains a place of torture and slaughter, where the instinct to kill is passed onto the next generation. It is the site of a massacre where Olds' voice is silenced by 'the steel cracking of those clenched jaws, the bright glaze of blood on the children'.

The other comparable writer is Stevie Smith. Bishop's process of coming to know the fish – allowing him the dignity of his otherness, but also placing him in a discourse that respects his achievement in human terms and acknowledges his history as an individual – is the exact reverse of the process by which Smith's protagonist in her pre-war novel *Over the Frontier* summons the necessary detachment to kill one of the enemy. She has to dehumanise him – transforming him from individual to just another 'rat-face' seen in a crowd: 'the nostrils splayed and broken at the edges, the flat nose, the saliva dripping from too slackly open lips, the teeth, long, yellow, filthy, like dog's fangs'.[14]

In her poem 'Fish, Fish',[15] Smith, like Bishop, acknowledges the fish's otherness that resists human attempts to 'catch' him: 'Underneath the brook dim / Sits the fish, / He sits *on* the hook / It is not *in* him.' But her encounter with the fish is really an excuse for an escapist fantasy. She wants the fish's freedom: to leave her entrapment in this world to go to him, to be 'happy...in the watery company of his kingdom'. The fish is another of her incarnations of welcome death. The encounter with the fish enriches Bishop's world. It provides her with an emblem of heroism and survival. It helps her recover a sense of the oneness that is lost at the moment of birth, and reach out to a sense of a nurturing power within and beyond the material. It counters her aggressive instincts – the desire to dominate and possess – with sympathy and understanding. The last sentence of Smith's novel is: 'Power and cruelty are the strength of our life, and in its weakness only is there the sweetness of love.' In 'The Fish' Bishop comes to a radically different conclusion. Power in the poem resides not in capturing and killing a fish but in releasing it and letting it live. What triumphs is the feminine instinct towards life.

'Filling Station' is a much lighter poem but it also ends with a transcendent sense of maternal nurture and love. Like 'The Fish' it is located in a place traditionally occupied by men: a space that is not just 'dirty' – the word is repeated three times in the poem – but potentially dangerous:

> Oh, but it is dirty!
> – this little filling station,
> oil-soaked, oil-permeated
> to a disturbing, over-all
> black translucency.
> Be careful with that match!

The final warning reinforces the illusion, achieved partly through the use of the present tense, that we are there with the poet, making the same discoveries. The overall oiliness is reminiscent of the boat in 'The Fish'. It also connects with the forge of 'In the Village'. Like Nate, the blacksmith, with his 'sooty black face', the 'Father' and 'several...greasy sons who assist him / (it's a family filling station)' are 'all quite thoroughly dirty'. The garage is filled with things that would normally be in a home. These objects have all become impregnated with oil and dirt – 'a set of crushed and grease- / impregnated wickerwork; / on the wicker sofa / a dirty dog, quite comfy'. But as with the forge, the blackness and dirtiness seems to contribute to the feelings of homeliness and comfort.

The more the narrator elaborates the details of what she sees – 'a big hirsute begonia', comic books lying on 'a big dim doily' that on closer inspection is 'embroidered in daisy stitch / with marguerites... and heavy with gray crochet' – the more strange, even bizarre are her discoveries. In this normally unquestionably male space, permeated with grease and filth, there are not just the necessary objects of domesticity but those objects that are 'extraneous' to it, that are part of the inexplicable human desire not just to create shelter and comfort but to be "at home".

In a wonderfully witty last stanza, Bishop draws the conclusions from the evidence the poem has presented that

> Somebody embroidered the doily.
> Somebody waters the plant,
> or oils it, maybe. Somebody
> arranges the rows of cans
> so that they softly say:
> ESSO—SO—SO—SO
> to high-strung automobiles.
> Somebody loves us all.

Of course it is a joke that in such an oily place somebody maybe oils the plant. It is a joke that the cans of oil are placed in such a way as to read 'ESSO—SO—SO—SO' – the phrase, Bishop explained that 'people use to calm and soothe horses'.[16] It is a witty continuation of this line of humour that the automobiles, like thoroughbred horses, are 'highly strung'. But, as the surprising last line of the poem conveys, it is also serious. 'Somebody loves us all' has meanings on a range from the most banal to the most profound. 'Somebody' could be anyone from a mum to a supernatural power. The poem is ambiguous. There is certainly no mention of a mother. But there is a sense of maternal nurture. 'Filling Station', although the domain of the male, is gendered as female space – through the

domestic details but also by less overt features that I would argue
help create a sense of a wombscape. The oiliness of the poem
operates like the oiliness in 'The Fish'. It touches and sanctifies
everything like holy oil. The 'ESSO—SO—SO—SO' whispered by the
cans – that sound that soothes horses – a sound already prepared
for in the sibilant repetitions of 'someone' – is like the comforting
ssshushing to sleep sound made to small child.

There's a painting of a filling station by the American painter
Edward Hopper – 'Gas' (1940). It is set on a lonely road that is
bordered by a forest of close-packed firs. The only human figure
is the pump attendant but the light coming from the pumps and
from the illuminated sign and the windows of little white clap-
board building with its unnecessarily decorative red roof suggests
a welcoming homeliness. It's almost as if Bishop had entered that
filling station and set her poem there. I mention it because the final
poem I want to look at, 'The Moose', also connects with Hopper's
image of rural mid-20th century America. Its moment of epiphany
occurs at the moment that the moose emerges onto the road from
an 'impenetrable wood' that I imagine as being exactly like the
forest in the painting.

Again the subject of the poem – a journey on the open road –
is ostensibly a male one. Kerouac's *On the Road*, published in 1957,
was just a development of the quest/journey theme that is a con-
stant in male literature from *The Odyssey* onwards. However, the
emphasis in Bishop's poem, begun in the 1940s [17] but not finished
and published until 1972, is not on the heroic or picaresque adven-
tures of the poet, or the growth of the poet's mind, but on the
immediate, intense sensual experiences of the journey. This is not
a pilgrimage or spiritual quest. It is the everyday journey of a
provincial bus: the record of Bishop's actual return journey from a
visit to the Great Village of her childhood in 1946. If it ends with
a sense of revelation, of having discovered something as amazing
as the Holy Grail, it is simply because Bishop has stuck to her
process of 'endless heroic *observation*'.

There are many commentaries on the poem. I intend only to
focus on what interests me most in the context of this paper: the
element of female space. From the moment, at one of the bus's
stops, a woman is glimpsed shaking 'a tablecloth out after supper'
a sense of female experience as central begins to creep into the
poem. Another woman 'climbs in / with two market bags, / brisk,
freckled, elderly.' We hear her voice: '"A grand night. Yes, sir, /
all the way to Boston"' – a voice that uses a word like 'grand' in
the colloquial sense and context in which it would never be used

in literature. Then we hear 'Snores. Some long sighs.' Then

> A dreamy divagation
> begins in the night,
> a gentle, auditory,
> slow hallucination....

As in the previous poems there is a womb-like space (in this case
the dark capsule of the night bus), and a sense of sound that is
rhythmical, incantatory, outside logical discourse. Again there is a
sudden slippage, a transformation by which the overheard mur-
mur of the passenger's voices become 'Grandparents' voices /
uninterruptedly / talking, in Eternity', discussing the tragedies and
disasters of life: 'deaths, deaths and sicknesses;' and the things
that particularly blighted Bishop's life, alcoholism and madness:

> He took to drink. Yes.
> She went to the bad.
> When Amos began to pray
> even in the store and
> finally the family had
> to put him away.
>
> "Yes..." that peculiar
> affirmative. "Yes..."
> A sharp, indrawn breath,
> half groan, half acceptance,
> that means "Life's like that.
> We know *it* (also death)."

That 'yes' – the affirmative 'yes' to life of Molly Bloom's soliloquy,
the 'yes' that here isn't even a word (that doesn't belong to lan-
guage of lack and desire) but is just 'a sharp indrawn breath' –
somehow redeems the catalogue of human sorrow. As Bishop
revealed in a letter to James Merrill, it is the reassuring sound
characteristic of the Nova Scotia voice that she had remembered
from childhood:

> But one thing struck me – calling on the woman who now lives in my
> grandparents' house. She was entertaining the lady who runs the vil-
> lage telephone switchboard for tea – so there were five ladies, with my
> aunt, cousin and me. They ALL, except me, did that queer thing with
> the indrawn breath, saying "ye-e-es" to show sympathetic understand-
> ing. I wish I could imitate it better – it is almost an assenting groan.[18]

It is typical of Bishop's skill as a poet that she could incorporate
this 'indrawn breath' into her poetic, subverting but also enriching
it, creating a sense of rhythmical trance, of a secure space in which
it is 'all right now / even to fall asleep'.

It is just at this moment that 'the bus driver / stops with a jolt, /

turns off his lights' and the moose appears:

> A moose has come out of
> the impenetrable wood
> and stands there, looms, rather,
> in the middle of the road.
> It approaches; it sniffs at
> the bus's hot hood.

In a poem where the language is of the utmost simplicity the word 'impenetrable' stands out, halting the narrative almost as much as the emergence of the moose. 'Impenetrable' implies the physical denseness of the wood. But it also implies a space that it is impossible to enter: a space of unfathomable mystery. It's a 'wood' rather than forest because of the rhymes with 'road' and 'hood'. But 'wood' anyway is the simpler word, the word that Freud associated with women in dreams,[19] that for Jung was the symbol of the Great Mother,[20] the word for the place that in our culture and literature is a space of darkness and mystery and also of transformations and enchantments.

The moose that emerges from this female space[21] is 'Towering, antlerless, / high as a church, / homely as a house / (or, safe as houses).' In phrases that show our dependence on and need for the reassurances of language that is repeated until it is almost meaningless the moose is given both sacred and homely associations. It is huge, appearing as much larger than it in fact is: like the imago of a parent in a child's psyche, like a god, or goddess it turns out – ' "Look! It's a she!" ' someone 'childishly, softly' exclaims.

It's interesting to compare Bishop's account of the appearance of the moose in her letter because it reveals how important it was to her that the creature in the poem was female:

> Early the next morning, just as it was getting light, the driver had to stop suddenly for a big cow moose who was wandering down the road. She walked away very slowly into the woods, looking at us over her shoulder. The driver said that one foggy night he had to stop while a huge bull moose came right up and smelled the engine. "Very curious beasts," he said.[22]

The extraordinary image of the bull moose smelling the engine – a creature's negotiation by smell and touch – was too good to miss out. But in one of the few instances in Bishop's poems where "the facts" can be seen to be altered, the detail was transposed to the cow moose.

The sense of childish wonder is not confined to a few of the passengers. As the moose, 'taking her time,...looks the bus over, / grand, otherworldy', the poet asks 'Why, why do we feel / (we all feel) this sweet / sensation of joy?' Significantly, 'grand' repeats the word of the woman passenger who earlier applied it to the night. It is a word from colloquial speech that can't be directly translated but that implies 'wonderful'. It's used here in a sense that takes on as well the multiple meanings in the dictionary: 'of the most or great importance', 'imposing', 'impressive', 'great and handsome', 'dignified'. 'Otherworldly' might strike us as farfetched if it wasn't that it has already been established that the moose has emerged from an 'impenetrable wood', a place of mystery, that her scale is "out of this world". But why the 'sensation of joy'? Bishop doesn't answer the question. It's left to hang in the air until the quiet driver comes in with the more down to earth comment – ' "Curious creatures…Look at that, would you" ' – that Bishop "lifted" from her letter. What follows are more pure sounds – the driver 'rolling his *r*'s', the shifting gears – rather than rational explanations. To try and answer the question, the poem suggests, is as impossible as it is to enter 'the impenetrable wood'. I don't know either: except perhaps that there is a sense of a "visitation" from another world. A creature greater, grander than us has stopped the bus, a creature that is female (but with none of the pejorative associations of lack, or inferiority associated with the female), and has done it at a point when already – in the lulling whispers of the night bus – Bishop has created a sense of the nurturing and redeeming power of female space.

Finally, as the bus moves on the moose is left behind on the 'moonlit macadam'. All that is left is 'a dim / smell of moose, an acrid / smell of gasoline.' It could be argued that the 'acrid / smell of gasoline' is introduced as a way of bringing the poem back from the 'otherwordly' to an unpleasant reality. But I would argue, that as with the oil and grease and dirt of the other poems, a smell that might normally be repugnant here becomes sanctified by association with the female smell of the moose. Bishop leaves us with the smell because it is one of the strongest aids to memory. As incense is used in a church, the lingering mingled smells of moose and gasoline allow the 'sweet sensation of joy' to go on.

'The settings, or descriptions, of my poems are almost invariably just plain facts – or as close to the facts as I can write them', Bishop wrote. But she prefixed this statement by the acknowledgement: 'It takes an infinite number of things coming together, forgotten, or almost forgotten, books, last night's dream, experiences, past and present – to make a poem.' [23] What I have tried to do in this paper is to suggest ways in which the 'plain facts' of these poems are assembled in a way that is not just determined by language and form, or the ostensible subject, but, as Bishop recognised, by the coming together of other things, 'forgotten, or almost forgotten'. I have tried to show how Bishop, half consciously, or maybe entirely unconsciously – constructs a space within a traditionally male domain that in various aspects – shape/sound/the emphasis on touch – is a kind of wombscape.

It is a space in which Bishop achieves what she described in an early notebook, in relation to Marianne Moore's work, as 'using the poet's proper material, with which he's equipped by nature, i.e., immediate intense physical reactions, a sense of metaphor and decoration in everything – to express something not of them – something I suppose, spiritual'.[24] It is a truly creative space: a space of transformation. No new image is involved: just a way of seeing or interpreting what is already there – 'the plain facts', or material evidence – in a way that changes the image from the material to the marvellous and in doing so generates transcendent emotions of sympathy or joy or love.

The three poems, 'The Fish', 'Filling Station' and 'The Moose', are poems that both reassure and shake up received values. They question the nature of heroism and love and the relation between human and animal. They blur the boundaries of male and female space and of feminine and masculine characteristics and subvert limited phallocentric divisions of gender. The emphasis on oil and grease and touch conjures the experience of a child before it is introduced to language and challenges culture-bound classifications of "nice" or "nasty" substances. They are poems of healing: of restoring the rift between infant and mother that occurs at birth, and again in acquiring symbolic language. For Bishop – who never saw her mother after the age of eight when she was committed to an asylum and whose early experience of home was traumatised by her mother's madness – they are poems in which she is able to reclaim the nurturing space of the lost mother, even perhaps, in 'The Moose', the mother herself.

> A moose has come out of
> the impenetrable wood
> and stands there, looms, rather,
> in the middle of the road.
> It approaches; it sniffs at
> the bus's hot hood.
>
> ...
>
> Some of the passengers
> Exclaim in whispers,
> Childishly, softly,
> "Sure are big creatures."

"It's awful plain."
"Look! It's a she!"

Taking her time,
she looks the bus over,
grand, otherworldly.
Why, why do we feel
(we all feel) this sweet
sensation of joy?

"Curious creatures,"
says our quiet driver,
rolling his *r*'s.
"Look at that, would you."
Then he shifts gears.
For a moment longer,

by craning backward,
the moose can be seen
on the moonlit macadam;
then there's a dim
smell of moose, an acrid
smell of gasoline.

*

NOTES

Unless otherwise cited, quotations of published works are from Bishop's *Complete Poems: 1927-1979* or *The Collected Prose*, and of letters from *One Art*.

1. Acceptance speech for the 1976 *Books Abroad*/Neustadt International Prize for Literature.
2. *One Art*, p.87.
3. In a letter to Robert Lowell from Key West, dated 1 January 1948 (*One Art*, p.153), Bishop thanked him for sending her Isaac Walton's *The Compleat Angler*, commenting 'it is wonderfully soothing reading & wonderfully "precious" reading here in the land of big game fish and Hemingway'.
4. Ernest Hemingway: 'On the Blue Water' in Robert O. Stephens' *Hemingway's Nonfiction: the Public Voice* (University of North Carolina Press, 1968), p.312. It is even possible that Bishop was told the story. She visited Hemingway's ex-wife Pauline several times as is revealed in a letter to Marianne Moore, 21 May 1940, *One Art*, p.90.
5. *One Art*, p.79.
6. 'I did as you suggested about everything except "breathing in" (if you remember that) which I decided to leave as it was. "Lousy" is now "infested"...' Letter to Marianne Moore, 19 February 1940, *One Art*, p.88.
7. Helen Vendler: 'Domestication, Domesticity, and the Otherworldly' in *Part of Nature, Part of Us* (Cambridge, MA and London: Harvard University Press, 1980).
8. Cited by Anne Stevenson in *Elizabeth Bishop* (New York: Twayne, 1966), p.66.

9. 'Boxes, cases, chests, cupboards and ovens represent the uterus, and also hollow objects, ships, and vessels of all kinds. Rooms in dreams are usually women; if the various ways in and out of them are represented, this interpretation is scarcely open to doubt...' See Sigmund Freud's *The Interpretation of Dreams* (London: Penguin, 1976), pp.470-73.

10. 'Avec Ardeur' in *The Complete Poems of Marianne Moore* (London: Faber, 1967), p.237.

11. A similar effect is created at the end of 'The Sandpiper' where looking for 'something something something' (again the rhythmical repetition) in the 'shifting grains' of sand, the bird is rewarded by a vision of the drab beach transformed into a jewelled pavement: 'The millions of grains are black, white, tan, and gray, / mixed with quartz grains, rose and amethyst'.

12. I can't help comparing the "casual perfection" of this passage with Luce Irigaray's attempt to describe the inter-uterine birth of colour in her critique of Merleau-Ponty: '(Color) pours itself out – stretches itself out, escapes itself... imposes itself upon me as a recall of what is most archaic in me, the fluid. That through which I have received life, have been enveloped in my prenatal sojourn, have been surrounded, dressed, fed, in another body. That by the grace of which I could see the light, could be born, and moreover, see: the air, the light...' Taken from 'The Invisible of the flesh' in *An Ethics of Sexual Difference*, translated from the French by Carolyn Burke and Gillian C. Gill (London: Athlone Press) p.158.

13. From *The Sign of Saturn* (London: Secker & Warburg, 1991), p.13.

14. From *Over the Frontier* (London: Virago), p.250. First published in 1938.

15. From *The Collected Poems of Stevie Smith* (London: Penguin, 1986), p.453.

16. Letter to John Frederick Nims, 6 October 1979. *One Art*, p.638.

17. Bishop describes the trip in a letter to Marianne Moore, 29 August 1946. *One Art*, p.139-41.

18. *One Art*, p.573.

19. 'Wood seems, from its linguistic connections to stand in general for female "material". The name of the Island of "Madeira" means "wood" in Portuguese.' See Freud, *Interpretation of Dreams*, p.472.

20. Jung claims that the 'tree is a symbol of the Great Mother', in *Memories, Dreams, Reflections* (London: Collins, Routledge & Kegan Paul, 1963), p.239; and that 'the forest, like the tree, has mythologically a maternal significance' in *Psychology of the Unconscious* (London: Routledge & Kegan Paul, 1919), p.169.

21. I find Patricia Yaeger's essay 'Toward a Female Sublime', in which she discusses both 'The Fish' and 'The Moose', in general very illuminating. See *Gender & Theory*, edited by Linda Kauffman (Oxford: Blackwell, 1989). But I don't agree with her description of Bishop's wood as 'the "impenetrable forest" of masculine discourse'. I prefer to think of it as another 'female space' – a 'sacred wood' not of phallocentric logic but of a mystery that is much more instinctual and primitive.

22. Letter to Marianne Moore, 29 August 1946. *One Art*, p.141.

23. Letter to Jerome Mazzaro, 27 April 1978, *One Art*, p.621.

24. Cited by David Kalstone in *Becoming a Poet* (London: The Hogarth Press, 1989), p.15.

PETER ROBINSON

Pretended Acts: 'The Shampoo'

Elizabeth Bishop's poem 'The Shampoo' approaches a conclusion with what seems an invitation to wash someone's hair, but one which is as much a request for permission: ' – Come, let me wash it in this big tin basin, / battered and shiny like the moon.' However, the phrase 'Come, let me wash it' must also be neither of these things, because this apparent speech act makes up most of the penultimate line in a poem, whose verbal role is not actually to invite someone to have a hair wash nor to be granted permission. To tease out implications in the double aspects of such phrases in poems, I will read Bishop's 'The Shampoo' and analyse the nature of its close in the light of John R. Searle's essay on 'The Logical Status of Fictional Discourse'. At the end of that chapter in his book *Expression and Meaning: Studies in the Theory of Speech Acts* (1979), Searle notes:

> Literary critics have explained on an ad hoc and particularistic basis how the author conveys a serious speech act through the performance of the pretended speech acts which constitute the work of fiction, but there is as yet no general theory of the mechanisms by which such serious illocutionary intentions are conveyed by pretended illocutions.

My aim is not to propose a general theory, and I'm not sure that 'mechanisms' can be the right word for the innumerable strategies that writers have and will continue to find for doing something by pretending to do something else, while, further, I wonder if any such theory would be of much abiding use to writers or readers. Yet Searle's final point does invite a consideration of exactly what serious illocutionary intentions are performed by the pretended speech act at the end of 'The Shampoo'.

Composed about nine months after settling with Lota de Macedo Soares in Brazil, 'The Shampoo', was rejected in 1952 by *The New Yorker*. Writing to Pearl Kazin on 19 July of that year, Bishop enclosed the poem with these comments:

> Here is the little poem Mrs White couldn't understand. I have changed three words, though, since she returned it. I wonder if I am in honor bound to return it to them because of the three words before I send it someplace else? & do you remember those tin basins, all sizes, so much a part of life here? (*One Art*, p.241)

On the basis of evidence from the three typed final drafts of 'The Shampoo' held at Vassar College, evidence generously provided by Barbara Page, there seem to be two possibilities for the 'three words' which Bishop changed at this late stage. Of these three typed drafts, the last two also contain the poet's return address, suggesting that they may have been submitted for publication. In these two drafts, three small rewordings do occur: 'you were, dear friend' becomes 'you've been, dear friend'; 'These shooting stars' is changed to 'The shooting stars'; and there's a dither between 'Well, let me wash' and 'Come, let me wash'. On the basis of the fact that these 'three words' were altered after its rejection by *The New Yorker* and because only distinctly minor changes would likely prompt Bishop to her moral qualm about being 'honor bound' to resubmit it (she had a first refusal deal with the magazine at this time), I'm inclined to believe that these are the late changes.

However, Barbara Page also tells me that in the third, and probably earliest, of the typed drafts (which does not include Bishop's return address) there are several words significantly different from those in the published poem. These are carried over from handwritten drafts, but have been changed in the final two typed texts to the wording in the published version. They are, in line 10, 'demanding and too voluble' (instead of 'precipitate and pragmatical'), and, in line 14 'in swift formation' (instead of 'in bright formation'). In this probably third-to-last draft, Bishop has written 'bright' in the margin. On the basis of this evidence, Page suggests that the revised words in question may be 'demanding and too voluble', perhaps because they might seem too personal and critical, certainly less in the spirit of the metaphysical conceit sustained throughout 'The Shampoo'. My own instincts would incline me to guess that this revision, made between a typescript without a return address and one with, took place before the poem was submitted – for the very reason that the phrase is too 'personal and critical' both for the poem (about which more later) and for the public domain of *The New Yorker* or *The New Republic*, where 'The Shampoo' finally appeared in 1955.

'Here', anyway, 'is the little poem' in its definitive reading which 'Mrs White couldn't understand':

> The still explosions on the rocks,
> the lichens, grow
> by spreading, gray, concentric shocks.
> They have arranged
> to meet the rings around the moon, although
> within our memories they have not changed.

And since the heavens will attend
as long on us,
you've been, dear friend,
precipitate and pragmatical;
and look what happens. For Time is
nothing if not amenable.

The shooting stars in your black hair
in bright formation
are flocking where,
so straight, so soon?
– Come, let me wash it in this big tin basin,
battered and shiny like the moon.

Though the rosettes of moss and the rings around the moon may
have come to the poet as a pair of suitably discreet, dark and light
erotic images of stimulated nipples, their primary role in the opening
stanza is as emblems of a gradualist approach to growth and change
– the oxymoronic 'still explosions' and the 'gray...shocks' (punning on
shocks of hair) figuring dramatic processes that are not even noticed.
These changes are said to take place so slowly that we don't have
occasion to remember the past forms as different from the present
ones, and so 'within our memories they have not changed'. Yet the
paradox of this is implicit in the preparatory rhyme word 'arranged',
a word which like 'shocks' points forward to the impulsive practical
move that in the second verse the friend is implied to have made.

There, the valued sense of a benefit in slow maturing time's
actions is overtly applied to human affairs, for 'the heavens will
attend / as long on us' and 'Time is / nothing if not amenable.'
It's in the context of this natural and cosmic time that the 'pre-
cipitate and pragmatical' actions of the 'dear friend' are implicitly
criticised for having brought matters to a head when they might
have been left to mature more tactfully. Yet in so far as this is an
after-the-fact poem by a coy mistress feeling pushed into some-
thing, yet glad to have been pushed, the phrasing delicately fails
to decide about the behaviour and its consequences – for 'and
look what happens' can be bridling at the emotional turmoil
which has resulted, or exclaiming at the extraordinary changes
that have been wrought.

In the final stanza, the opening sentence, which continues the
heavenly bodies theme, turns abruptly from what the word order
of subject and verb had made seem a statement into a pair of un-
answerable questions, questions whose pitch is raised late in the
day by the appearance of the question mark. This too exemplifies
the play of aspects that gives dynamic shifts of feeling to lines of
poetry: what had appeared to be a statement about the dear friend's

hair turns out to be a question asking about the location of these fast-moving stars.

Just as Bishop's 'shooting stars' evoke something fallen to her from heaven, so the discovered question ('flocking where...?') invites the speculation 'in her heart?' – but the question itself and the hint of premature ageing in 'so soon' point towards an interwoven *carpe diem* theme that further mitigates the criticism of the friend's precipitate acts. Rather than state where the shooting stars are flocking, or answer the question that's posed, the poem's syntax cuts across its drift of metaphysical speculation, to resolve the emotional dilemma, not by a synthesis of seemingly incompatible options, but by demonstrating its resolution through a putting of love into action by means of the hair washing offer and request. ' "Love should be put into action!" / screamed the old hermit' in 'Chemin de Fer'. So the poem's successful conclusion comes in overcoming the speaker's quarrel with herself by rising to an enacted transformation of how the other person is accommodated into her imagined affective life. The poem preserves its uneasiness right until the offer and request of the final two lines, their dash introducing the pretended speech act rounded off by a 'battered and shiny' simile that gently deflates the sustained metaphysical conceit aligning the couple with astral and lunar forces.

The trajectory of a large number of lyric poems involves such a movement towards the point where one or more pretended speech acts (such as inviting, questioning, ordering, or exclaiming) can raise the pitch of attention and feeling. A model for the ending to 'The Shampoo' is plainly one of the many George Herbert lyrics (lyrics such as the two 'Jordan' poems or 'The Collar') which interrupts its described conflicts with a formally resolving irruption of dramatised divine communication. Bishop adopts the opening words of Herbert's 'Love Unknown' ('Dear Friend, sit down') to call – with a trace of archness – upon the interlocutor in 'The Shampoo'. Recalling the brief parentheses in the same Herbert poem, Bishop inserts a parenthetical self-command at the close of her villanelle 'One Art': 'the art of losing's not too hard to master / though it may look like (*Write* it!) like disaster.' 'One Art' also praises the '(the joking voice, a gesture / I love)' and the gesture which brings 'The Shampoo' to an end has its own vein of comedy in the "winning" bathos of finessing that request for permission to perform an intimate act by comparing the battered tin basin to the shiny moon.

If this makes for a jokey ending, it doesn't mean that 'The Shampoo' isn't attempting to utter something which is not a joke. 'One Art' loves the joking voice because it provides a way of managing in art and life emotional difficulties between people, whether they

be the poet's private friends, the inscribed subject and the inter-
locutor, or the publishing author and her readers. 'The Shampoo'
ends by performing a real act, in the guise of an obviously pre-
tended one – so obvious that understanding the poem's end requires
and expects a reader to see through the pretence. And this is some-
thing that we become so expert at that we barely notice the poem
making an offer, taking it instead as a way of expressing a feeling in a
poem. Doubtless, it's doing this too, but the point at issue is that
poets so often choose to end their poems not with the direct expres-
sions of feeling but the performance of some action that may deliver
the feeling but doesn't directly express it. Poems rightly go in fear
of such assertions unsupported by contexts of action and exchange.

In English the word 'act' has a curious double usage – because
it means to pretend to do something and really to do it. So if I
say, you must act decisively, I'm suggesting that you must really
do something without uncertainty which we hope will make a
significant difference; but if I say that you must act convincingly
I'm suggesting that you must pretend, and this could be because
you are an actor on a stage, or because you are in a real situation,
like a job interview, but feel you lack the qualities required to face
it. What this ambiguity tells us about how English views 'acts'
and 'action' is that pretending to do something and really doing it
are intimately related.

This is certainly true about learning and education. Ambitious
young people have to risk being called pretentious, because the only
way to succeed in doing something is to pretend that you can do
it, until, with luck and perseverance, you really can. Pretending is
also essential to the workings of social institutions: children use bits
of paper and card to pretend to buy things in a pretend shop; but
what we call "real money" involves the learned ability to under-
stand and believe that a particular type of printed paper really func-
tions as money. Pretending is part of imagining, and imagination is
not just a special quality added on to life by creative people, but a
necessary requirement for life to continue for every one of us.

Searle's idea of pretended speech acts in fictional works such as
novels and poems also serves to underline the role of fact in liter-
ature. He gives a description of what is involved in pretending to
do something:

> It is a general feature of the concept of pretending that one can pretend
> to perform a higher order or complex action by actually performing
> lower order or less complex actions which are constitutive parts of the
> higher order or complex action. Thus, for example, one can pretend to
> hit someone by actually making the arm and fist movements that are

characteristic of hitting someone. The hitting is pretended, but the movement of the arm and fist is real. Similarly, children pretend to drive a stationary car by actually sitting in the driver's seat, moving the steering wheel, pushing the gear shift lever, and so on. The same principle applies to the writing of fiction.

It might be added that as far as the punch is concerned, if you are on the receiving end of an unsignaled pretend one that has all the arm and fist movements with the relevant bodily and facial gestures, then you will really flinch. Poetry may make things happen in a related way. You may well be unable to prevent yourself flinching, to some lesser extent, even if you are told in advance that it's going to be a pretend punch. You're instincts are such that the prior explanation won't override them. Understanding what is about it come, a pretended punch for instance, allows you a safe occasion to examine what your reactions to such an occurrence would turn out to be.

This can follow for reading too. The response of the reader to pretended speech acts is at the heart of how, as Wittgenstein put it in *Zettel* (1981), section 155: 'A poet's words can pierce us. And that is of course *causally* connected with the use that they have in our life.' An essential requirement for this response would have to be a degree of conviction on the reader's part that something real is meant, and such a sense is conveyed, in part, by the persuasive role of an admixture of fact. Searle describes the process of mixing facts with fictional elements and brushes aside the 'fictional world' idea of literary space as he does so:

> Theorists of literature are prone to make vague remarks about how the author creates a fictional world, a world of the novel, or some such. I think we are now in a position to make sense of those remarks. By pretending to refer to people and to recount events about them, the author creates fictional characters and events. In the case of realistic or naturalistic fiction, the author will refer to real places and events intermingling those references with the fictional references, thus making it possible to treat the fictional story as an extension of our existing knowledge.

In *Modern Poetry: A Personal Essay* (1938), Louis MacNeice suggested that 'All poetry probably contains an element of wish-fulfilment and a certain recognition of hard facts', and poems can effect such an intermingling through their use of deictics, figures of speech, and pretend versions of speech acts. One distinction between much fiction and lyric poetry would involve the degree of expected naturalisation. Many lyrics work by keeping both naturalising and disjunctive aspects of the reading experience in full view; much fiction expects its readers to imagine a complete and continuous natural scene.

The third and final verse of 'The Shampoo' appears, then, to ask a question and to make an offer in the form of a request for permission. Two essential facts are indicated by the deictics in '*your* black hair' and '*this* big tin basin' (emphases added). A third crucial fact is, by the way, signified by the first pronoun in 'let me wash it'. That Bishop revised out of this last stanza one such deictic when she changed 'These shooting stars' to 'The shooting stars' indicates how in a poem such words can function in relation with other determiners to produce an increase of fictive presence as a reader progresses through the final verse. To have such a deictic in the stanza's opening line might well give the impression of protesting too much about the presence indicated, pre-empting thus the decisive shift of emphases in the concluding speech act.

Though in Yeats's 'Politics' the hair colour of 'that girl standing there' is of no relevance to the poem, and asking what it actually was would be nonsensical, here, the colour is a crucial element in a poem whose working title was 'Gray Hairs'. The 'you' in this poem has black hair with 'shooting stars' in it. These stars are also 'flocking' in an unspecified place 'so straight, so soon'. The poet's companion Lota had straight black hair which was prematurely streaked with white strands – as can be plainly seen from the black and white fig. 20 of Brett C. Millier's *Elizabeth Bishop: Life and the Memory of It* (1993) or fig. 45 in Fountain and Brazeau's *Remembering Elizabeth Bishop: An Oral Biography* (1994). In 1952, Bishop, the 'me' of 'let me wash it', still had troublesomely wavy red hair. Referring as she does to the fact of the black hair with the premature white streaks is part of Bishop's way of implying to the reader that something serious is at stake. Referring to the streaks as 'shooting stars' in the dark heavens of the hair adds a playful level of pretended assertion to the sentence.

The shooting stars are a metaphor with the first term, the grey hair, suppressed. Transforming the premature greyness to an image of the constellations performs an act of affection, an act whose lesbian implications are carefully deflected by leaving the place where the stars are flocking as a question. So with her fact-related deictics and her metaphor 'the shooting stars' and simile 'battered and shiny like the moon', Bishop mixes together hard fact and wish-fulfilment. This love poem resolves conflicts of feeling artic-ulated in the previous verse ('you've been, dear friend, / precipitate and pragmatical') by expressing a commitment to, and care for, the other person through the issuing of this pretended speech act: ' – Come, let me wash it in this big tin basin, / battered and shiny like the moon.'

Helen Vendler asserts in the introduction to her edition and commentary *The Art of Shakespeare's Sonnets* (1997) that

> Since the person uttering a lyric is always represented as alone with his thoughts, his imagined addressee can by definition never be present. Lyric can present no 'other' as alive and listening or responding in the same room as the solitary speaker.

Yet the pretended speech act which concludes 'The Shampoo' illustrates the slip in Vendler's polemical overstatement: sometimes, certainly; but not always and not never. Quite a large number of lyric poems are dedicated to named people, and many more have unnamed addressees – because if these poems are to perform a real act by performing a pretended one, they need to signal a relationship between people of some kind in which such acts can be imagined to be taking place. More frequently than Vendler cares to consider this named or unnamed person is being imagined as present in the poem's space of action. The conclusion of 'The Shampoo' would not instance the poet's 'joking voice', but merely her battily talking to herself, if readers did not respond naturally to the assumption that the addressee, the 'dear friend', is present at the poem's occasion and ready to respond to her offer. What response does she make?

Here the altered title comes into play: not 'Gray Hairs' but 'The Shampoo'. No one, I assume, reading Bishop's poem imagines that the 'dear friend' responds to its concluding offer by, for example, laughing cruelly into the face of the poet and walking away. The reader's assumption is that the offer is accepted. Why? As a title, 'The Shampoo' might conceivably prepare us for a poem à la Francis Ponge's 'Le savon'; but it refers, of course, to the action of giving someone a hair wash. Yet no such act is described as taking place in the poem. So the title starts the assumption, which reading the poem's conclusion reinforces, that a bit of hair washing is set to go on involving poet and interlocutor. The title then prepares the implication that 'The Shampoo' dramatises the delivering of a 'happy' performative – to use J.L. Austin's term, from *How To Do Things With Words* (1976) – for an utterance of this kind which 'comes off'. The interlocutor accepts this offer, at once maternal and erotic, by giving permission for the shampooing to happen.

'The Shampoo' is the final poem in *A Cold Spring* (1955). On the facing page in *The Complete Poems: 1927-1979*, you find the title page for *Questions of Travel* (1965) with its dedication to Lota de Macedo Soares. 'The Shampoo' is also a happy note to end the earlier book on. The making of such a poem is itself a type of act, and its publishing will involve some others, such as coping with the fact that the poetry editor of *The New Yorker* didn't want to publish it, and sending it out to *The New Republic* – while its placing in a collection of poems involves yet another. These acts, while they involve the institutions of the literary world and publishing also take place and have meaning in the private life of the author. Placing 'The Shampoo' at the end of her book helps to make it into a tribute to and gift for the person who has helped to put her life back together, to give it a stability that lasted rather longer than any of Bishop's other sustained relationships. A few months after reporting that 'The Shampoo' had been rejected and lightly revised, on 16 September 1952 Bishop wrote to her doctor, Anny Baumann, dedicatee of *A Cold Spring*: 'the drinking and the working both seem to have improved miraculously. Well no, it isn't miraculous really – it is almost entirely due to Lota's good sense and kindness. I still feel I must have died and gone to heaven without deserving to' (*One Art*, p.246). While 'The Shampoo' may thus exemplify the poet's gift, and draw upon generosity in the given circumstances of its imagined context, the poem is itself, via those acts of making public, a gift to Lota Soares and to us.

My book *In the Circumstances: About Poems and Poets* (1992) addresses the idea that poetry could perform reparative acts, the idea of poems as trying to make amends, forming thus a counterweight to negative experience; and critics such as Joanne Feit Diehl in her *Elizabeth Bishop and Marianne Moore: The Psychodynamics of Creativity* (1993) have applied similar ideas to Bishop's writings. Making amends doesn't mean putting things back the way they were before the bad event happened. That really is impossible. It means making some symbolic or emblematic acts and gestures that represent regret and the wish that what has befallen had not occurred. The emblematic gesture stands in place of the imaginable 'undoing' of the past, and points forward, changing the way the past is seen by altering the future through an act performed in the present.

'The Shampoo' is, in its discreet way, also performing such an act, for its conclusion not only resolves the emotional dilemma in which the poet finds herself, it also makes amends for the shadow of ingratitude that hangs over the faint air of criticism for the addressee in 'precipitate and pragmatical' or 'and look what happens'. The drafts at Vassar also make clear that this critical note had been more personal and stronger in the poem's gestation: 'demanding and too voluble' makes the 'dear friend' sound like a pushy chatterbox. Not only is 'precipitate and pragmatical' more distanced in its abstract diction, it is also more properly poised in its ambivalence. You can also hear that something is not quite right with the earlier phrase because the '-uble/-able' rhyme is comically clumsy, at a point where satirical irony is not called for. The revision lightens the chiming and increases the sense that its stanzas rhyme as if by chance – a felicitous chance meeting, as it were. The speaker can be grateful for these 'precipitate and pragmatical' qualities as well as faintly flustered in being overwhelmed by them; 'demanding and too voluble' are characteristics hard to square with the final warmth for the love object that the poem seeks to imply.

The sense that a mending of divided responses has taken place by the end of 'The Shampoo' is emblematically represented by the stanza's casually improvised closing rhyme. This too is a device that Bishop may have learned from Herbert who uses it overtly in the 'And mend my rhyme' close to 'Denial'. I am convinced that works of art, and especially poems, can perform such types of emblematic act. Just so, there's an attempt going on in 'The Shampoo' to construct an imaginative relatedness to stand in for the momentarily attenuated relationship with the loved one. The hope is, of course, that if this sort of object works for the writer and her 'dear friend', then it can also work for others – and thus institute a further firm relationship out of a more attenuated one, that between poet and reader.

That's one more example of the kind of pretended acts that I have been thinking about today. But in the case of the poem being offered to the reader, it seems to me that it's not a 'pretended' act, but the act itself, one especially evident when I'm in front of you saying the poem out loud. The description of the relationship in 'The Shampoo' involves pretended assertions; I say the deictics in 'your black hair' and 'this big tin basin', but Lota Soares is obviously not 'here', and you can't see her even when you read the poem, you have to imagine her as present, and the same is true for the battered basin whose real existence is recalled in Bishop's letter to Pearl Kazin. So when I read the poem out loud today and make the poem's closing offer, it's really a poem being read, and through me that's what 'The Shampoo' does: it occasions a real act involving other people by performing a congruent series of pretended ones.

JO SHAPCOTT

Confounding Geography

we are driving to the interior
(Elizabeth Bishop, 'Arrival at Santos')

In the late 70s, in my first week at Harvard, I took the street car down to Boston University to hear Elizabeth Bishop read her poems. I had been reading and studying her work for the previous two years, and to hear her deep rich voice and the strange, precise, profound poems emerging from this small, plump, well-dressed woman (she dressed like the sort of woman who lunches) was sheer pleasure and the fulfilment of a private excitement. At that time, her work wasn't widely known or appreciated at home in England; I had felt pretty much a lone fan. I was far too shy to approach her after the reading and stole off back to Cambridge full of the poems.

I was taking a poetry class taught by Seamus Heaney, who offered to intercede for me with the notoriously private Bishop, and pretty soon I received a charming letter from her in reply to my own, offering to meet me. But I was to miss her. On 7 October I crossed the quads to hear her read at Harvard. The hall was packed; everyone else there seemed to know what I didn't know, that she had died suddenly the day before, at her apartment overlooking Boston Harbor. I was slow to grasp what was going on, still expecting her to appear, as a collection of her friends and fellow-poets came to the microphone in turn to read her poems as a tribute. The understanding and sorrow hit me like a wave.

I had lost two things: not only the possibility of direct connection with one of very few major women poets writing at that time, but also the possibility of direct connection with the contemporary poet (of either sex) whose work I admired most. I was also haunted by the idea that I was part of the first generation of poets for whom both these statements could be true at once – given that the door had only just started to open beyond a crack to women poets – which compounded my sense of loss.

All poets will tell you of the importance of their predecessors.

The poets who have gone before are the ones who teach us our business, help us refine our craft, and carve out our territories. We quarrel with them, rebel against them, restate their positions, assert our own. We have imaginary conversations and arguments with them; we write (but do not send them) letters in which we arrogantly try to correct the mistakes in their writing and their lives. In this way, Elizabeth Bishop has been my teacher. More particularly she has been my geography teacher, or perhaps even my anti-geography teacher.

When I wrote the poem 'Phrase Book' in 1991, I had just tripped over the following sentences in an old *Collins Italian/English Phrase Book* dating from 1963. 'Let me pass please. I am an Englishwoman.' I was stunned and amused. I couldn't think where in the world that order would actually work now. Pulled this way into the phrase book, I combined its world and language with language of the technology of warfare and so the poem was born. The encounter with the English-woman of the phrase book also caused me to pause and think about her. Who was, or is she? The word even sounds colonial. It carries far more connotations than simple gender and place of habitation, making it almost too difficult, too uncomfortable to use, to the point where it has died as a word in common currency. There are layers of meaning which make the designation of her original country just as much an evocation of time and political context as of place.

Any poet has to think hard about her origins. When I was first trying my wings as a writer, the tyro poet was always told, first, to write about what you know and, second, to 'Dig where you stand', to delve into the language and landscape of your own territory. In a writer like Seamus Heaney the landscapes and place-names of his home could become, in the poem 'Anahorish', 'soft gradient / of consonant, vowel meadow'.[1] As a young writer I felt at a disadvantage. I grew up in a new town, Hemel Hempstead, where there were absolutely no vowel meadows and where the spoken language was flat, a version of London watered down by a mild accumulation of the various modes of speech of the many people who had moved there from all over the place. My own parents, from England's West Country, were a case in point. Over the years I heard their rich Forest of Dean accents and phrase-ology fade. To my ear the speech mixture around us was milk and water rather than, say, the tang of language you hear on London streets today. In addition, and if it was true then, it is even more true now, the best poetry in English was by writers from other countries or, at least, with strong links back to other countries, cultures and languages.

Since then, my quest has been to discover how to be a different kind of writer, for whom place and language are less certain, and for whom shifting territories are the norm. It's no wonder that from the start I found a model in the reluctantly American poet Elizabeth Bishop; her travels through geography and poetry led my own steps. I am not the only writer to feel this way about her. Robert Lowell famously said that 're-reading her suggested a way of breaking through the shell of my old manner. Her rhythms, idiom, images, and stanza structure seemed to belong to a later century.'[2] I suspect there is a hint of early post-modernism in her work which speaks to writers who want to make an aesthetic of the fragmentary and rootless experience which now seems the norm. Julia Kristeva spoke of the theorist as 'an impertinent traveller' passing across 'whole geographic and discursive continents'. It is in this context that Englishness, the meaning of being English – and yes, an Englishwoman, because gender certainly has something to do with it – has nagged at me, and has cropped up in many of my poems. Who is this Englishwoman?

Part of the answer to the question of how to engage with the material of my own country came from Bishop. Reared in Nova Scotia, she was a reluctant American, describing herself as 'kidnapped' from Canada when, as a small child, she was taken by her grandparents to the United States. In her moving essay, 'The Country Mouse', she gives an account of the move, and at one point describes the wrench from the language of her old home. This early dislocation would ensure that she could never be a poet of the 'vowel meadow' and would have to find another way.

> I had been brought back unconsulted and against my wishes to the house my father had been born in, to be saved from a life of poverty and provincialism, bare feet, suet puddings, unsanitary school slates, perhaps even from the inverted *r*'s of my mother's family. With this surprising set of extra grandparents, until a few weeks ago no more than names, a new life was about to begin. It was a day that seemed to include months in it, or even years, a whole unknown past I was made to feel I should have known about, and a strange unpredictable future. (*Collected Prose*, p.17)

Most interestingly, she decided at once that she did not want to be American and her relationship with her second country remained ambivalent for the rest of her life, large parts of which were spent living abroad:

> The War was on. At recess we were marched into the central hall, class by class, to the music of an upright piano, a clumping march that has haunted me all my life and I have never yet placed. There we pledged allegiance to the flag and sang war songs: "Joan of Arc, they are ca-all-lll-ing you." I hated the songs, and most of all I hated saluting the flag.

I would have refused if I had dared. In my Canadian schooling, the year before, we had started every day with "God Save the King" and "The Maple Leaf Forever." Now I felt like a traitor. I wanted us to win the War, of course, but I didn't want to be an American. When I went home to lunch, I said so. Grandma was horrified; she almost wept. Shortly after, I was presented with a white card with an American flag in colour at the top. All the stanzas of "Oh, say, can you see" were printed on it in dark blue letters. Every day I sat at Grandma's feet and attempted to recite this endless poem. We didn't sing because she couldn't stay in tune, she said. Most of the words made no sense at all.
(*Collected Prose*, pp.26-27)

A life spent travelling, living for long periods in other countries, a distaste and longing, for political or emotional reasons for one's homeland. These aspects of Bishop's life felt familiar to me and, as I came to understand, more typical of western contemporary experience than rootedness. Imagine my glee, on first opening *The Complete Poems* to find the names of Bishop's books – *North & South; A Cold Spring; Questions of Travel:* 'Brazil' and 'Elsewhere'; and then, turning to the first page, an exquisite poem called 'The Map', which read to me like formal permission to put travel, rootlessness, even lost identity, at the centre.

When, in 1993, I was commissioned to write a version of Marina Tsvetaeva's poem 'Motherland' [3] I surprised myself by starting to explore some of these issues. For Tsvetaeva, the motherland is Mother Russia. Her poem movingly evokes its landscapes and its history with nostalgia and passion from the perspective of her exile in Paris in the 1920s. My Motherland is England, and I found my version evoking quite a different emotional tone:

Motherland
after Tsvetaeva

Language is impossible
in a country like this. Even
the dictionary laughs when I look up
'England', 'Motherland', 'Home'.

It insists on falling open instead
three times out of the nine I try it
at the word Distance: 'Degree
of remoteness, interval of space.'

Distance: the word is ingrained like pain.
So much for England and so much
for my future to walk into the horizon
carrying distance in a broken suitcase.

The dictionary is the only one
who talks to me now. Says, laughing,
'Come back HOME!' but takes me
further and further away into the cold stars.

I am blue, bluer than water
I am nothing, for all I do
is pour syllables over aching brows.

England. It hurts my lips to shape
the word. This country makes me say
too many things I can't say. Home
of me, myself, my motherland.

Such a viewpoint need not always be tragic. In 1952 Bishop wrote
to Anny Baumann: 'It seems to be mid-winter, and yet it is time to
plant things – but my Anglo-Saxon blood is gradually relinquishing
its seasonal cycle and I'm quite content to live in complete confusion,
about seasons, fruits, language, geography, everything.' The critic
Anne Shifrer thought this made Bishop sound 'refreshingly post-
modern and not like Crusoe, moribund with lost meaning and
collapsed symbolic systems...she seems content with occasionally
numinous secular objects and events that may well be disconnected
or connected only by "and" and "and." Perhaps this attitude of
nonmastery, of accepting bafflement is less imperial...[4]

The reference here is to 'Crusoe in England', Bishop's most
ambitious poem of travel. The poem is spoken by the old Crusoe,
reflecting on his life on the desert island from the safety – and
prison – of England. The question now is what is left after travel,
what is memory, what is loss, what is home. Crusoe's – and Bishop's
– worst nightmare changes during the course of the poem from
the dream of infinities of islands, all to be described in detail, to
its opposite: the nightmare of exile – in England, the so-called
motherland – exile from travelling, and a subsequent shrivelling of
the imagination.

Changes in the outer world have been just as important to what
is left of the Englishwoman as changes in her inner world. Gillian
Beer has written on the effect of the coming of the aeroplane on
the essentially island story of England looking, in particular, at the
writing of Virginia Woolf:

> Woolf's quarrel with patriarchy and imperialism gave a particular com-
> plexity to her appropriations of the island story. At the same time her
> symbolising imagination played upon its multiple significations – land
> and water margins, home, body, individualism, literary canon – and set
> them in shifting relations to air and aeroplane.[5]

The wars of the last century, the end of empire, the aeroplane, the channel tunnel, the World Wide Web, the role of women, the power of multi-national conglomerates, the preponderance of great literature in English from elsewhere, our many changed viewpoints as we enter the new century, all these unite to tell us that the island story of England, little England, is finished. Borders and edges of territory and language, home and body, land and water have always offered some of the most attractive hide-outs for women writers who have long understood that the secret might be simply to let the other in or to sift through whatever flotsam washes up.

*

NOTES

Unless otherwise cited, quotations of published works are from Bishop's *Complete Poems: 1927-1979* or *The Collected Prose*, and of letters from *One Art*.

1. Seamus Heaney: 'Anahorish', Wintering Out (London: Faber & Faber, 1972).

2. Robert Lowell: 'On Skunk Hour', in Lloyd Schwartz & Sybil P. Estess in *Elizabeth Bishop and Her Art*, edited by (Ann Arbor: Michigan University Press, 1983), p.199.

3. Jo Shapcott: 'Motherland', *Her Book* (London: Faber & Faber, 2000).

4. Anne Shifrer: 'Elizabeth Bishop as Delicate Ethnographer', New Readings symposium at Vassar College, 22-25 September 1994, http://projects.vassar.edu/ bishop/Shifrer.html.

5. Gillian Beer: 'The Island the Aeroplane: the case of Virginia Woolf', in *Nation and Narration*, edited by Homi K. Bhabha (London: Routledge, 1990), p.268.

MICHAEL DONAGHY

The Exile's Accent

Ever play that parlour game where you answer one snatch of song
with another? Listen:

As I walked out one evening
Walking down Bristol Street
The crowds upon the pavement
Were fields of harvest wheat.

- Wheat, not oats, dear. I'm afraid
if it's wheat it's none of your sowing,
nevertheless I'd like to know
what you are doing and where you are going.

Two stanzas by – you might say – two very different poets. But
this trick works because Auden and Bishop share a tone – that
'dear' could have easily come from Auden. We normally associate
Bishop with Lowell and Marianne Moore, and we know she had
sections of Stevens' *Harmonium* by heart and we can readily see
these influences in her work – but they don't account for that arch,
intimate tone, that formal flourish. Bonnie Costello has suggested
Bishop learned more from Auden than any of her contemporaries.

In 1974, Bishop wrote 'A Brief Reminiscence and a Brief Tribute'
on Auden for the *Harvard Advocate*. She concludes:

These verses and many, many more of Auden's, have been part of my
mind for years – I could say, part of my life...When I was in college,
and all through the thirties and forties, I and all my friends who were
interested in poetry, read him constantly. We hurried to see his latest
poem or book, and either wrote as much like him as possible, or tried
hard not to...We admired his apparent toughness, his sexual courage –
actually more honest than Ginsberg's, say, is now, while still giving
expression to technically dazzling poetry. Even the most hermetic early
poems gave us the feeling that here was someone who knew – about psych-
ology, geology, birds, love, the evils of capitalism – what have you? They
colored our air and made us feel tough, ready, and in the know, too.

Bishop plays a similarly pivotal role in my development as a
writer. As a young poet sending my work about, I'd get 'encour-
aging' rejections from American magazine editors who found my
work promising but 'affected', who felt I hadn't 'found my natural

voice'. This was the 70s, and the contents page of most school anthologies of 20th century American poetry started (and in a sense ended) with William Carlos Williams. They tended to document the 'natural' and 'confessional' and downplay or reject the influence of Auden – that arch elegance, that courageous affectation – a tone I recognised in the work of two of the poets I most revered: James Merrill and Elizabeth Bishop – a somewhat campy note of displacement resolved by conspicuous technique, a mode defined by wit – in the Renaissance sense – irony, seduction, and playfulness alloyed with reserve. I've heard it said that artists often emigrate as a strategy to disguise a chronic private exile. I thought of all those poets whose craft is driven not by a desire to express a confidently anchored 'natural' self, but by a need to create a self through the work. Bishop provided a model.

Bishop's poetic 'accent' was forged by a very real exile. In 'A Country Mouse' she tells of her childhood rejection of American identity after she'd been taken from her grandparent's home in Canada. (Contrast this with William Carlos Williams' childhood experience and subsequent literary nationalism.) Perhaps this crisis helped her escape the two-party system of American poetry. It's hard to steer your own course when the river keeps channelling into Whitman's yawp or Dickinson's centripedal concision, especially if you're seeking a current that's 'dark, salt, clear, moving, and utterly free'. And maybe it helped her access more freely the tradition of English poetry.

Costello has discovered in the Vassar library Bishop's unfinished 1937 review of Auden's *Look, Stranger!* which she calls 'The Mechanics of Pretense: Remarks on W.H. Auden'. Pretense, she argues, is a way of bringing something into being (children pretend to speak a foreign language and grow up linguists; small nations pretend grandeur and become empires). So a poet facing a different world from that of his forbears pretends the existence of a language to match a reality or feeling that is not yet articulate. Bishop writes:

> In his earlier stages the poet is the verbal actor. One of the causes of poetry must be, we suppose, the feeling that the contemporary language is not equivalent to the contemporary fact; there is something out of proportion between them, and what is being said in words is not at all what is being said in "things". To correct this disproportion a pretence is at first necessary. By "pretending" the existence of a language appropriate and comparable to "things" it must deal with, the language is forced into being. It is learned by one person, by a few, by all who can become interested in that poet's poetry.

Pretense is a mechanism by which a self is invented for every poem, either a persona like Robinson Crusoe, or a housemaid, or the Riverman, or 'an Elizabeth' who inhabits us for the duration of the poem. American poetry at the end of this century seems less rigidly "fundamentalist" and more open to true poetic decorum, that continuous negotiation between subject and style. Looking back, though, I'm grateful to all those hostile editors and critics who, appalled by my propensity for rhyme and metre, rejected my poems and gave me time to develop my own range of 'unnatural' voices.

I'd like to conclude by looking at one of Bishop's most admired lyrics, 'The Shampoo'. She wrote this in 1952 – first included in a letter to Marianne Moore, but it made the rounds of umpteen magazines including *The New Yorker* and *Poetry* before it was finally published in *The New Republic* in 1955. A true metaphysical love lyric, its conceit – a contrast between human and natural time scales – built like a ribcage about its emotional core.

> The still explosions on the rocks,
> the lichens, grow
> by spreading, gray, concentric shocks.
> They have arranged
> to meet the rings around the moon, although
> within our memories they have not changed.

On the one hand time's cyclical, immeasurably slow as the grey concentric shocks of lichen on the boulders which have – listen for the social nuance here – arranged to meet the rings around the moon. On the other hand it can be linear. In the second stanza Bishop addresses her dear friend (Lota, of course):

> And since the heavens will attend
> as long on us,
> you've been, dear friend,
> precipitate and pragmatical;
> and look what happens. For Time is
> nothing if not amenable.

Precipitate and pragmatical – an odd pairing of adjectives. Surely, we say, she means to oppose these qualities: rash but practical. But, as she told her writing class at Harvard: 'Always use the Dictionary; it's better than the critics.' If precipitate connotes rash, the obsolete pragmatical can mean meddlesome. So this is a gentle rebuke: 'And look what happens' – time 'nothing if not amenable' appears to comply with this attitude and hasten its pace. And what form does it take as it streaks through space? The shooting stars in your black hair which recalls precipitate and the

suggestion of a chemical precipitate falling out of its solution to
rest at the bottom of a glass.

> The shooting stars in your black hair
> in bright formation
> are flocking where,
> so straight, so soon?
> – Come, let me wash it in this big tin basin,
> battered and shiny like the moon.

What goes without saying? The bleak answer to where those stars
are flocking? The tenderness and simplicity of the gesture in the
last two lines? Or the way Bishop invites her beloved to step out-
side of time with her and meet the rings around their own battered
and shiny artificial moon?

Bishop's Birds

In a letter to the critic Jerome Mazzaro, Elizabeth Bishop writes that her poem ' "Santarém" *happened*, just like that, a real evening & a real place, a real Mr Swan who said that – it is not a composite at all.' She ends her reply by stating that 'the settings, or descriptions, of my poems are almost invariably plain facts – or as close to the facts as I can write them. But, as I said, it is fascinating that my poem should arouse in you all those literary references!' In another poet this insistence on 'plain facts' might be disingenuous, but it's one of the virtues of Bishop's poems to convince us that they did indeed *happen* more or less as she said they did, even if they didn't, and to convince us that Bishop is a poet – the same could be said of her as a letter writer – for whom the 'real' takes precedence over the literary. And so for her to name another poet within one of her poems almost amounts to a breach of decorum. It makes sense, then, to take such references as signals that these poems are especially concerned with the art of poetry – though it's obvious that no poem is going to be truly unconcerned.

There's no shortage of explicit literary references in Bishop's poems – 'The Gentleman of Shalott', the wittily incomplete quotation from Wordsworth in 'Crusoe in England', the line 'The boy stood on / the burning deck' from Felicia Hemans, broken in half, in 'Casabianca', as well as some occasional poems, and the direct address to Marianne Moore, the unnamed Ezra Pound in 'A Visit to St Elizabeth's' and so on. Bishop is not the kind of parochial poet who would subscribe, at least in her practice, to any kind of simple opposition between life and literature. But the only two occasions where she names other poets in her poems are to be found in 'The Bight' and 'The Sandpiper'. In both, the references, respectively to Baudelaire and to Blake (as though her own poems were sandwiched alphabetically between them) are affectionately mocking, and in both, I'd argue, for all their lightness of touch, their air of being *en passant*, the references alert the reader to an aesthetic quarrel within the poem: they serve as poems which not only differentiate her own procedures from the poet named but also enquire into her own practice as a poet.

After its self-dedication in miniscule, bracketed italics '*(On my birthday)*', 'The Bight' begins:

> At low tide like this how sheer the water is.
> White, crumbling ribs of marl protrude and glare
> and the boats are dry, the pilings dry as matches.
> Absorbing, rather than being absorbed,
> the water in the bight doesn't wet anything,
> the color of the gas flame turned as low as possible.
> One can smell it turning to gas; if one were Baudelaire
> one could probably hear it turning to marimba music.

Several critics (including Bonnie Costello and David Kalstone) have noted how, later in the poem, the line 'The bight is littered with old correspondances', as well as referring to the foregoing 'torn-open, unanswered letters', takes on another meaning from its association with Baudelaire's signature poem 'Correspondances'. But why is Bishop conscripting the French symbolist for a poem which describes a stretch of Floridan coastline? 'The Bight' is wonderfully painstaking in its description – it also takes pain as being of the nature of the scene: the 'ribs protrude and glare'…'Pelicans crash'… the boats are 'bristling with jackstraw gaffs and hooks', even the water itself, in one of Bishop's unobtrusively violent wrenches of perspective and of 'plain fact', is imagined as hard and dry. Nothing could seem further from Baudelaire's synaesthetic 'forêt de symboles', his taste for the exotic and his remembered voyages, which Bishop wittily sums up as 'marimba music'. Her use of the impersonal in 'One can smell it turning to gas' has a plummy formality she immediately sends up: 'if one were Baudelaire / one could probably hear it turning to marimba music' – that possibility depends on the improbable conditional of being the great French poet. But even if she makes fun of the exotic props of Symbolism, the poem is still troubled, it seems, by the need to come up with something, to be unlike the pelicans 'rarely coming up with anything to show for it', or like the dredge which, at the end of the poem, 'Brings up a dripping jawful of marl'.

The poem is Bishop's witty, slightly desolate ('awful but cheerful') birthday present to herself, and it scrutinises, by displacing it onto the birds and the boats, the whole 'untidy activity' of writing at the same time as it observes the seemingly pointless maritime bustle of the bight. That this lies at a substratum of the poem (to extend the delving and digging similes she uses) and remains undeclared but for the Baudelaire marker is part of the poem's preference for reality, for the primary status of what 'happened'. This counters the symbolist aesthetic – even if the poem were to fail to retrieve anything from it, we sense that she would prefer 'the dry perfectly off-beat claves' of 'the little ochre dredge at work' to marimba music. But the irony that distances her own work from Baudelaire's is also a kind of homage.

From the first line's demonstrative 'this', Bishop attends to the here and now of the scene. Even the dry, short 'i' of the first line's 'this' and 'is' is sounded emphatically through the poem, especially in her similes, her own 'correspondances': *pickaxes, scissors, glinting like little plowshares, littered with.* The sound is heard deliberately at the end: 'Click. Click. Goes the dredge' followed in the last lines by 'brings up a dripping...' and 'activity continues'. The similes, unlike Baudelaire's, are largely drawn from the everyday, from a domestic setting or workplace – matches, gas flame, pickaxes, scissors, retrievers, plowshares, litter. If I'm right that the poem contains an uneasiness as to whether its descriptions are enough and that they suggest a drying up, a 'low tide', of the imagination, there is still a brave persistence in her method and a refusal to stray into a 'forest of symbols' for more heightened effects.

Aside from the bracketed self-dedication and an almost parenthetic personal appearance in the lines 'Pelicans crash / into this peculiar gas unnecessarily hard, / it seems to me, like pickaxes', the poem is scrupulously impersonal as we've seen also in her arch use of 'one'. The poem, for all that it suppresses the personal, is strewn with muted indications that the personal still subsists, like the birthday dedication and like the 'torn-open, unanswered letters' where the violent eagerness of 'torn-open' suggests loneliness whilst the 'unanswered' points to a degree of personal chaos. As Costello points out, Bishop describes the Bight after a storm in a letter to Robert Lowell, adding 'It reminds me a little of my desk'. Her later prose poem '12 O'Clock News' which again links landscape and writing, only this time the other way round, elaborates its analogues in a far more stated and static manner.

Rather than serving the kind of maritime pastoral they easily might have, the poem's details (matches, gas flame, pile of stove-in boats, litter) amount to something closer to an imminent conflagration, a sacrificial pyre. Bishop doesn't seem to be a great enjoyer of her own birthdays, as indeed her letters record. The reference to her birthday also makes of the poem an unobtrusive meditation on mortality, which is implicit in the clay of the second line's 'White, crumbling ribs of marl' and reappears again at the end in 'a dripping jawful of marl', framing the entire poem with a subliminal skeleton image, a memento mori with a formal equivalence to the anamorphic skull in Holbein's *The Ambassadors*. And the

hard clicking sounds throughout, as well as particular details such as
the 'blue-gray shark tails hung up to dry' and 'the little white boats
...still piled up' do much to reinforce this image of the skeleton, a
figure memorably present in several Baudelaire poems, notably 'La
Squellette laboureur'. For the marl itself, Costello adduces the
'burning marl' of *Paradise Lost* – 'Key West's marl being that
black sediment of dead coral which Milton used to construct hell',
only here it isn't black but white. A more likely prompt for Bishop,
though, is the derivation of the name Key West from the Spanish
Cayo Hueso meaning Callus (and by extension, Hill) Bone. But even
though the images of clay and bone inevitably evoke mortality,
Bishop steers the poem away from anything lugubrious in the comic
way that the 'jawful of marl' becomes acoustically transformed
into the final line: 'awful but cheerful'. The word 'bight', meaning
a wide bay, is finally made to jostle with and suggest the homo-
phonic 'bite' by way of the word 'jawful'. (In the only recording of
Bishop reading this poem, she spells out the title so the audience
doesn't confuse the word with its homophone.) Incidentally, the
last line 'awful but cheerful' was Bishop's favourite line from her
poems: she taught it to her mynah bird, Jacob, who seems, from
the evidence of one of her letters, to have added a comma 'Awful,
but cheerful', and also asked for it to be inscribed onto her head-
stone. The line has a brisk stoicism to it, the jaw set behind that
drab word 'cheerful'. The poem also lives up to this motto, and
through its unflagging descriptions of 'untidy activity' finally
comes up with something to show for it: not just a 'moral' but an
extraordinarily precise account of *this* scene and also a disguised
enquiry into an aesthetic.

                                   *

The amused, slightly distanced perspective with which Bishop
observes the labour-intensive pelicans in 'The Bight' is also em-
ployed in her description – characterisation might be a better word
– of the wader's antics in 'Sandpiper'. A degree of self-identification,
however, becomes more apparent as the poem proceeds. And, as
often in Bishop's poetry, where a sense of scale is radically chal-
lenged, this distance of perspective is offset by the extraordinarily
close-up optics of the descriptive effects. The first lines bring the
reader into startling proximity with the sandpiper's view of the
world:

The roaring alongside he takes for granted,
and that every so often the world is bound to shake.
He runs, he runs to the south, finical, awkward,
in a state of controlled panic, a student of Blake.

Many commentators on the poem have noted that the lines from
Blake which have most bearing on the poem, are from the opening
of 'Auguries of Innocence':

To see a World in a Grain of Sand,
And a Heaven in a Wild Flower,
Hold Infinity in the palm of your Hand,
And Eternity in an Hour.

The sandpiper's microscopic scrutiny of the shoreline is ironically
equated with that of the visionary poet who insisted on the 'minute
particulars' of vision. The word 'state' is a peculiarly Blakean term
– as in his description of the *Songs of Innocence and Experience* as
'SHEWING THE TWO CONTRARY STATES OF THE HUMAN SOUL'.
Even the name 'Sandpiper' is reminiscent of the poet's vocation as
it appears in the introductory poem of Blake's *Songs of Innocence*:
'Piper, pipe that song again'. (Sand, the other component of the
bird's compound name, is the object of the bird's and the poet's
scrutiny.) And yet the reference makes fun of both Blake and the
sandpiper in their shared obsessive questing. I think Kalstone is
right to draw attention to the differences between Bishop and Blake
here: 'Bishop lets us know that every detail is a boundary, not a
Blakean microcosm' and to see Bishop's poem as 'a critique of
Blake's auguries of innocence'. Almost inadvertently, and seemingly
unbeknownst to himself, the sandpiper at the end of the poem
does chance on, or come up with 'something' – not too far from a
'World' or 'Heaven' – in 'the millions of grains of sand', though
the effect occurs as a weird by-product to his act of 'obsessed'
attention.

It is as though her poem were enacting the drama that in a cel-
ebrated letter to Anne Stevenson she noted in Darwin:

– But reading Darwin one admires the beautiful solid case being built
up out of his endless, heroic observations, almost unconscious or auto-
matic and then comes a sudden relaxation, a forgetful phrase, and one
feels that strangeness of his undertaking, sees the lonely young man,
his eyes fixed on facts and minute details, sinking or sliding giddily off
into the unknown. What one seems to want in art, in experiencing it,
is the same thing that is necessary for its creation, a self-forgetful, per-
fectly useless concentration.

Her phrase 'controlled panic' is seemingly a criticism of the whole visionary enterprise – the will to control the world through one idée fixe. But even here there may be more self-projection than the tone would suggest. Panic, we remember, is derived from Pan, the god of music and wild places as well as the instigator of fear. Bishop herself, in *Efforts of Affection: A Memoir of Marianne Moore*, defends Moore's poems by seeing panic as crucial to the making of art:

> Lately I have seen several references critical of her poetry by feminist writers, one of whom described her as a "poet who controlled panic by presenting it as whimsy." Whimsy is sometimes there, of course, and so is humor (a gift these critics sadly seem to lack). Surely there is an element of mortal panic and fear underlying all works of art?

Commenting on the poem, Seamus Heaney claims that it 'has about it a touch of comedy and a hint of self-portraiture'. In a way, it is the comic distance that maintains the self-portraiture at the level of a hint, and it is typical of Bishop that the bard should take a back seat to the bird. Yet, as with the Baudelaire reference in 'The Bight', the presence of Blake in the first stanza of this poem alerts the reader to the ways in which the poem is concerned with the art of writing. The poem continues:

> The beach hisses like fat. On his left, a sheet
> of interrupting water comes and goes
> and glazes over his dark and brittle feet.
> He runs, he runs straight through it, watching his toes.
>
> – Watching, rather, the spaces of sand between them,
> where (no detail too small) the Atlantic drains
> rapidly backwards and downwards. As he runs,
> he stares at the dragging grains.
>
> The world is a mist. And then the world is
> minute and vast and clear. The tide
> is higher or lower. He couldn't tell you which.
> His beak is focussed; he is preoccupied,
>
> looking for something, something, something.
> Poor bird, he is obsessed!
> The millions of grains are black, white, tan, and gray,
> mixed with quartz grains, rose and amethyst.

The seismic presence of the Atlantic alongside is heard rather than seen – its 'roaring' in the first and hissing in the second stanza. The ocean's edge is then perceived as 'a sheet / of interrupting water' which 'glazes over his dark and brittle toes'. Subliminally, this sheet with the implied marking of bird tracks recalls the act of writing. The presence of the ocean, or the macroscopic, is 'taken for granted' and the bird, and by extension the writer, or this particular kind of writer, couldn't tell whether 'The tide / is higher or lower'. It is as if, insofar as the bird stands for Bishop, the poem is reproaching the writer's craft for its massive exclusions, its insensitivity to external events. The peculiar kind of seeing that the bird is capable of is at once a miraculous magnification and a comic occlusion. The exact admixture of these two elements crucially depends on how the reader interprets the poem's last lines:

> Poor bird, he is obsessed!
> The millions of grains are black, white, tan, and gray,
> mixed with quartz grains, rose and amethyst.

These lines have a diminuendo quality characteristic of Bishop's endings. Another striking feature is the way the poem's rhyme scheme which has been in a consistently *abcb*, full-rhymed pattern turns slant-rhymed only in this final quatrain with 'obsessed' and 'amethyst'. The acoustic effect is to make the ending less clinching and sounded. At the same time, the lines subtly weave together two sound patterns which have been created earlier in the poem: *aw<u>kw</u>ard...back<u>w</u>ards and down<u>w</u>ards...(<u>black</u>, <u>w</u>hite)... <u>qu</u>artz* and *hisses...mist...vast...focussed...obsessed...amethyst*. The penultimate line, with its more or less monochrome and monosyllabically itemised shades 'black, white, tan, and gray' (the superfluous comma after 'tan' slows down the verse and emphasises the separateness of the shades), is quietly infiltrated in the final line by the mineral splendour of 'quartz grains, rose and amethyst'. The bird who has been 'looking for something, something, something' – presumably food, though the poem pretends not to have thought of this obvious fact – may well be unaware of the 'something' that the poem has made visible to the reader, and yet these semi-precious grains are all the more dazzling for the drabness of their setting. That vertigo of numbers that we sense in 'The millions of grains' (which Baudelaire visits in 'Le Gouffre': 'Je ne vois qu'infini par tous les fenêtres, // Et mon esprit, toujours du vertige hanté /... / – Ah! Ne jamais sortir des Nombres et des Êtres!'), a queasy sense of Blake's 'Infinity', seem finally to be sifted and ends up with the beautiful specificity of 'rose and amethyst'. The word 'rose' is so often in Bishop erotically charged (as in her extraordinary, unpublished poem 'Rock Roses' which, again, employs a crystalline image) that it may account for a residue of this emotion in the final line.

Everything in this poem validates a remark which Kalstone makes in another context: 'all of Bishop's poems about seeing are critiques of the act of seeing'. There is something self-delighting but never self-congratulatory about the precision of Bishop's observations –

and certainly, here, the sandpiper's excluding focus is problematic. The ambivalence of the ending and the humour directed at the 'Poor bird' – which includes the poet to the extent to which we allow Bishop's identification with the sandpiper – as well as the shift from full to slant rhyme make the ending muted and unemphasing, but the effect is paradoxically the stronger for that.

*

If Blake is invoked at the outset with irony, the poem may well have delivered more in the way of 'minute particulars' and found more 'detail' in each minutely observed grain of sand than Blake himself achieved with his more symbolic and visionary approach to the exterior world. Although the poem puts Blake *in primo piano*, there's reason to consider that Baudelaire's 'L'Albatros' is at least as much to the fore of Bishop's mind in composing it. In this poem, also in quatrains, Baudelaire describes the albatross on the ship's deck and contrasts its clumsy floundering there with its majestic flight. And then, in the fourth and final stanza, he explicitly makes a comparison with the role of the poet:

> Souvent, pour s'amuser, les hommes d'équipage
> Prennent des albatros, vastes oiseaux des mers
> Qui suivent, indolents compagnons de voyage,
> Le navire glissant sur les gouffres amers.
>
> À peine les ont-ils déposés sur les planches,
> Que ces rois de l'azur, maladroits et honteux,
> Laissent piteusement leurs grandes ailes blanches
> Commes des avirons trainer à côté d'eux.
>
> Ce voyageur ailé, comme il est gauche et veule!
> Lui, naguère si beau, qu'il est comique et laid!
> L'un agace son bec avec un brûle-gueule,
> L'autre mime, en boitant, l'infirme qui volait!
>
> Le Poète est semblable au prince des nuées
> Qui hante la tempête et se rit de l'archer;
> Exilé sur le sol au milieu des huées,
> Ses ailes de géant l'empêchent de marcher.

The two poems, Bishop's and Baudelaire's, apart from the quatrain form and the bird as poet analogy, seem very remote from each other. The greatest distance is perhaps in the method of analogising – where Baudelaire's fourth stanza makes the comparison explicit, Bishop's comparison is both implicit and subsidiary. The effect of the crew's cruelty to the bird – these deckhands are indulging in a bit of Shelley-baiting – invokes a kind of pity, which finally seems close to self-pity as well as being a triumphant assertion of the poet's storm-tossed grace. Their mimicry of the bird's clumsiness is something that Bishop does on a formal level with the repetition of 'He runs, he runs' – the phrase is like a refrain or a tic, occurring five times, and imitating the bird's stop-start, hasty movements. The repetition of 'something' serves a similar function and gives the impression of obsessive, repetitive, almost involuntary movement. It's notable how daring, and effective, these repetitions are in such a short poem. Though different in kind, the comic element in both links them, as does Bishop's epithet 'awkward' which is emphatic in Baudelaire in the two words 'gauche' and 'maladroit'. In Bishop's poem we've seen already how a sound-pattern almost alchemically transforms 'awkward' into 'quartz'; which in a way is equivalent to the albatross who is the butt of jokes on dry land but, in the air, 'se rit de l'archer' (laughs at the bowman). Both poems make large claims for the poet, Baudelaire's overtly and Bishop's far more cagily.

But it's perhaps in the contrasts that we can see the affinity, or at least the kind of engagement, Bishop has with her predecessor. Baudelaire's albatross, with its Coleridgean ancestry, is ultimately a stand-in and justification for the poet – socially ridiculous, but empowered in his own element. Bishop's bird, on the other hand, hardly even seems to have wings, and far from being a prince of the clouds is utterly earthbound, hugging the shoreline. Baudelaire's explicit 'semblable' makes a symbol of the bird, where Bishop resists this kind of allegorising, and – though the poem is richer for its seam of associations with the poet's role – never lets the bird itself leave the foreground of the poem, never, as it were, lets it leave the ground and doesn't make it subservient to its symbolic properties.

Like 'The Bight', it seems to me, the poem is both a homage to and criticism of the French poet's procedures. Bishop states in one letter that, alongside of Herbert, Baudelaire is her favourite poet, and in another, to Robert Lowell, that 'The Swan' is 'one of my favourite Baudelaire poems'. 'La Cygne' is another bird poem which takes Baudelaire's symbolist strategies to far subtler and more explorative extremes than does 'L'Albatros' and includes his declaration that 'Tout, pour moi, devient l'allégorie', a personalised version of Goethe's 'Alles ist Symbol'. The central image of the swan spawns a series of recursive variants on the theme of exile, change and loss – a series that includes Paris itself as setting and source, Andromaque, a tubercular negress and so on, as the poem itself concludes: 'Je pense aux matelots oubliés dans une île, / Aux captifs, aux vaincus!... à bien d'autres encor!' – whoever, in short, has lost what can never be regained: 'À quiconque a perdu ce qui ne se retrouve / Jamais! jamais!' The plangent repetition of 'jamais' implies that the poet himself shares the suffering of his examples. This repetition is reminiscent of Bishop's bird which is 'looking for something, something, something' – an obsessive search which implies the lack of an essential, if not necessarily an essential ever possessed. Again the first person pronoun which structures the entire poem ('je pense à...') highlights the plight and primacy of the poet who assembles these images of his own sense of exile, whereas Bishop's presence in her poem is left delicately unstated and indeterminate. (As an indicator of the continuing importance of this poem by Baudelaire, it's interesting to see Paul Muldoon's affectionately exaggerated and parodic, and this time passive, re-working of its 'je pense à' format in his poem to the French sym-bolist poet Gérard de Nerval 'Something Else': 'he hanged himself from a lamp-post / with a length of chain, which made me think // of something else, then something else again'.)

The presence of the words 'something' and 'quartz' alerts the reader to another allusion, this time to Robert Frost's poem 'For Once, Then, Something' (first published in 1920). If this kind of intertextual triangulation seems too suppositious, I can only say that Bishop started it with her reference to Blake. Frost's poem is even more evidently than Bishop's a kind of manifesto and justi-fication as well as both a poem about seeing and an exploration of what brings a poem into being. Frost allows his critics to mock him for his poetry's narcissism – of staring into wells, and seeing his own reflection deified:

> Others taunt me with having knelt at well-curbs
> Always wrong to the light, so never seeing
> Deeper down in the well than where the water
> Gives me back in a shining surface picture
> Me myself in the summer heaven, godlike,
> Looking out of a wreath of fern and cloud puffs.

This image allows the poet to appear as at once 'always wrong' and 'godlike', and (jokingly) allows the anxiety of 'never seeing / Deeper down' to attach itself to his writing. This is a comic way of going along with what 'Others taunt' him with, of showing them that they may be right and that he doesn't care if they are. Or else it could be seen as someone who exaggerates a fault, of which they stand accused, in a nonchalant self-parody which is meant to disarm further criticism. The poem continues:

Once, when trying with chin against a well-curb,
I discerned, as I thought, beyond the picture,
Through the picture, a something white, uncertain,
Something more of the depths – and then I lost it.
Water came to rebuke the too clear water.
One drop fell from a fern, and lo, a ripple
Shook whatever it was lay there at bottom,
Blurred it, blotted it out. What was that whiteness?
Truth? A pebble of quartz? For once, then, something.

The three 'something's here scattered through the poem are reprised all together in Bishop's poem. If Frost's poem begins with a taunt to the writer it ends up with the writer teasing the reader, teasing the reader's urge to find at last 'something' substantial to settle on which would validate the attention of writer and reader. This 'something' is uncertainly glimpsed by the poet, like the boasted catch of a fisherman '– and then I lost it'. That the whole poem should be constructed out of something so fugitive, and possibly inconsequential, is too disappointing a prospect for the reader to be at ease with, and therefore the poem encourages the reader to invest this 'uncertain' something with meaning – again, part of Frost's play is to put the abstraction and the actuality ('Truth? A pebble of quartz?') in the reverse order of expectation, and both in an interrogative form. Richard Poirier who, in his fine study *Robert Frost: The Work of Knowing*, devotes very little space to this poem about the nature of 'knowing', enlists the sinister whiteness of Melville's whale to explain the effect of 'What was that whiteness?' – and in doing so enacts the way the poem toys with the reader's need to alight on larger meanings. Frost's readers also bring to this 'whiteness' the explicitly sinister and tainted whiteness of his later poem 'Design' in which the whiteness is that of a sepulchre and where the Thomist argument from design is deliberately subjected to the part Satanic, part Darwinian, stresses of a vicious 'design of darkness to appall'. Certainly there is something unsettling here about 'something white' which is 'more of the depths', as though the darkness we would associate with the deep has entered into the white. But those two proposals – 'Truth? A pebble of quartz?' – which veer between the abstract and the concrete, the absolute and the particular, are left hanging and only seemingly resolved by the final phrase which also supplies the title – a phrase that leaves the reader no closer to 'knowing' or understanding anything. Though to some, the critics that 'taunt' him, this games-playing might seem too pleased and coy, the way the poem has been constructed out of (almost) nothing – a glimpse, an uncertainty – reveals much about poetry's interest in inklings and intimations and, beyond that, the way the mind latches onto the insubstantial and gives credence to the fugitive. Frost is characteristically drawn to the indefinite, starting three poems with the word 'Something' which here he ends on – notably 'Mending Wall' with its famous and unexplained opening 'Something there is that doesn't love a wall' – plus another which begins 'Some things are never clear'. It's possible that both Frost's and Bishop's 'something' hark back to the ending of George Herbert's 'Prayer' where in its final appositional phrase 'Something understood' – the exhausted contentment of the voice seems sure of some counter-response available neither to the playfully sceptical Frost nor to Bishop's questing and fidgety bird. However the presence of quartz and three somethings in both poems suggests a deliberate reference on Bishop's part, though Bishop might well reply with polite discouragement, as she did to Mazzaro, 'but...it is fascinating how my poem arouses in you all those literary references!' Even if unconscious, which seems to me doubtful, there is a sense in which poems may enter into critical dialogue with their predecessors without their author's express permission.

Whereas in Baudelaire the albatross had served as a symbol on which to hang the handicaps and consolations of the poet's vocation, Bishop's 'Sandpiper', whilst subtly introjecting the concerns of the poet, nevertheless gives primacy to the bird itself, and the poem could be appreciated well enough, even if incompletely, without the allegoric running alongside. I'd say that there's also a conscious element of reference to, and of self-differentiation from, Frost which enters into Bishop's poem. What is found at the end of both poems has an element of ambiguity. In Frost, it may be truth (but then we wonder what the poem which has 'lost' sight of it amounts to and how the poem might have grasped it) or it may be quartz (and would that give the poem a quality of artistic durability like Horace's 'aere perennius' or would the stone just be an image of natural beauty?), but is it really, then, something? In Bishop's poem it is uncertain whether the bird – and so the poet also – gets much joy from the quartz and amethyst, but at least the poem, and therefore the reader, does. By contrast with the Frost poem in which the poet's presence permeates, or supersaturates, the whole structure ('Me myself'), Bishop's presence in her poem is elusive and disguised, and far from 'godlike'.

*

The muted effect of the off-rhyme at the end of 'Sandpiper' is not an isolated example of Bishop subverting the formal structures she employs, making it a device to explore a dialectic between order and chaos, liberty and determinism. In 'The Map', the first poem of her first book with its geographer's title *North & South*, Bishop sets up for the first and last stanza a regular *abbacddc* rhyme-scheme (where *a* and *c* are identical rhymes) whilst leaving the middle eight-line stanza unrhymed. So the enclosed rhyme scheme (*abba*) itself encloses an unrhymed stanza. Rigid enclosure or order around what continues to break out from it is very much the subject of the poem. The continent described in the middle stanza is not without its order but it is one which resists human schemata or mapping. It runs over its edges (and line-endings): 'its edges / showing the line of long sea-weeded ledges' as she notes in the first stanza – 'The names of sea-shore towns run out to sea...' The order here is more susceptible to touch than to sight: 'where the oily Eskimo / has oiled it' or 'These peninsulas take the water between thumb and finger / like women feeling for the smoothness of yard-goods'. And this discriminating subtlety of texture and perception is what makes her finally commend one kind of mapping over another: 'More delicate than the historians' are the map-makers colors'.

In 'Sunday, 4 A.M.' – a poem which from the title alone, diary-like in its particularity, we would guess to be about insomnia – Bishop has contrived an unusual alternation between masculine and feminine rhymes which is maintained (with slight variants) until the final stanza, where it changes into alternating feminine rhymes in the same *abab* structure. The poem is a strange confusion of conflicting thoughts and voices ('Dream dream confronting') with a sense of increasing menace and sudden hypnagogic clarities. The penultimate stanza ends with the tone of a curdled fairy-tale:

> The cat's gone a-hunting.
> The brook feels for the stair.

Only in the last stanza does the threat finally diminish:

> The world seldom changes,
> but the wet foot dangles
> until a bird arranges
> two notes at right angles.

The alternation of masculine and feminine rhymes is the temporal equivalent of the spatial image of 'two notes at right angles'. The final change to all feminine rhymes in the last stanza is something of a resolution to the pattern, particularly two rhymes so close visually, the 'g' hardened by the addition of the 'l' in the second and fourth lines. The bird's notes, like the arrival, or at least the promise of dawn, offer at once a reprieve from the rising water of the dream landscape and a consolatory music. This rhyme of 'changes' and 'arranges' is the same one Bishop uses at the end of 'North Haven', her elegy for her friend, the poet Robert Lowell, a poem that we would expect to be concerned with the craft of poetry, and those two words in both poems have to do with artistry, the bird's and the poet's, between which, again, she makes an equivalence:

> You can't derange, or re-arrange,
> your poems again. (But the Sparrows can their song.)
> The words won't change again. Sad friend, you cannot change.

In that additional rhyming word 'derange', it's hard not to hear both a reference to Lowell's intermittent manic condition as well as to his obsessive rewriting – and underneath both, connecting them, that phrase from Rimbaud's 'lettre du voyant' which speaks of a 'un long, immense et raisonné *dérèglement de tous les sens*' (to Paul Demeny, 15 May 1871). 'North Haven' begins with another harbour view:

> *I can make out the rigging of a schooner*
> *a mile off; I can count*
> *the new cones on the spruce. It is so still*
> *the pale bay wears a milky skin, the sky*
> *no clouds, except for one long, carded horse's-tail.*

These natural observations are framed by the auxiliary verb 'I can' which seems oddly redundant, a rather listless declaration of power, until the last stanza highlights the contrast between what Bishop, being alive, can still do and what Lowell, now dead, 'can't'. Bishop even imagines the islands 'drifting... / a little north, a little south or sideways', pretending that they are endowed with a mobility implicitly denied to her friend. The third and fourth stanzas record the names of flowers and birds – all capitalised like the 'Sparrows' of the final stanza as though they were the names of fellow poets, or else the works of Nature:

> Nature repeats herself, or almost does:
> *Repeat, repeat, repeat; revise, revise, revise.*

This continuing repetition and revision – for better or worse – both in life and in literature is what her friend Lowell 'can't' any longer take part in.

*

Although I've been amassing the kind of 'literary associations' which Bishop quietly discourages in her letter to Mazzaro, I don't mean to suggest that to make sense of her poetry it must be refracted through the work of other poets nor, for that matter, that only these poems which mention other poets are poems which scrutinise the process of writing – what purpose the poem serves, its *raison d'être*. A comparable ending to that of 'Sandpiper' – a last minute adjustment or reversal (in this case a vocal one) – can be found, for example, in 'Under the Window: Ouro Prêto'. Its status as one of her 'Uncollected Poems' may betray some doubts Bishop had as to whether it was truly finished. And at a first reading, the poem would seem merely to describe the jumble of events taking place 'Under the Window' and around the fountain in this Brazilian gold-mining town, with that air of continuing 'untidy activity' which 'The Bight' records. In this case: conversations, gossip, the various animals that come for water, the black boy under a pile of laundry and the lorries, with their stickers, in their way as 'talkative / and soiled and thirsty' as the townsfolk. One truck 'grinds up / in a blue cloud of burning oil' – a stray image which prepares us for the transformation of oil at the end of the poem. Tom Paulin, in his essay 'Dwelling without Roots: Elizabeth Bishop', traces the original and charged uses to which oil is put in her poems – blending the natural and the industrial in unexpected ways, and challenging a traditional hierarchy of values: 'Oil is a sacral symbol of dwelling in her poems...an emblem that is insistently artificial, unnatural, technological, commercial.' Here too spilt oil instead of being a pollutant takes on an almost redemptive, celestial quality, not the antithesis of water but its complement. If the water supplies a human and animal thirst, the oil quenches, it seems, at least momentarily, another thirst, a symbolic and transcendent one. The place-name Ouro Prêto means, in Portuguese, 'Black Gold' and was originally called Villa Rica du Ouro Prêto ('Town Rich from Black Gold') in reference not to the slave trade – another valence of the phrase – but to its mining history: the town grew around the discovery of alluvial gold and when that was exhausted they mined from the ground gold that was mixed with silver, the silver blackening on contact with the air. Something of this history may linger in the word 'soiled' which in turn both phonetically and by association suggests the image of oil. But the prominence of the oil imagery especially at the end may have to do with 'black gold' being U.S. slang for oil – a phrase that will be familiar to those who still remember the song at the beginning of *The Beverly Hillbillies* in which petrol is described as 'Black Gold. Texas Tea'.

These are the last two stanzas of the poem:

> The seven ages of man are talkative
> and soiled and thirsty.
>   Oil has seeped into
> the margins of the ditch of standing water
>
> and flashes or looks upward brokenly,
> like bits of mirror – no, more blue than that:
> like tatters of the *Morpho* butterfly.

Bishop, in that first line-and-a-half, offers up a resumé of the pro-
longed foregoing description. But instead of ending on this note,
the poem takes another turn, breaks off mid-line by noticing a small,
marginal detail, something at the edge both of the scene and of
the poem, some fragment that can carry the weight of all the
accumulated details. It is interesting that the oil 'flashes or looks
up brokenly' in a kind of defeated aspiration. There are several
different types of metallic blue Morpho butterfly in Southern Brazil,
but this is most likely the *Morpho electra*. In *Beautiful Butterflies*,
J. Moucha writes that this family of butterflies can be captured by
waving small coloured flags or 'by flashing a mirror in the sunshine'.
He describes their appearance: 'Their wings reflect the endless
blue of the skies – they are jewels on the wing...' A poem which
has been at such inclusive pains to describe what happened, that
would seem essentially mimetic in its relation to the world, finally,
and I'd argue typically, moves beyond the mimetic with that simile
of 'bits of mirror'. The mirror that reflects the world is broken,
but not in the debased manner of Stephen Dedalus's symbol of
Irish art: 'the cracked lookingglass of a servant' – an image that
Bishop would handle very differently, as when she writes about
the black servant 'Cootchie' and her grave marked by 'pink wax
roses / planted in tin cans filled with sand'. On the contrary this
mirroring oil, even though in 'tatters' which effectively ground the
creature, takes on the colour of one of the most dazzling butterflies
and so the final simile rather than being merely reflective is subtly
transformative.

*

Bishop's absorption in and minute attention to the world she
describes is one of the most striking characteristics of her poems.
Bishop was delighted when Randall Jarrell compared her poems to
Vermeer's paintings. Though her own paintings include several
interiors, by far the best are some of the landscapes, in which,

though without any of his technical virtuosity, there's an almost Adamic kind of pleasure in landscape for its own sake that's reminiscent of Dürer's watercolour sketches. John Berger's *Dürer* quotes the German artist's credo 'The more accurately your work represents life, the better it will appear.' Berger comments on this 'key tenet' of Dürer's:

> it accounts for his love of seemingly insignificant detail, apparent not only in his studies of plants and his portrait sketches, but also...in the muzzle of an ox, or the attempt at drawing a walrus.

Elsewhere Berger writes:

> Never before had anyone dared to paint anything as insignificant as a piece of turf. Dürer was later to account for his avant-garde sense of the real in his *Four Books of Human Proportions*: 'Life in Nature reveals the truth of things.'

We've come to expect from artists after Dürer, at least up until the age of photography, this kind of attention to the details of the natural world. With poets, it has been often seen as an encumbrance and a failure to respect the boundaries between the arts. Most notably, G.E. Lessing in his essay 'Laocoön' (1766), sees pictorialising description more or less as a dereliction of the poet's duties. In poetry, he writes, 'the detailed pictures of physical objects...has always been recognised by the best judges as a frigid kind of sport for which little or nothing of genius is demanded'. This argument is based on his belief that 'the verbal delineations of bodies fail of the illusion on which poetry particularly depends...for the reason that the *co-existence* of the physical object comes into collision with the *consecutiveness* of speech'. It is precisely 'the consecutiveness of speech' that Bishop uses to such effect at the end of 'Under the Window: Ouro Prêto' with the interrupting qualification of 'like bits of mirror – no, more blue than that: / like tatters of the *Morpho* butterfly'. It has the same quality which M.W. Croll noted in the writers of Baroque prose, and which Bishop copied out in a letter she wrote at the age of twenty two: 'Their purpose was to portray, not a thought, but a mind thinking...'

The *consecutive* nature of experience as a poem transmits it – as opposed to its spatial extension in painting – is a recurrent concern in Bishop's descriptions. Her strong pictorialising impulse (her 'settings' as she puts it in her letter to Mazzaro) frequently come up against the passing of time – not just in the formal sense that in a poem phrase follows phrase, as in the case of the ending of 'Under the Window: Ouro Prêto', but also conceptually. We've already seen how in the last line of 'The Map' time is set against space in the comparison: 'More delicate than the historians' are the map-makers' colors' and how a temporal image of 'consecutiveness' has been converted into a spatial figuration at the end of 'Sunday 4 A.M': 'until a bird arranges / two notes at right angles'. 'At the Fishhouses', one of her most meticulously and beautifully descriptive poems, concludes with a Heraclitean image of the water that the poem has so patiently depicted suddenly perceived as free and mobile in time:

> It is like what we imagine knowledge to be:
> dark, salt, clear, moving, utterly free,
> drawn from the cold hard mouth
> of the world, derived from the rocky breasts
> forever, flowing and drawn, and since
> our knowledge is historical, flowing, and flown.

In 'Poem', a poem which is ostensibly about a painting but which, as its title reminds us, is aware of the difference of its own art form, Bishop again confronts the temporal via the pictorial. The poem begins:

> About the size of an old-style dollar bill,
> American or Canadian,
> mostly the same whites, gray greens, and steel grays
> – this little painting (a sketch for a larger one?)
> has never earned any money in its life.
> Useless and free...

The poem records a sudden recognition ('Heavens, I recognize the place, I know it!') of the Nova Scotian scene within the painting made by her great-uncle, and the strangeness and intimacy of meeting the spirit of place in this 'minor family relic': 'life and the memory of it so compressed / they've turned into each other. Which is which?' She ends by returning to the question of scale that she began with, only this time 'the size' has become duration, and 'Not much' at that:

> – the little that we get for free,
> the little of our earthly trust. Not much.
> About the size of our abidance
> along with theirs: the munching cows,
> the iris, crisp and shivering, the water
> still standing from spring freshets,
> the yet-to-be-dismantled elms, the geese.

But in those last five lines the size of that 'Not much' has become infinitely expanded to include the cows, the flowers, the trees and the birds alongside of the human – time being their common element.

There ought to be a rhetorical term to describe this central (and, as far as I know, uncommented-on) trope in Bishop's poetry, in which a pictorialising impulse cedes to a sense of time, what Lessing would call the 'consecutive' nature of experience as it's perceived in a poem. There is – at least for the reverse effect in 'Sunday, 4 A.M.' – where the sound of the bird's notes are translated into a visual (or geometric) image which could be termed 'synaesthesia'. But essentially Bishop has expanded the reach of this device to shift perception not just from one sense to another but from one axis or dimension to another, from time to space, or, in the other examples, vice versa. It is a recurrent figure, often signalled by the word 'free', whereby Bishop manages to conflate space and time, picture and poem, and so escapes beyond the determining limits of Lessing's categories.

*

Bishop's poetry, as we have seen, has one foot in the symbolist camp, but her attitude to nature is essentially distinct from that of a poet like Baudelaire, for whom nature, despite his odd respectful reference to 'the temple of nature', is there to be improved on by art. But to say this, risks making her descriptions belong to a mimetic, representational tradition that is prominent in painting, whereas her poems question how we perceive, not only through language but through the whole spectrum and gamut of the senses. They are not content with mere representation – they push through towards that sense of mystery she noted in her passage about Darwin.

In her introduction to *The Diary of 'Helena Morley'*, Bishop quotes at length a letter by Hopkins to Robert Bridges about a book, Richard Henry Dana Jr's *Two Years Before the Mast* (1840):

> "a thoroughly good one and all true, but bristling with technicality – seamanship – which I most carefully go over and even enjoy but cannot understand; there are other things, though, as a flogging, which is terrible and instructive *and it happened* – ah that is the charm and the main point." And that, I think, is "the charm and the main point" of *Minha Vida de Menina*. Its "technicalities," diamond digging, say, scarcely "bristle,"... But – *it really happened*; everything did take place, day by day, minute by minute, once and once only, just the way Helena says it did.

This passage is such a close repetition of the phrasing – down to the italics – of her letter to Mazzaro, that there's no mistaking its importance for Bishop. Here she is writing of a diary (a form she was fascinated by and taught as one of her courses) and this is the kind of expectation a reader would naturally bring to the form, whereas from a poem we might legitimately expect something more.

Her poem 'In the Waiting Room' which charts an inner event begins 'In Worcester, Massachusetts' and ends repeating the place, adding the date 'it was still the fifth / of February, 1918'. The statement of the external place and time have a talismanic importance as though the gulf into which the girl that she was falls could only be re-approached through the actuality of its setting – that 'everything did take place...once and once only'. Only thus could the poem be adequately equipped to confront the internal journey with its ontological vertigo, its questions of belonging, of gender, of identity, that make the world she started from and returned to something henceforth dangerous and unfathomable. The waiting room and the solid world of separate facts, dates, places and identities have slid 'beneath a big black wave, / another, and another'. This aesthetic of what really happened is at a considerable remove from reportage and from straight description. As Kalstone suggests 'she would use observation as a kind of tentative anchorage, as a way of grasping for presence in the world'. Her attitude towards the actual far from consuming it, or turning it for consumption, is marked by a reverence, sometimes an appalled delight (awful but cheerful), that what happened happened. Though that, perhaps, isn't 'the charm and the main point' of her poems.

NICHOLA DEANE

'Everything a Poet Should Be': Elizabeth Bishop in Her Letters

'Perfectly sensible crystal fish'; Key West plants with 'violent names' such as 'Rose of Hell', 'Woman's Tongue' and 'Crown of Thorns'; 'ices in the shape of ballet dancers': the letters of Elizabeth Bishop teem with a fantastic array of objects, flora, fauna, landscapes, buildings and people. From the Brazilian *Menaca* tree, with its 'big, separate flowers of white purple and pale lavender' to the disappointing Mexican fireworks that 'make a great deal of hissing and sputtering and a long *whoosh* and trail of smoke, and then a very mild report and no light at all', everything is delivered to the recipients of her letters with prodigious gusto and good humour.[1] Each scene she describes, each object and person, seems 'sensitive and alive all over'. More than this, the letters often leave a sting behind them in the mind of the reader, of the kind that creates a 'taste or appetite for what it sees'.[2]

The same gusto that characterises her poems also distinguishes her correspondence. It is as if the letters are, to a very great extent, an extension of Bishop's poetic work. And it is in this light that her critics generally tend to see them. I don't wish to challenge this consensus, but I do intend to re-evaluate the relationship between the letters and poems. The commonplace assumption in literary studies is that letters are material to be combed through by scholars, critics and biographers, in their attempt to discover the precise origins of published poems, novels, plays etc. Letters themselves are scarcely written about *as letters*. Even when a writer's correspondence is thought to be exceptional (as is Keats's, for example), it will almost certainly be the case that one or two critics will set down a standard Writer-in-his-Letters article, which calls the correspondence a 'vivid' or 'accurate' self-portrait, and excerpts examples of entertaining subject-matter to illustrate the point. Occasionally, a letter-writer such as Keats may provoke one or two attempts at thematic analysis.[3] But generally, literary familiar letters seem conspicuously resistant to this kind of inquiry, and probably for good reason.

Consider the letters of a literary titan such as Coleridge, whose every scrap of extant writing is in print. Even dedicated Coleridgeans must pause and take a *very* deep breath before they embark on a journey though all five volumes of Earl Leslie Griggs's *Collected Letters* in search of sources for poems, essays, or biographical incident. His correspondence is often entertaining, but frequently it is also prolix, to say the least. To write a thematic characterisation of it, as a few have done with Keats's letters, would be a bewildering and daunting task. Very few would attempt such an enterprise on the collected written detritus of a life. The tacit assumption seems to remain that such an undertaking – to organise these scraps into a narrative and interpret them – remains the proper activity of the biographer alone.

Bishop's letters have, in part, suffered from this apparently standard measure of neglect. A few articles exist which focus on the letters, and half of these are reviews of Robert Giroux's 1994 edition, *One Art: Selected Letters*.[4] Yet, Bishop's letters are far from being a "standard" literary correspondence, as Robert Lowell was not slow to recognise:

> When Elizabeth Bishop's letters are published (as they will be), she will be recognized as not only one of the best, but also the most prolific writers of our century.[5]

Even before her death, it was felt by this recipient of her letters that they are *already* works of art. What Richard Wollheim might call the 'aesthetic attitude' of the writer is conspicuous to this reader.[6] It is also conspicuous to Robert Giroux, who titles his selection of her letters *One Art*, thereby definitively categorising the correspondence's status as a work of art. Giroux's action in doing so is, so far as I am aware, if not unprecedented, extremely unusual. Of the literary Selected Letters that tend to be published, very few are given a title of this order. The writer's name: Lord Byron, say, or John Keats, is usually in the largest type on the spine, with 'Selected Letters and Journals' or 'Letters of' in smaller print.[7] In these cases, the biographical significance is held by the editors and publishers to be paramount, and the aesthetic interest secondary. But not so in Bishop's case: the aesthetic rather than the biographical interest is felt to be key.

Bishop herself, in conjunction with her letters' recipients, publishers and reviewers and readers makes her correspondence into a work of art. It is as if Bishop's epistolary habits of composition cause her to evolve or invent a new sub-genre within the wider genre of literary correspondence. This is a sub-genre which comes to appear like a brand-new art form. But before I move on to celebrate the achievement this represents, I hope to piece together some of the comments Bishop makes on letters, in an attempt to *suggest* (and I feel I can do no more) how she sees the familiar letter and the practice of letter-writing.

I use the verb 'to piece' deliberately here. Nowhere in *One Art* is there any systematic attempt to defend the practice of letter-writing, and there is a quality of 'lofty vagueness' in her comments on the subject. There is ample evidence that she held the genre in high regard, but there is little exploration of the reasons for that regard. It is well known that Bishop was an enthusiastic collector and reader of published editions of correspondence, but it is not clear how this enthusiasm originates. What *is* clear, however, is the extent of the enthusiasm. In his introduction, Giroux notes that Bishop possessed collections of letters by, among others: 'The Elizabethans, George Herbert, Lady Mary Wortley Montagu, Jane Austen, Sydney Smith, Gerard Manley Hopkins, Oscar Wilde, Virginia Woolf, etc.' I can also find in *One Art*, references to Bishop reading the letters of Hart Crane, Edna St Vincent Millay, Flannery O'Connor, Henry James, Keats and Coleridge, and my list is not exhaustive.

When Bishop records her reactions to reading such correspondence, she is frequently highly enthusiastic (although less so in the case of Millay and Crane). And occasionally, she shows herself to be more than enthused. One letter to Randall Jarrell begins:

> Those two volumes of Coleridge's *Letters* arrived last night, and I read until two and woke up at six to start in again – and only the pleasant and relieving prospect of writing you can tear me away from that adorable man. As Alice J. says of Henry James: "His intestines are *my* intestines; his tooth-aches are *my* tooth-aches." I'd never realized how wonderful the letters could be in bulk like that, and how contemporary he sounds.[8]

With her interest in the letters 'in bulk', maladies, verbosity and all, Bishop is vigorous in her unqualified enthusiasm. In this she surpasses the majority of commentators on the subject. Virginia Woolf, for example, feels that the letters often degenerate into incoherence, as Coleridge's 'meaning dwindles and fades to a wisp on the mind's horizon'. Even Griggs, Coleridge's editor, finds large portions of the correspondence to be 'burdened with laborious detail and pedantic expression'.[9] But Bishop seems to be utterly entranced.

Between October 1956, when she writes to Jarrell, and December of the same year, she continues to plough through Coleridge's letters.

Writing to Lowell on December 2nd, she praises his (Lowell's) prose
memoir '91 Revere Street', and adds:

> I'm glad ['91 Revere Street'] came along now, because for several
> weeks I've been completely absorbed in Coleridge's *Letters* – that new
> edition. (Maybe I was when I wrote you last; I can't remember how
> long it's been going on now.) ...I want very much to write some sort
> of piece, mostly about Coleridge, but bringing in Fitzgerald's *The
> Crack-Up*, Dylan Thomas, Hart Crane, etc.[10]

Brett Millier records that an essay on Coleridge's letters was in fact
written in October 1956 for 'a monthly column on U.S. writing
for a new Rio magazine', although the essay was probably never
published.[11] The essay projected in the letter to Lowell may, or
may not be an extension of the piece on Coleridge: Bishop's letter
does not make this clear.

Bishop appears to have thought better of making that case in
public, and so her thoughts on letters, and the role of disasters and
disintegration in the lives of writers remained a private matter, for
the duration of her lifetime at least. This near-legendary insistence
on privacy, which probably caused her to abandon the work on
Coleridge *et al*, is also clearly in evidence when she writes to Lowell
to remonstrate with him over the use he makes of his ex-wife
Elizabeth Hardwick's letters in *The Dolphin* (1972).

On March 21st of that year, after struggling with more than
one draft of her letter, she finally writes to Lowell to express her
anxieties. She asks whether in quoting from Hardwick's letters, he
isn't 'violating a trust'. She also feels that the betrayal of using
what she calls 'personal, tragic, anguished letters' is compounded
by the fact that the letters have been *'changed'*. And the changes
do not work to portray Lowell's second wife to advantage: Bishop
writes that they have the effect of 'loading the dice' against Hard-
wick, something which Bishop feels is cruel. In the case of Lowell's
other works, she had been able to applaud or criticise his poetry
on a technical level. But here, she faces the excruciatingly uncom-
fortable task of criticising, not simply the writing, but also the
ethics of Lowell's actions. Her tactic in dealing with the difficulty
is to invoke comments made by Thomas Hardy and Henry James
about the ethics of using private correspondence in fictional work,
alongside Hopkins's observation (to Robert Bridges) that the 'idea
of the gentleman' is 'the highest thing ever conceived – higher
than a "Christian", even, certainly than a poet'.[12]

What is disputed is the misuse of letters, of Lowell *inappropri-
ately* turning them into art. And she bolsters her response through
the use of several quotations about, and taken from, familiar letters

from the correspondence of these writers. The most extensive quotation comes directly from a letter written by Hardy in 1911 about:

> "an abuse which is said to have occurred – that of publishing details of a lately deceased man's life under the guise of a novel, with assurances of truth scattered in the newspapers." [13]

Where her argument becomes difficult and painful to make, and her criticisms severe, letters are used to buttress her position. As she does so, the familiar letter begins to emerge something of an aesthetic. Her argument in the letter to Lowell places privacy and social intimacy, trust and personal honour above art in her scheme of values – the privacy, intimacy and trust that are entailed in keeping any epistolary friendship afloat. It is a value system which Bishop reiterates more publicly in her prose memoir of Marianne Moore, 'Efforts of Affection'. Here, the Hopkins letter makes another appearance. It prefaces the closing paragraphs of the piece, where Bishop writes:

> But I am sure that Marianne would have "vehemently agreed" with Hopkins's strictures: to be a poet was not the be-all and the end-all of existence.
> I find it impossible to draw conclusions or even to summarize. When I try to, I become foolishly bemused...I catch myself murmuring, "Manners and morals; manners *as* morals? Or is it morals *as* manners?" Since like Alice, "in a dreamy sort of way," I can't answer either question, it doesn't much matter which way I put it; it *seems* to be making sense. [14]

In a dreamy sort of way, letters seem to be associated in her mind with her ethical sense of what it means to be an artist. The link is not made explicit, but it is there. Letters seem to act as a reminder to Bishop of the fuzzy connection between morals and manners. They are *emblems* of that indistinct connection. Samuel Johnson in his *Rambler* essay, 'Criticism on Epistolary Writings', observes:

> No man was ever in doubt about the moral qualities of a letter. It has always been known that he who endeavours to please must appear pleased, and he who would not provoke rudeness must not practise it. [15]

As Johnson's comment reveals, the connection between good morals and good manners is conflated when it comes to letter-writing. But letters might also be emblems for Bishop, not only of the fact that being a poet is not the be-all and end-all, but also emblems of what she believes her art can and should aspire to do. On the subject of the *Life Studies* poems, she writes to Lowell:

> I am green with envy of your kind of assurance. I feel that I could write in as much detail about my Uncle Artie, say – but what would be the significance? Nothing at all. He became a drunkard, fought with his

wife, and spent most of his time fishing. It is sad; slightly more inter-
esting than having an uncle practicing law in Schenectady maybe, but
that's all. Whereas all you have to do is put down the names! And the
fact that it all seems significant, illustrative, American, etc., gives you,
I think, the confidence you display about tackling any idea or theme,
seriously, in both writing and conversation.[16]

Bishop, of course, does come to write about Artie, her Grandmother,
Uncle Neddy and even her mother and her own life experiences
and makes them supremely illustrative – despite her anxiety. But
she does so in a way that makes use of that anxiety about the
smallness of her enterprise; she somehow transforms the perceived
debility into a kind of victory. And, I would suggest, this comes
about partly because of her habit of seeing letter-writing as an
aesthetic benchmark. I refer back to Johnson's clear-sighted essay
on letters at this point, not because there is evidence that Bishop
read the piece, but because Johnson's perception is illustrative of
what I think the letter *might* mean to Bishop:

> When the subject has no intrinsic dignity it must necessarily owe its
> attractions to artificial embellishments, and may catch at all advantages
> which the art of writing can supply. He that, like Pliny, sends his friend
> a portion for his daughter will, without Pliny's eloquence of address,
> find means of exciting gratitude and securing acceptance. But he that
> has no present to make but a garland, a ribbon, or some petty curiosity,
> must endeavour to recommend it by his manner of giving it.
>
> The purpose for which letters are written when no intelligence is
> communicated or business transacted is to preserve in the minds of the
> absent either love or esteem. To excite love we must impart pleasure,
> and to raise esteem we must discover abilities. Pleasure will generally
> be given as abilities are displayed by scenes of imagery, points of con-
> ceit, unexpected sallies, and artful compliments. Trifles always require
> exuberance of ornament; the building which has no strength can be
> valued only for the grace of its decorations. The pebble must be polished
> with ease and care which hopes to be valued as a dia-mond; and words
> ought surely to be laboured when they are intended to stand for things.[17]

As Bishop seems to feel that Lowell's particular brand of rhetorical,
Pliny-like authority and Pliny-like grandeur of subject-matter is
beyond her reach, she reaches instead for apparently homelier
models for what she feels her art should be. What evolves from
this is an aesthetic which is as sociable, genial, and modest as letters
can be, and as careful and detailed. And in practising letter-writing
as much as she did, she also practises, over and over again, the
process of making the pebble seem as valuable as the diamond; of
conferring dignity on the curiosities she describes.

That the familiar letter is a benchmark of her aesthetic is suggested
in at least one other defining letter. On 28 May 1975, Elizabeth

Bishop wrote to a Miss Pierson, giving advice about the process of poetic composition:

> Read a lot of poetry – all the time – and *not* 20th-century poetry. Read Campion, Herbert, Pope, Tennyson, Coleridge – anything at all almost that's any good, from the past – until you find out what you really like, by yourself. Even if you try to imitate it exactly – it will come out quite different. Then the great poets of our own century – Marianne Moore, Auden, Wallace Stevens – and not just 2 or 3 poems each, in anthologies – read ALL of somebody. Then read his or her life, and letters, and so on. (And by all means read Keats's Letters.) Then see what happens.[18]

Her formula for learning to write includes, as might be expected, the recommendation to read 'all of' the poems of writers such as 'Moore, Auden [and] Wallace Stevens'. Distinctive here is the emphasis she places on reading the 'life and *letters*' of the poets concerned. For the aspiring poet, she implies, familiarity with the lives of exemplary writers is an important part of becoming a poet.[19]

But Bishop takes this enthusiasm for letters one stage further, and in 1971 teaches a course on 'Letters' at Harvard. The summer prior to the course, she asks Arthur Gold and Robert Fizdale:

> Did I tell you about that? Bobby should be interested, and any ideas you have on the subject would be welcome. Just *letters*, as an art form or something. I'm hoping to select a nicely incongruous assortment of people – Mrs Carlyle, Chekhov, my Aunt Grace, Keats, a letter found in the street, etc. etc. But I need some ideas from you both – just on the subject of letters, the dying "form of communication".[20]

She sets out no theory about what she intends to teach. Only her love for incongruity, and her conviction that letters are an art form of some kind is articulated. Bishop's class is not a course of study in social history, but what she found to be a 'very sociable' exercise in the reading and *writing* of letters.[21] And this does not just mean studying literary letters, but all forms of correspondence. Just as her attitude to preparing the class is sociable and practical, as the earnest request to Gold and Fizdale for them to write letters to her on the subject of letters suggests, so is her approach to teaching it.

In the opening pages of this essay, I suggested that Bishop's achievement as a reader and writer of, and also enthusiast about letters had caused her to evolve a brand-new art form, a new sub-genre in the wider genre of the literary familiar letter. I hope I have already been able to suggest just how profoundly the letter shapes her ideas about what it means to be a poet. I hope I have also shown that Bishop sees the letter *as* an art form, and values it so much as an art form that she devises a class to teach it. But what remains to be emphasised about that teaching exercise is what, precisely, the 'incongruous' syllabus shows about what she perceives epistolary art to be. For it is this list that marks out her attitude towards the art of letter-writing as something new, something modernist.

From the 16th century onwards, the practice of letter-writing had been governed by ideals set out in innumerable *secrétaires* or collections of model letters. According to Roger Chartier:

> by announcing the prescriptions to be observed and the examples to be imitated, manuals on writing fulfilled a dual function: they established strict control over the production of written matter – even in its ordinary forms; and they distinguished between the learned, who complied naturally with the conventions that civility required, and the uncouth, whose use of writing was as yet untamed.[22]

The distinction that the *secrétaires* marked out is something that Bishop recognises when she labels her list 'incongruous': her syllabus mixes learned with unlearned letter-writers. What marks her out as modernist, though, is her insistence on exploring the art of *both* the supposedly primitive letter-writers (Aunt Grace, the anonymous writer of the 'letter found on the street'), *and* the art of the 'high' stylists, like Chekhov and Keats. All types of letters, from the 'cultivated' to the 'uncouth' are seen as art. Richard Wollheim argues:

> For the central case, which must be our starting point, is where what we regarded as a work of art has in point of fact also been produced as a work of art. [...] This is not to deny that we can regard objects that have not been made as works of art, or for that matter pieces of nature that have not been made at all, as though they had been: we can treat them as works of art. For once the aesthetic attitude has been established on the basis of objects produced under the concept of art, we can then extend it beyond this base [...] Such an extension in the case of art can occur temporarily: as, for instance, in Valéry's famous reflection on the sea shell. Or it can occur permanently – as, for instance, in the event, which has had such far-reaching effects on the whole of modern art, when, around the turn of this century, in response to an aesthetic impulse, there was a wholesale transfer of primitive artefacts from ethnographical collections, where they had hitherto been housed, to museums of fine art, where it was now thought, they were more appropriately located.[23]

The modernist sensibility that Wollheim describes, where the 'concept of art' is extended beyond the base of those 'objects produced under the concept of art', is one which informs Bishop's choice of syllabus in her letters course. She extends the 'concept of art' beyond those letters that were produced by writers who saw their practice of letter-writing as an art. She extends it to those letters which she regards as possessing an alternative aesthetic value. The artefact – the family letter, the letter found on the street – becomes art object, whose meaning is both *intransitive*, and transitive. Wollheim explains Wittgenstein's distinction between the two terms very usefully:

> Let us begin, as [Wittgenstein] does, with the word "peculiar". Talking about a piece of soap (Wittgenstein's example) I might say that it has a peculiar smell, and then add something like "It is the kind we used as children": alternatively I might say "This soap has a *peculiar* smell", emphasising the word, or "It really has a most peculiar smell". In the first case, the word is used to introduce the description that follows it, and indeed, when we have the description, is altogether replaceable. In the second case, however, the word is more or less equivalent to "out of the ordinary", "uncommon", "striking": there is no description whose place it takes, and indeed it is important to see that in such cases we aren't describing anything at all, we are emphasising or drawing attention to whatever it is, without saying, perhaps without being in a position to say, what it is. [...] Wittgenstein calls the first usage of these words "transitive", the second usage, "intransitive" [...] [24]

Whatever the text says, whatever descriptions it contains, and however much its conventions may influence the composition of poems, the letter has an additional intransitive value: it is also a symbol, or perhaps more accurately still, a talisman.

The term 'talisman' is an extremely serviceable one when applied to Bishop's letters. Talismans, or objects possessing magic power for the owner or bearer, appear often in Bishop's poetry. Michael Donaghy identifies one of them as Crusoe's knife in 'Crusoe in England'; the Man-Moth's palmed tear is another.[25] But letters, too, act as talismans. The Hopkins letter about the value of gentlemanly conduct is one epistolary talisman. Jimmy O'Shea's letter is another. O'Shea is one of Bishop's students during her brief employment at the exploitative 'U.S.A. School of Writing'. His letter to her is copied into Bishop's notebook of 1934, and recurs in two prose pieces, the story 'The Sea & Its Shore' and the memoir 'The U.S.A. School of Writing'.[26] It acts as a kind of talisman in both cases, because O'Shea had asked 'Mr Margolies' (Bishop's alias at the U.S.A. School) one question she struggled to answer throughout her professional career:

> Mr Margolies, I am thinking of how those Authors write such long stories of 60,000 or 100,000 words, and where do they get their imagination and the material to work upon? [27]

In 'The Sea & Its Shore', the same question is addressed to Bishop's narrator, Boomer, who then reflects:

> Although Boomer had no such childish desire, he felt the question posed was one having something to do with his own way of life; it might almost be addressed to him as well as the unknown Mr Margolies. But what was the answer? The more papers he picked up and the more he read, the less he felt he understood.

The question is something that Bishop later calls a 'self-riddle', and this is at the heart of its importance for her: its intransitive resistance to explanation. And the letter itself comes to stand for that unanswerable riddle.

The Hopkins and O'Shea letters are not the only epistolary talismans that exist for Bishop; Keats's letters, as a whole, are another. In March 1959, Bishop writes to Lowell:

> [I] am now finishing the new edition of Keats's letters [...] Except for his unpleasant insistence on the *palate*, he strikes me as almost everything a poet should have been in his day.[28]

Bishop does not explain what she believes a poet 'should have been', but perhaps the benefit she gains from these letters is some additional insight into the question of what a poet should be. After all, this is exactly what Keats uses the writing of his own letters to do. Unlike his contemporary, Wordsworth, Keats did not publish any equivalent of the Preface to *Lyrical Ballads*. He did not declare in public what he believed poetry should be and what the poet should do. Instead, he worked out what he believed, less systematically, in letters to friends, and his letters are the vehicle of his aesthetics, as much as they are of his life story. But this is mere speculation. Whatever she admired in Keats's letters, his *example* remained talismanic for her for many years. Keats's letters are on the syllabus of her 'Letters' course of 1971, and they are also recommended reading in the letter to Miss Pierson of 1975.

What letter-writing allowed Bishop to do was to weigh up her experience, and to try and find more potential talismans, in her continued efforts to solve the 'self-riddle' Jimmy O'Shea's letter represents. And it is to Bishop's practice of letter-writing that I would like to turn in the concluding section of this essay.

A quilt, a cage of owls, and a very curious creature

From the very beginning of her adult life, Bishop's letters can be seen to contain talismans. As far back as 1929, objects are described in such a way that they appear to 'reek with meaning'. She writes to her friend Frani Blough during an unhappy stay with relatives at Harwich Port, Massachusetts, on 5 September 1929:

The other day I got for myself out of the attic a patchwork quilt, one that my great-grandmother made. It's the *Sunflower Pattern* – big orange wheels on a white ground, and so many thousands of little white stitches that it pains one to look at it. I'd love to hang it on the wall of my room at school – a spur to conscientiousness, you know – but then I'm afraid it might make it rather like a padded cell. Well, I shall huddle under it in January and bless my great-grandmother. It should look well placed artistically near a bowl of calendulas.[29]

The quilt invites her meditation almost as if it were a mandala. The *Sunflower Pattern*, in italics, suggests she could be thinking of Van Gogh. And then there's the fact that it has a connection with family and affection; a connectedness that seems to have been lacking for her on the trip to Harwich Port. There's a suggestion of primitive art in all that painful stitchwork, and the lifelong preoccupation with her perceived lack of conscientiousness makes an early appearance too. In addition, the fact that her room at school might look like a padded cell should the quilt be hung on its walls hints at the continuing distress she suffers over her mother's breakdowns and confinement in an asylum. But once again, this is speculation based on biographical knowledge. Bishop, of course is unlikely to be conscious of this as she writes. What is of ultimate interest in this passage, however, is not the potential it has to be re-described, but simply the way in which Bishop is able to make the quilt's existence as an object stubbornly intransitive and luminously real. My paraphrase seems to me to diminish Bishop's evocation of the quilt's essential mystery: its intransitive life is lost, or in some way diminished, in the translation.

The same would be the case if I attempted to suggest *why* it is that Bishop ends this paragraph of a letter to Marianne Moore, (dated 24 November 1937, and sent from Rome) in the way that she does:

At present Louise [Crane] and I are planning to sail for New York with from two to eight owls. I think I described to you the kind we saw in Morocco – stubby, fluffy, placid little owls that you see along the side of the road. They sell them in a shop here for a horrible purpose – to be used to attack other birds, for the hunters. They are very friendly, although when we asked the man what they ate, he replied "Hearts!"[30]

The paragraph is perfectly calculated to give a small, humorous shock, a closing kick. It may also be a way of suggesting something about the dangers of sentimentalism; or perhaps Bishop sees in the owls an emblem of *human* love, much in the same way as the 'Five remote red lights' on the Navy Yard aerials become 'witnesses for love' in 'Late Air'.[31] Either, both or neither of these possibilities could be true. But what is undoubtedly important for Bishop is the act of describing them and bringing them to life in a way which is *exactly* suited to the taste of the fastidious Marianne Moore.

The owls also seem to accrue still more meaning in at least one subsequent letter. From on board the SS *Exeter*, bound for New York, Bishop recounts one anecdote on December 10 of that year, in which they appear for Frani Blough's benefit:

> This boat is so *silly*. But our manner of making it was a little undignified too – the night before leaving Florence we all ate oysters. They have the quaintest system there, my dear. The restaurants themselves don't serve fresh seafood, but a few old men go around with little trays and buckets of ice and a couple of lemons. They wander in and out of the bars and restaurants with all kinds of ancient and decaying shells on their trays. The sweetest old man served us – and wore three vests and a woolly sailor's coat, and long black fingernails which he used to flip the oyster before serving. The result was that Louise and Nina were horribly sick all night, and I was not quite myself. We started off, very pale and hollow-eyed, in a taxi with eight pieces of luggage, two paper parcels with loose strings, an umbrella and the owls in a cage – and poor Nina was sick in the taxi. At Genoa it was pouring. We were the only people getting on the boat and even we weren't expected, I guess – and we staggered down long slippery docks, no porters, no signs, no gangplank. Then it immediately grew rough (much rougher than the oysters) and from seven last night till this morning we have clung in agony to our very hard and narrow beds. The owls have retained their composure…They balance beautifully, but as Louise says, "They are probably used to branches." [32]

The comical owls could now also stand as emblems of composure, when set against the indignity of the passengers. And, as any reader of Bishop is aware, finding dignity and composure in the midst of chaos and disaster is an extremely important theme. The passage reads like a comical version of a spiritual allegory, and in itself has a fine sense of balance; exuberant detail, a deft touch of the grotesque (the old man's fingernails) and a sharp steadying up at the close of the paragraph with Louise Crane's pithy observation. So many paragraphs of description in Bishop's letters end with this kind of punch, that the cumulative effect of reading the correspondence is staggering. Her prose is masterly, even when she appears to be 'working without really doing it', and her ability to construct paragraphs on this model allows her to *test* what she observes by describing it in this superbly ironic way. Objects, people, and experience are weighed up and described as if to find out their level of suggestiveness. I chose the examples of the quilt and the owls because they do not find their way into a major public work. They are minor talismans, if you will, that ultimately do not prove suggestive enough. The major talismans; Crusoe's knife, the *National Geographic* of February 1918, the female moose, to name but three, emerge as such because they come to bear a huge weight of suggestion if they are to occupy a place in a finished poem. One of the talismans that does emerge in this way, the moose, begins her symbolic life in a letter to Marianne Moore, where Bishop describes a return trip to Nova Scotia and her relatives in 1946:

> I came back by bus – a dreadful trip, but it seemed most convenient at the time – we hailed it with a flashlight and a lantern as it went by the farm late at night. Early the next morning, just as it was getting light, the driver had to stop suddenly for a big cow moose who was wandering down the road. She walked away very slowly into the woods, looking at us over her shoulder. The driver said that one foggy night he had to stop while a huge bull moose came right up and smelled the engine. "Very curious beasts," he said. [33]

This is a marvellous piece of description in itself, a perfectly balanced paragraph with a similar structure to the one which contains the description of the owls that eat hearts. But it's also a paragraph that is attuned to Moore's poetic sensibility as much as it is to her own. It would famously take until 1972 before the encounter with the moose would transform itself into its final shape, and come to stand so powerfully for Bishop's enterprise as a poet. Twenty-six years would pass until the talisman could assume its full meaning, and Bishop could come to answer the self-riddle of why that beast had proven so curious to her. The dreamy divagation of the poem leads through the endless talk of the grandparents' voices, through the recounted disasters, and on to the turning point marked by the 'indrawn yes':

> "Yes..." that peculiar
> affirmative. "Yes..."
> A sharp, indrawn breath,
> half-groan, half acceptance,
> that means "Life's like that.
> We know *it* (also death)."

The poem relaxes in the next stanza as the voices talk on peacefully, and the narrator is lulled towards sleep. Then, suddenly all are jolted awake as the bus driver 'stops with a jolt, / turns off his lights':

> A moose has come out of
> the impenetrable wood
> and stands there, looms, rather,
> in the middle of the road.
> It approaches; it sniffs at
> the bus's hot hood.

Towering, antlerless,
high as a church,
homely as a house
(or, safe as houses).
A man's voice assures us
"Perfectly harmless...."

Some of the passengers
exclaim in whispers,
childishly, softly,
"Sure are big creatures."
"It's awful plain."
"Look! It's a she!"

Taking her time,
she looks the bus over,
grand, otherworldly.
Why, why do we feel
(we all feel) this sweet
sensation of joy?

"Curious creatures,"
says our quiet driver,
rolling his *r*'s.
"Look at that, would you."
Then he shifts gears.
For a moment longer,

by craning backward,
the moose can be seen
on the moonlit macadam;
then there's a dim
smell of moose, an acrid
smell of gasoline.[34]

From the elegantly-constructed near-whimsy of the letter looms this
beast, its size, its plainness, even its smell. And the equally elegant
closure of Bishop's prose paragraph eventually cedes to a sharper,
more exquisitely concrete sense of closure; that 'dim / smell of moose'
and (even sharper) the '*acrid* / smell of gasoline' (my emphasis). All
of which leaves us, like the passengers on the bus, to turn back to
the moose of the title, to look at her: look and look again. This is an
image of an animal that also 'presents an intellectual and emotional
complex in an instant of time'.[35] A lifetime of associations seem to
stand behind it. The moose of the poem is much more than the
'petty curiosity' it seems to be in the letter. And yet, it might not be
an overstatement to argue that Bishop's ability to perform this feat is
sharpened and perfected, as she looks steadily *at* and *into* the essences
of a myriad of objects, flora, fauna, landscapes, buildings and people
in letter upon letter.

*

NOTES

Unless otherwise cited, quotations of published works are from Bishop's *Complete Poems: 1927-1979* or *The Collected Prose*, and of letters from *One Art*.

1. *One Art*, pp.30, 67, 271, 273.
2. 'On Gusto', William Hazlitt, *Selected Writings* (Harmondsworth: Penguin, 1970), pp.201 & 202.
3. To illustrate this point there follows a short bibliography of articles on Keats's letters: Nichola Deane, 'Keats's Lover's Discourse and the Letters to Fanny Brawne', *Keats-Shelley Review*, no.13 (1999); David Luke, 'Keats's Letters: Fragments of an Aesthetic of Fragments', *Genre*, 11 (1978); Robert Pack, 'Keats's Letters: Laughter as Autobiography', *New England Review and Broadhey Quarterly*, 7 (Winter 1984); Lionel Trilling, 'The Poet as Hero: Keats in His Letters', *The Opposing Self: Nine Essays in Criticism*, (New York: Viking, 1968); Timothy Webb, ' "Cutting Figures": Rhetorical Strategies in Keats's Letters', in *Keats: Bicentenary Readings*, edited by Michael O'Neill (Edinburgh: Edinburgh University Press, 1997); 'Keats the Letter-Writer: Epistolary Poetics', *Romanticism Past and Present*, 6 no.2 (1982).
4. Langdon Hammer, 'Useless Concentration: Life and Work in Elizabeth Bishop's Letters and Poems', *American Literary History*, 9 no.1 (1997), pp.162-80; Victoria Harrison, 'Recording a Life: Elizabeth Bishop's Letters to Ilse and Kit Barker', *Contemporary Literature*, 29 no.4 (Winter 1988), pp.498-517; Lynn Keller, 'Words Worth a Thousand Postcards: The Bishop/Moore Correspondence', *American Literature*, 55 no.3 (October 1983), pp.405-29; Cristanne Miller, 'Bishop Studies: Questions of Biography', *New England Quarterly*, 67 no.3 (September 1994), pp.487-99; Barbara Page, 'The Rising Figure of the Poet: Elizabeth Bishop in Letters and Biography', *Contemporary Literature*, 37 no.1 (Spring 1996), pp.119-31; Elizabeth Spires, 'One life, one art: Elizabeth Bishop in her Letters', *The New Criterion*, 12 no.9 (1994), pp.18-23; Donald Stanford, 'From the Letters of Elizabeth Bishop, 1933-34', *Verse*, 4 no.3 (November 1987), pp.19-27. Of these Barbara Page's review characterises Bishop most positively. Langdon Hammer attempts to write about the letters more thematically, but perhaps tends to characterise Bishop too much as a victim.
5. *One Art*, p.vii.
6. Richard Wollheim: *Art and Its Objects* (Cambridge: Cambridge University Press, 1980), pp.91-98.
7. *Letters of John Keats*, edited by Robert Gittings (Oxford: Oxford University Press, 1970); *Lord Byron: Selected Letters and Journals*, edited by Leslie A. Marchand (London: Pimlico, 1992).
8. *One Art*, p.324.
9. *The Collected Letters of Samuel Taylor Coleridge*, edited by Earl Leslie Griggs (Oxford: Clarendon, 1956), I, p.xxxvi.
10. *One Art*, p.333.
11. Brett C. Millier: *Elizabeth Bishop: Life and the Memory of It*, (Berkeley, Los Angeles, Oxford: University of California Press, 1993), p.288.
12. *One Art*, pp.561-62.
13. *One Art*, pp.561.
14. *Collected Prose*, p.156.
15. Samuel Johnson: *The Rambler*, edited by S.C. Roberts (London: Everyman, 1953), p.244.

16. *One Art*, p.351.
17. Johnson: *The Rambler*, pp.245-46.
18. *One Art*, pp.595-96.
19. *One Art*, pp.595-96.
20. *One Art*, p.544-45.
21. Millier, p.453.
22. Roger Chartier: 'Introduction: An Ordinary Kind of Writing', in Roger Chartier, Alain Boureau & Cécile Dauphin, *Correspondance*, translated by Christopher Woodall (Cambridge: Polity Press, 1997) p.7.
23. Wollheim, pp.97-98.
24. Wollheim, pp.94.
25. Michael Donaghy: *Wallflowers: A Lecture on Poetry with Misplaced Notes and Additional Heckling* (London: The Poetry Society, 1999), p.31.
26. Millier, p.71.
27. 'The U.S.A. School of Writing', *Collected Prose*, p.48. See also 'The Sea & Its Shore', *Collected Prose*, p.177.
28. *One Art*, pp.371-72.
29. *One Art*, p.5.
30. *One Art*, p.64.
31. *Complete Poems*, p.45.
32. *One Art*, p.65.
33. *One Art*, p.141.
34. *Complete Poems*, pp.172-73.
35. *Wallflowers*, p.37.

LINDA ANDERSON

The Story of the Eye: Elizabeth Bishop and the Limits of the Visual

The Blindness of Seeing

In 1938, when she was touring Europe with her friend Louise Crane, Elizabeth Bishop saw Pieter Brueghel's painting of the 'Parable of the Blind' in the National Museum in Naples.[1] Bishop had already encountered some of Brueghel's paintings in Brussels in 1935, including the famous 'Landscape with the Fall of Icarus', and her Naples visit was preceded in her 'Travel Notes' by a vivid conjoining of the painter's eye with her own vision: 'A Peter Bruegel view of Naples with that wonderful running effect on the surface water'.[2] Brueghel seems to have been one of the painters who served as an important reference point for her own observations and whom she turned to much later and in very different landscape, to help her ruminate on the odd – and emotionally charged – effects of distance. This is from the notebook she kept during her unhappy stay in Washington in 1950 as Consultant in Poetry at the Library of Congress:

> The television aerials – not those on the next roof-tops but those at a distance against the sky, look unfortunately perhaps to me like some of those dreadful Bruegels – landscapes – some of wars or aftermaths of wars in which in a silent, beautiful countryside one notices Icarus (Auden's poem) – men on wheels, raised on poles, against the sky – or, more exactly, the crucifixion taking place, the spidery little crosses off on a hill.[3]

The 'dreadful Bruegels' that she refers to – 'Landscape with the Fall of Icarus', 'The Triumph of Death', 'The Procession to Calvary' – all display Brueghel's characteristic juxtaposition of two different modes of seeing: landscapes perceived from a high viewpoint and the closely observed details of life going on against the panoramic background.[4] Brueghel's attention to naturalistic detail refused to be subsumed into an Idealism which concentrated only on the most important figures in a composition to the exclusion of 'some untidy spot' which is Auden's phrase in his 'Icarus' poem;[5] rather he bestows his attention equally, even reversing, as in the Icarus picture, the expected hierarchy of foreground and background. Brueghel's vision is not at odds with a 16th-century moral and religious emphasis on the frailty of human life and the obliviousness or blindness of the human subject to his fate. However, it was also resonant for Bishop of a more modern and existential sense of tragedy, where vision and meaning do not necessarily cohere.

From the very outset of her career, critics frequently remarked on the importance of the visual to Bishop's writing. Randall Jarrell, reviewing her first book, *North & South*, in 1946, noted that 'her work is unusually personal and honest in its wit, perception, and sensitivity – and in its restrictions too; all her poems have written underneath, *I have seen it.*'[6] Bishop, herself, expressed the belief, in an interview in 1966, that she was 'more visual than most poets', adding that she had been particularly flattered by the art critic, Meyer Shapiro's view that she wrote poems ' "with a painter's eye" '.[7] Yet, gradually, commentators also noticed that there was also something odd, even disturbing, about Bishop's way of seeing. For David Kalstone, writing in 1977, too much emphasis on her 'famous eye' avoided the 'larger issues' to do with seeing; how her 'precise observations' become a way of 'countering and encountering a lost world'.[8] For Frank Bidart, four years later, there was always a 'drama of perception' going on beneath her descriptions, which involved 'cost' as well as 'pleasures'.[9] If one thinks, too, about the list of artists in whom Bishop expressed an interest – the Surrealists, in particular Max Ernst and de Chirico, the 'primitive' painter Gregorio Valdes, Brueghel, Vermeer, Vuillard, Paul Klee and Alexander Calder, it is evident that not only was 'the painter's eye' capable of wide variations of vision but that her interest in painting was particularly focused on work which interrogated – with greater or lesser self-consciousness – traditional perspectives and forms. Her tribute to Gregorio Valdes, the only painter, apart from her friends Loren McIver and Wesley Wehr, as Lorrie Goldensohn has pointed out, that Bishop chose to write about at length,[10] notes how his very failure to reproduce the 'classical ideal of verisimilitude' also 'unwittingly' helped to create 'a peculiar and captivating freshness, flatness and remoteness'.[11] Valdes brings a fresh eye to painting because he naïvely changes the privileged, unified perspective through which 'reality' has been conventionally represented in Western post-Renaissance art. Distanced from this tradition and its sense of a shared perspective, his paintings embody that 'remoteness' as an estrangement or flatness.

Bishop, though never naïve, shared Valdes' inability to see in prescribed ways. Her fascination with seeing is linked to her exploration of shifting and uncertain perspectives and her embodiment of vision in speakers who can neither forget, nor totally understand, their 'place' in the world. In her prose poem, 'Rainy Season; Sub-Tropics', completed in 1967, where she seems to join her poetic self to displaced and awkward animal bodies, she has her giant toad complain: 'My eyes bulge and hurt. They are my one great beauty, even so. They see too much, above, below, and yet there is not much to see' (*CP*, p.139). For this speaker – and perhaps for Bishop too – seeing does not transcend the body but is subject to the physical eye as sensation or travail. The toad offers a grotesque and melancholy commentary on the idea that vision can be self-sufficient: instead the visual conveys both too little and too much, both knowledge of its own limitations and the difficulty of either comprehending or enduring what one sees.

Perhaps most disturbing of all, Bishop seems to be asking here and in other poems, how can perception be separated from both 'introspection' and 'retrospection';[12] how does one draw a line or boundary between the conscious and unconscious or memory. Indeed, one of the most pervasive preoccupations of Bishop's earliest work is the way an oddly angled gaze can reflect back on the subject, displacing them not only across space but across time as well. In 'The Man-Moth', for instance, a poem inspired by a newspaper misprint, Bishop explores the occluded perspective of a creature whose knowledge is limited to the night-time world. If the man-moth's aspiration is to push through the 'clean opening' of the moon into visibility or legibility, 'forced through, as from a tube, in black scrolls on the light', his failure condemns him to a repetitive backwards journey, where he 'dare not look out of the window', for fear of the 'unbroken' connection with the 'poison' which is both temptation and destiny. At the end of the poem the man-moth caught in a momentary gaze which seems to reveal a non-seeing eye, an eye which retains its physicality and is not subsumed in a reciprocal gaze, can yet hand over a tear – a revelation of 'depths' existing beyond vision – but only to the 'you' who watches or pays attention (*CP*, p.15) In this, as in other poems of the period – 'The Weed', for instance or 'Love's Lies Sleeping' – Bishop invokes a complicated rhetoric of seeing, where sight must also include 'the black space' where vision falters, and revelation, if it comes at all, may emerge from the eye's capacity for blurred or 'distorted' vision (*CP*, p.20, pp.16-17). For Bishop, inner and outer vision are not clearly aligned and the subject, drifting between perspectives and worlds, will see only against the background of – and as a substitute for – the blindness they can never escape.

Physical blindness, so powerfully represented by Brueghel, in his 'Parable of the Blind', the picture Bishop saw in 1938, is, of course, an analogy for the spiritual blindness his hapless peasants refuse to acknowledge. 'Can a blind person guide a blind person? Will not both fall into a pit?' [13] For Bishop, however, blindness, as this extract from her notebooks demonstrates, can help to reveal the partiality of sight:

> Mrs G's old mother, who has had 2 "strokes", is senile and almost blind – when she started going blind she kept complaining that how foggy it was all the time – Mrs G and I'd agree with her because I wanted her to think *we all saw the same.* [14]

It is a consoling fantasy that we all see the same, and that the old lady's befogged vision has accurately construed poor weather. Though the fog here is an illusion, it is interesting to note how sensitive Bishop was to conditions in which it was difficult to see and how often she returned to descriptions of fog in her notebooks. On her journey back to Nova Scotia, the coastline of her childhood in 1951, she wrote: 'The fog came & went rapidly – sometimes one could glimpse the island, then it would disappear in an instant.' [15] Towards the end of her life, North Haven Island became a favourite place to visit, and she again experienced the obfuscating qualities of the East-coast fog. As she described in her notebook, in the mixture of sun and fog, the bay became 'removed, vaporous, dream-like or unknown' whilst the fir trees were 'real', highlighted 'next to, against the sudden change to an atmospheric, imaginary world'. [16] The dissolving of the visible world into fog could open up a dream space, 'an atmospheric, imaginary world', but it could also threaten her sense of boundaries and hold on reality. On another trip, this time to Carolina in 1940, she contrasted the misty mountains unfavourably with 'all the bright, detailed flatness' of Key West. In foggy weather the mountains were 'all around us, big blue shapes, coming and going through the mist – like recurring thoughts rather depressing'; 'I hate masses of things you can't see the shape of, no formality anywhere,' she commented. Continuing the analogy between inner and outer worlds, she then went on to note:

> Every time I look at the mountains I think of the expression "at the back of my mind". This suggestion they give me is so strong that I feel a physical compulsion to turn my back and then with them there, to go on looking at the ferns, roots, etc. [17]

This very interesting passage reveals how Bishop's fascination with detail could also be construed as a form of displaced attention, a way of diverting her gaze from the mountains of her unconscious

memory. Hopkins undoubtedly resonates in this metaphorical trans-
formation of the mountains of Carolina into an invisible landscape
of the mind. By concentrating on seeing, Bishop is also, it could
be argued, providing a screen for what she cannot bear to look at;
her sense of detail becomes a kind of compensatory vision, keeping
her 'I' more or less securely situated in the present. However, the
immensity and amorphousness of the invisible still looms some-
where else and the mist, like the fog in other descriptions, both
obscures visibility and haunts it with all it cannot see, with the
pervasive spectre of its own blindness.

Dreaming and Looking

The 1930s marked the period in Bishop's life when she was most
directly interested in the unconscious; her notebooks from this time
reveal her carefully attempting to record her own dreams; at the
same time, her poetic tastes veered away from the 'self-conscious-
ness' she found in Wallace Stevens' writing and had been influenced
by as a student, to a preference for poetry with 'more of the un-
conscious spots left in'.[18] Some of her most disturbing dreams, for
instance her dream of a Hell inhabited by people in 'Bedlam-like
uniforms' [19] or her dream of being dead, 'or at least in some other
form of existence' and 'arranged on a card, like buttons' [20] evoke a
peculiar psychic territory where creativity is imprisoned or endan-
gered, instead of being liberated into new realms. Whilst Bishop
knew and was influenced by the work of the Surrealists in her early
career, she was later critical of their association of art with the 'mind
being broken down'. She preferred, she told Anne Stevenson in a
much-quoted letter, 'the always-more-successful surrealism of
everyday life' with its sidelong glimpses into the unconscious, its
'peripheral vision of whatever it is one can never really see full-
face'.[21] What these dreams may well have indicated to Bishop was
that the mind released from the constraints of the conscious mind
could encounter the compulsiveness and repetition of the death
drive instead of a desired freedom, a destructive unconscious already
fixated on death. The automatism which André Breton placed at
the centre of Surrealism, through his attention to hypnotic states
and automatic writing, contained a contradiction, as Hal Foster
has shown, turning the subject into an automaton, mechanically
driven rather than free. For Foster 'the question of the constraints
of the conscious mind obscured the more important question of
the constraints of the *unconscious* mind'.[22]

In Bishop's poem 'Sleeping Standing Up', a poem which has its origins in the same notebook as the dreams cited above, the sinister, mechanical 'armored car' in which she is carried through the dream landscape, still allows her some degree of self-determination, the capacity to steer, however 'stupidly'; it also offers a protective, as well as dangerous, contrivance or vehicle for her journey:

> The armored cars of dreams, contrived to let us do
> >so many a dangerous thing,
> >>are chugging at its edge
> all camouflaged, and ready to go through
>
> >>>>(*CP*, p.30)

Bishop was certainly intrigued by the mechanical as her poem 'Cirque d'Hiver' from this same period, reveals; however, the mechanical toy she describes in this poem is also significantly split between a mannequin and a 'more intelligent' horse who, unlike the dancer, can return the poet's gaze, and contemplate its progress as something more than mere repetition:

> The dancer, by this time, has turned her back.
> He is the more intelligent by far.
> Facing each other rather desperately –
> his eye is like a star –
> we stare and say, "Well, we have come this far."
>
> >>>>(*CP*, p.31)

This poem could be registering 'desperately' an anxiety about the affinity between the human and the non-human, or machine, and the limits set for creativity and freedom or it could be finding a moment of authenticity, or even transcendence, within those limits. The reciprocity between poet and mechanical toy that the poem arrives at is also a kind of threshold moment, a moment of suspension, when either interpretation might be possible; it effects a kind of conjunction between the human and the mechanical, with each turning towards the other. For Bishop, such 'interstitial' moments uncannily presage another interior meaning, without closing the gap of uncertainty.[23] They refuse to obliterate separation, or destroy limits, in the way that was desired, if not achieved, by the Surrealists. For Bishop, it was these 'between' moments which represented the true 'lingua unconscious', where the 'factual' and 'the fabulous' and the 'perfectly natural' and the 'highly artificial' might meet or inhabit a 'realm of reciprocity', with neither being privileged over the other.[24] Characteristically she assigned the unconscious to borders, edges and folds – to intersecting planes of reality – rather looking for it in an undisclosed but desired interior.

Bishop's uneasy relationship with Surrealism had much to do with the nature of the 'look' that it cultivated: a hallucinatory or desiring look that could overcome conscious volition, and which displaced the mimetic with the visionary or spectral. 'As far as the eye can see,' Breton wrote, 'it recreates desire.'[25] Bishop's looking was always more reticent than this, less transgressive or erotic, and often focused on the interchange of looks or glances, as we have seen in both 'The Man-Moth' and 'Cirque d'Hiver', a look both ways. Bishop saw Surrealism as daring, even impudent, in what it was attempting: 'Is surrealism,' she wrote, 'just a new method of dealing, bold-facedly, with what is embarrassing?'[26] Embarrassment or shame suggests a surrender to the repression which the frankness or boldness of Surrealism overcomes; it is also, significantly, associated with a different kind of looking: a looking down or away. According to the American psychologist Silvan Tompkins, who sees shame as the most crucial of all the emotions, the shamed individual will drop 'his eyes, his eyelids, his head, and sometimes the whole upper part of his body' in an attempt to 'call a halt to looking at another person, particularly the other person's face, and to the other person's looking at him, particularly at his face'.[27] However, this look away is also ambivalent in that the other person is never renounced completely; the wish to look and be looked at continues, even as one looks away. Tompkins cites as example the child who 'covers his face in the presence of strangers' only to peek through his fingers 'so that he may look without being seen'.[28]

Some of Bishop's most famous poems have at their centre the pleasure, fear or strangeness of looking and being looked at. Whilst the fish's eye remains impassive under Bishop's detailed scrutiny in 'The Fish', the 'sweet sensation of joy' in 'The Moose' surely comes from the moose's enveloping gaze:

Taking her time,
she looks the bus over,
grand, otherworldly.
            (CP, p.173)

Here the moose's look returns the poet's inquisitiveness with her own: she looks with a mysterious and yet human responsiveness. The fact that this moment of strange empathy is arrived at through a journey which also takes the poet back to the Nova Scotian landscape of her childhood, hints at its origins elsewhere, in the forgotten look which is exchanged with the maternal figure. However its 'otherwordly' dimension also contains distance: the moose is both imposing and inapproachable. The moose's look in this sense returns as the avatar of an uncanny memory, estranged by time and the inevitable loss or repression of the maternal body. Bishop's memory of childhood in another poem, 'In the Waiting Room', contains a different but perhaps related disturbance about looking and being looked at. Here the child is 'too shy' to stop reading because she is afraid to look at what she has already seen, the 'horrifying' breasts of the women displayed in the *National Geographic*. When she then experiences a terrifying revelation about her own identity and gender as 'one of them', and finds herself to be complicit with an aunt she considers 'a foolish, timid woman', she also becomes afraid to raise her eyes to look at the other people in the waiting room:

> I scarcely dared to look
> to see what it was I was.
> I gave a sidelong glance
> – I couldn't look any higher –
> at shadowy gray knees,
> trousers and skirts and boots
> and different pairs of hands
> lying under the lamps.
>   (*CP*, p.160)

By looking no higher than the knees, she also avoids the faces or eyes, which might return her look and inflict on her the humiliating consequences of her own visibility. As Silvan Tompkins suggests, shame involves a linkage to the other which it attempts to disavow because the subject fears the withdrawal of interest or the contempt of the other, even as she hopes for the pleasure she once knew of being looked at. Shame stands at the boundary of inside and outside; in this way it is, according to Eve Sedgwick, 'the affect that mantles the threshold between introversion and extroversion'.[29] Bishop's inability to look as a child – which also seems to operate like, or even as, a kind of sexual taboo – has to do with the space which has opened up at the boundary of self and other and which exposes her to the disgust, contempt, or perhaps desire, of the stranger's look. She looks, and fears to look, with the eyes of a stranger, at herself. If 'The Moose' returns Bishop to the strangely familiar look of the mother, a moment of intimacy transposed on to the 'otherwordly' moose, which can temporarily assuage alienation with the 'sweet sensation of joy', 'In the Waiting Room' opens up the disquieting possibility that the unalienated gaze has disappeared forever, and that only the anxious 'sidelong' look which can bypass the fear of seeing (or not seeing), but also of being seen, can be tolerated.

In 1940 Bishop confessed rather curiously to Marianne Moore how fond she was of glass eyes. She explained this 'indelicate' propensity by referring to the fact that 'when I was small I used to have relatives with glass eyes'.[30] Glass eyes turn up again in a putative essay Bishop never finished entitled 'Grandmother's Glass Eye: An Essay on Style' [31] and in the autobiographical story 'The Country Mouse' which dates from much later, and which links her Boston grandfather's 'walleye' to the glass eye of her maternal grandmother in Canada, the grandmother whom she had been abruptly taken away from at the age of six, 'unconsulted and against my wishes', to be brought up by her father's family.[32] This prosthetic and sightless eye, which held a special significance for Bishop, would seem to sit quite easily with the perverse imagery of detached or mutilated eyes, which pervades Surrealist painting and which separates the look from the looker; it could also have helped to reinforce Bishop's knowledge of the weakness or singularity of what is thought of as 'natural sight'. In the 'Country Mouse' her grandfather's squint seems 'only right and natural' because she is already accustomed to the artificial vision of her grandmother.[33] However, there is a passage in her notebooks, dating from the 30s, which makes an interesting series of connections and provides a slightly different insight into the significance of this eye for Bishop. Here Bishop is, it seems, looking back to the period of her life also described in 'The Country Mouse' and her disorientating transposition from the warmth of her mother's family to the stricter, more formal regime of her Boston family:

> My family circumstances, my "good fortune", surround me so well and safely, and only *I* am wrong, inadequate. It is a a situation like one of those solid crystal balls with little silvery objects inside: thick clear appropriate glass, only the little object, me, is sadly flawed and shown off as inferior to the setting.
>
> It makes me think, where oh where is the god-ball – the god-ball that made me want a billy-goat more than anything else for eight years, my pocket idol, the fetish I held in my hand and rolled down the bed-clothes whenever I was sick.[34]

The 'good fortune' of her adoption by paternal grandparents, a phrase that clearly reflects their attitude to Bishop, involved them 'saving her from a life of poverty and provincialism' but condemning her to a childhood of loneliness and boredom: 'At night I lay blinking my flashlight off and on, and crying.' [35] She is, before all, exposed to a new rule-bound household and a correcting gaze (which ironically is itself askew) which both fixes and diminishes her. In the sequence of memories in her notebook, this loss

of home and happiness is replaced by a memory of a lost child-
hood toy and its association with a longing for creature comfort. It
could be this same billy-goat that reappears later in 'Crusoe in
England' – standing somewhere between hope and despair – as
the unsatisfactory companion of Crusoe's loneliness and whose
unexpressive eyes deny Crusoe recognition, an experience he him-
self then goes on rather cruelly to inflict on a baby goat:

> I'd grab his beard and look at him.
> His pupils, horizontal, narrowed up
> and expressed nothing, or a little malice.

                              (*CP*, p.165)

To return to Bishop's notebook, the detachable object with which
she replaces the crystal ball which she imagines trapped her all too
visibly inside, seems to offer, instead of the abjuring gaze, the blind
comfort of touch. Speculatively – and perhaps rather grotesquely
– it could recall her grandmother's glass eye and an earlier emo-
tional closeness. The glass eye as fetishistic object – associated
with her grandmother – could have allowed her to escape the anx-
iety of visibility and to imagine an eye which is both sightless and
benign.

Appropriately enough Bishop spent a short period in the 1940s
working in an 'Optical Shop'. Whilst she also enjoyed the oppor-
tunity to 'watch everything through magnificent optical instruments
of every kind, including periscopes', she also suffered from eye-
strain which made her 'seasick'.[36] Seasickness and the disorientat-
ing memory of childhood homesickness seemed interchangeable in
one trip she made in the thirties, the one form of disequilibrium
recalling the other.[37] For Bishop the traumas of her childhood cast
her into an uncertain space where she was always striving with the
utmost vigilance to keep her balance. The glass eye – recalled perhaps
again by the optical instruments which made her seasick – seemed
to close the fearful separation encountered in the other's look and
heal the uneasy spacings of vision At the same time it suggests a
body already fragmented, unable to experience wholeness, and a
memory bound forever to the contradictions of seeing and not seeing.

Lines and Traces

Bishop's interest in art, which is evident everywhere in her writing,
was carried over into her own explorations with painting. Through-
out her life she produced small, portable sketches which could
accompany her on her travels; they offer glimpses of scenes and

interiors she was only temporarily at rest in and seem to function as traveller's notes, like her journal jottings. Bishop often included traces of the subject in her paintings – luggage, for instance, and a carefully placed plant and book and pen in the painting entitled 'Cabin with Porthole' or a hastily propped bicycle in 'The Harris School' – but significantly she did not paint portraits. People and faces are all but absent, except in one painting 'Sleeping Figure', where the figure, though possibly poised at a moment of comic awakening, still has her eyes closed, her gaze turned inwards. Bishop was deprecating, even embarrassed, about her painting. In 1971 she acknowledged that 'from time to time I paint a small gouache or watercolour and give them to friends' but added emphatically: 'They are Not Art – NOT AT ALL.' [38]

Whatever their real significance to her, paintings also occupied Bishop's dream life. In the 30s she recorded a dream of paintings which refused to hold their shape but which moved disturbingly between different perspectives:

> I dreamed last night of paintings that wouldn't stay still – the colors moved up closer and then further back, the whole thing changed from portrait to scenery and then back again – keeping the same lines all the time. [39]

The *trompe l'œil* effect here reveals a face – or look – simultaneously inscribed in the 'same lines' as the scenery. Perhaps this is the same face that almost materialises in the oddly timeless description that begins Bishop's autobiographical story 'In the Village':

> A scream, the echo of a scream, hangs over that Nova Scotian village. No one hears it; it hangs there forever, a slight stain in those pure blue skies, skies that travelers compare to those of Switzerland, too dark, too blue, so that they seem to keep on darkening a little more around the horizon – or is it around the rims of the eyes? – the color of the cloud of bloom on the elm trees, the violet on the fields of oats; something darkening over the woods and waters as well as the sky. The scream hangs like that, unheard, in memory – in the past, in the present, and those years between. [40]

Not only does the searing sound of a scream metamorphose into the visual register of a stain to be permanently, though soundlessly, present, but the horizon or background also seeps into the foreground. The glimpse of eyes is held in parenthesis just as the originating subject of the scream is withheld from us. This story, which gets as close as Bishop ever got to the traumatic early memory of her mother's madness, displaces sound into vision and vision into sound. In his *Memoirs of the Blind* Jacques Derrida reminds us that the gorgon's gaze was sometimes accompanied by a terrible cry.[41] Bishop's story, with its oblique detail, also deals with an unbearable sight, the loss of the mother. In some ways it could be read as the story of a traumatic blinding and the consequent intensification of invisible waves of sound.

Bishop wrote two poems explicitly about paintings, 'Large Bad Picture' and the later 'Poem', and in both of them she engages a connection between painting and memory; at the same time the paintings she describes decidedly lack the permanence or grandeur of artistic memorials. In 'Large Bad Picture' the great-uncle's act of remembrance creates an artificial stasis where there is 'perpetual sunset' but no resolution of his meaning. Trying to interpret the reality figured by the painting, the speaker keeps experiencing its turn to abstraction. The 'commerce or contemplation' that she indecisively offers as the ships' destination, also suggests the painting's ambiguous and unsatisfying positioning between art and reality. However at the frozen centre of the poem, when the poet imagines the sounds of the birds' 'crying, crying' and hears the sighing of a 'large aquatic animal', the painting also gets close to the body and the emotions ready to surface in a time which is not so much arrested but, like the unconscious, endlessly present (CP, p.11). 'Poem' more successfully entwines the two 'looks' of the painter and viewer, and arrives at a complex sense of time as both held in memory and shifting and in process. What the painting vouchsafes is circumscribed – 'cramped, / dim, on a piece of Bristol board' – but also handed along the line 'collaterally', existing through time, to be looked at again or not (CP, pp.176–77). The poet experiences a moment of recognition when different visions 'coincide', hers and the painters, but as Bonnie Costello points out, 'coincide' is a carefully chosen word here, since it can move between spatial and temporal perspectives, as can the word 'abidance' later.[42] The coincidence is also a momentary fusion of time and place, 'life and the memory of it', as she recognises a place, assembled by means of different tenses, which can contain time without freezing its movement.

One is aware, of course, of the fragility of what is temporarily brought to rest in 'Poem'; in her dream quoted above and in this later entry in her notebooks, painting poses a risk precisely because it is not still but can undo the boundaries so carefully achieved and maintained, between conscious and unconscious, the visible and the invisible, and between the present and past. Bishop is writing about a time in the 1940s when she had been 'hysterically unhappy' after finally leaving Florida:

The past and present seemed confused or disturbed each other vio-
lently and constantly and the pool wouldn't "lie down". (I've felt the
same thing when I tried to paint – but this was mostly taught me by
getting drunk, when the same thing happens. For perhaps the same
reasons, for a few hours.[43]

The process of painting could produce a state, it seemed, not un-
like intoxication, where the boundary between past and present
becomes muddy, and the calm relation between surface and depth
in the 'pool' of her mind is lost. Bishop seems to be describing
the effect of intrusive memories, and a disorientation in terms of
time. The observation and imagining of space for Bishop was a
way of mapping out boundaries, of finding a relation to the other-
ness of objects, but the geographical territories of Bishop's poems –
and her paintings – were also a 'land of oblivion', in Julia Kristeva's
words,[44] where the lost contours of the past were always threaten-
ing to make themselves visible. Bishop was sensitive to the effect of
the use of different tenses in her poetry. 'Switching tenses always
gives effects of depth, space, foreground, background, and so on.' [45]
The opposite was also true: foreground and background, planes and
perspectives in space, could also reflect – or be haunted by – the
relations between present and past, conscious and unconscious.

If painting involved Bishop in figuring a complex relation to
memory, it is interesting to note how often she also exchanged
depth for surface by turning writing into inscription or visual sign.
In her poems she often likens objects or creatures to the physical
appearance of writing. The birds in 'Large Bad Picture' hang 'in
n's in banks' (CP, p.11); the unfortunate hen in 'Trouvée', run
over in West 4th Street, turns into 'a quaint / old country saying /
scribbled in chalk' (CP, p.150), whilst in 'The Bight', 'the little
white boats' which are 'not yet salvaged' are compared to 'torn-open,
unanswered letters' (CP, p.60). Her notebooks similarly contain
descriptions of nature taking on a resemblance to writing: the pat-
tern the waves leaves on the shore is like 'white-handwriting' [46] or
the crickets are like 'large white hieroglyphics when they jump'.[47]
By combining the visual and the verbal in this way, Bishop under-
mines the self-sufficiency and integrity of both: perception is also a
form of interpretation, a subjective reading of the external world,
whilst writing has no essential link to reality but may signify no
more than itself.

In an analogous way the lines which Bishop drew across her
paintings, or left tentatively etched there, are suggestive of the
mark or trace that writing left on her paintings. In 'Interior with
Extension Cable' an electicity wire is threaded across the ceiling;

in 'County Courthouse' wires are looped across telegraph poles, and power lines hang down, unattached; in 'Harris School' strings dangle from kites like question marks, their origin, or end, obscured by the imposing building in front of them.[48] In each of these paintings lines seem to lead beyond the frame to points of origin or energy which are not contained within it. In an early essay, written at Vassar, entitled 'Dimensions for a Novel', Bishop described how in writing 'from a vacant pinpoint of certainty start out geometrically accurate lines, star-beams, pricking out the past, or present, or casting ahead into the future'.[49] Lines, so she suggests, are invisible energies and connections, and in particular, can trace the temporal lines between past, present and future. Bishop knew the work of Paul Klee and mentioned him several times with enthusiasm.[50] Though Klee's use of line goes well beyond anything Bishop attempted in her painting, a comparison with Klee is an interesting one. Klee saw line as his own personal possession, a way of escaping from naturalism. 'A work of art goes beyond naturalism the instant the line enters the picture.'[51] Lines were a tracing, a black energy, an attempt to capture the 'expressive moment of the hand holding the recording pencil'.[52] They did not conform to what was visible but were an encounter with what escaped the field of vision. Derrida picks up this idea in *Memoirs of the Blind* when he likens the draughtsman to a blind man who reaches out with his hand into an unknown space, the space of blindness, which is shaped by the future – anticipation – and memory; it is a space which 'conjugates' different tenses.[53] In a resonant passage in his journal Klee wrote:

> To work my way out of my ruins, I had to fly. And I flew.
> I remain in this ruined world only in memory, as one occasionally does in retrospect.
> Thus, I am "abstract with memories".[54]

Bishop was never so directed towards transcendence as this, nor so confident about her own flights of imagination. Nevertheless the lines in her paintings – which she also invokes in her writing – lines without density or meaning, could be read as archival scribbles, traces of the very act of tracing an identity through the eye / I; they are lines that hover at the edges of visibility drawing our eye to all that remains invisible. In this they are also 'abstract with memory'. They lead us back to irretrievable origins, the vanishing point that eclipses vision, but also outwards along a chain or string of signifiers towards that airy freedom that sometimes beckoned in her poems. In this poem, written in the year of her death, Bishop was perhaps after all, like Klee, able to fly out of her ruins:

Freed – the broken
thermometer's mercury
running away;
and the rainbow-bird
from the narrow bevel
of the empty mirror,
flying wherever
it feels like, gay!
           (*CP*, p.192)

*

NOTES

Unless otherwise cited, quotations of published works are from Bishop's *Complete Poems: 1927-1979* or *The Collected Prose*, and of letters from *One Art*. Quotations of unpublished work are from the Elizabeth Bishop Papers in the Vassar College Library.

1. Vassar Archives, Box 77.2, p.41.
2. Vassar Archives, Box 77.2, p.37.
3. Vassar Archives, Box 77.4, p.46.
4. See Keith Roberts, *Brueghel* (London: Phaidon, 1971), p.9.
5. W.H. Auden: 'Musée des Beaux Arts', *Collected Shorter Poems 1927 –1957* (London: Faber, 1966, p.124.
6. Randall Jarrell: 'On *North & South*', in *Elizabeth Bishop and Her Art*, edited by Lloyd Schwartz and Sybil P. Estess (Ann Arbor: University of Michigan Press, 1983), p.181.
7. Ashley Brown: 'An Interview with Elizabeth Bishop, 1966' in *Conversations with Elizabeth Bishop*, edited by George Monteiro (Jackson: University of Mississipi Press, 1996), p.24.
8. David Kalstone: 'Elizabeth Bishop: Questions of Memory, Questions of Travel' in *Elizabeth Bishop and Her Art*, p.4.
9. Frank Bidart: 'On Elizabeth Bishop' in *Elizabeth Bishop and Her Art*, p.214.
10. *Elizabeth Bishop: The Biography of a Poetry* (New York: Columbia University Press, 1991), p.132.
11. 'Gregorio Valdes' in *The Collected Prose*, p.58.
12. 'Paris, 7 A.M.', *The Complete Poems*, p.26.
13. Luke 18: 42-43, *The New Oxford Annotated Bible* (Oxford: Oxford University Press, 1991).
14. Vassar Archives, Box 72 B.5, p.11.
15. Vassar Archives, Box 72.B.5, p.33.
16. Vassar Archives, Box 73.5, p.24.
17. Vassar Archives, Box 77.3, p.27.
18. Vassar Archives, Box 75.3, p.89.
19. Vassar Archives, Box 75.4A, p.27.
20. Vassar Archives, Box 75.4A, p.39.
21. See Anne Stevenson: *Elizabeth Bishop* (New York: Twayne, 1966); also quoted in *Elizabeth Bishop and Her Art*, p.288.
22. *Compulsive Beauty* (Cambridge, MA: MIT Press, 1995), p.5.

23. Vassar Archives, Box 75.3b, p.193.

24. Vassar Archives, Box 75.3b, p.63.

25. Quoted in Hal Foster, *Compulsive Beauty*, p.241.

26. Vassar Archives, Box 75.3, p.12.

27. *Shame and Its Sisters: A Silvan Tomkins Reader,* edited by Eve Kosofsky Sedgwick and Adam Frank (Durham and London, Duke University Press, 1995), p.134.

28. *Shame and Its Sisters,* p.137.

29. 'Shame and Performativity: Henry James's New York Edition Prefaces' in *Henry James's New York Edition: The Construction of Authorship* edited by David McWhirter (Stanford, CA: Stanford University Press), p.213.

30. *One Art,* p.88.

31. Vassar Archives, Box 75.4A, p.10.

32. The Collected Prose, p.17.

33. The Collected Prose, p.13.

34. Vassar Archives, Box 72 A.3, p.31.

35. 'The Country Mouse', in *The Collected Prose,* p.31.

36. *One Art,* p.115.

37. Vassar Archives, Box 72 A.3, p.32.

38. See Elizabeth Bishop: *Exchanging Hats: Paintings* edited by William Benton (New York, Farrar, Straus and Giroux, 1996; Manchester: Carcanet Press, 1997) for a published selection of Bishop's paintings. This quotation is contained in the 'Introduction' by William Benton, p.XVIII.

39. Vassar Archives, Box 75, p.39.

40. *Collected Prose,* p.251.

41. *Memoirs of the Blind: The Self-Portrait and Other Ruins* (Chicago and London: Chicago University Press, 1993), p.56.

42. *Elizabeth Bishop: Questions of Mastery* (Cambridge, MA: Harvard University Press, 1991), p.232.

43. Vassar Archives, Box 77.4, p.16.

44. *The Powers of Horror: An Essay on Abjection,* translated by Leon S. Roudiez (New York: Columbia University Press, 1982), p.9.

45. Ashley Brown, 'An Interview with Elizabeth Bishop, 1966' in *Elizabeth Bishop and Her Art,* p.298.

46. Vassar Archives, Box 77.3, p.6.

47. Vassar Archives, Box 77.3, p.27.

48. See *Exchanging Hats,* pp.43, 23, 24.

49. Vassar Archives, Box 70.9 p.8.

50. As with Brueghel, Klee was an important point of reference visual effects. The Andes, she tells James Merrill, are 'exactly like some of Klee's painting'. She also read Klee's journals (*One Art,* p.521, p.442).

51. *The Diaries of Paul Klee 1898–1918,* edited by Felix Klee (Los Angeles and London: University of California Press, 1964), p232.

52. *The Diaries of Paul Klee,* p.256.

53. *Memoirs of the Blind,* p.9.

54. *The Diaries of Paul Klee,* p.315.

NEIL ASTLEY

Elizabeth Bishop: A Bibliography

Works by Elizabeth Bishop

1. POETRY

North & South (Boston: Houghton Mifflin, 1946).

Poems: North & South – A Cold Spring (Boston: Houghton Mifflin, 1955; London: Chatto & Windus, 1956).

Questions of Travel (New York: Farrar, Straus and Giroux, 1965).

Selected Poems (London: Chatto & Windus, 1967).

The Battle of the Burglar of Babylon (New York: Farrar, Straus and Giroux, 1968).

Geography III (New York: Farrar, Straus and Giroux; London: Chatto & Windus, 1976).

The Complete Poems (Farrar, Straus and Giroux, 1969; London: Chatto & Windus, 1970).

Complete Poems: 1927-1977 (New York: Farrar, Straus & Giroux; London: Chatto & Windus, 1983). Paperback edition, *Complete Poems* (London: Chatto & Windus, 1991).

2. PROSE

The Diary of "Helena Morley" (New York: Farrar, Straus & Cudahy, 1957; London: Victor Gollancz, 1958), Alice Brant's *Minha Vida de Menina* (1942) translated by Elizabeth Bishop.

Brazil (with the editors of *Life*), Life World Library (New York: Time-Life Books, 1962).

'Three Stories of Clarice Lispector' ('A Hen', 'Marmosets' and 'The Smallest Woman in the World'), translated by Elizabeth Bishop, *Kenyon Review*, 26 no.3 (Summer 1964), 501-11.

An Anthology of Twentieth-Century Brazilian Poetry, translated with Emanuel Brasil (Middletown, CN: Wesleyan, 1972).

The Collected Prose, edited with an introduction by Robert Giroux (New York: Farrar, Straus & Giroux; London: Chatto & Windus/ The Hogarth Press, 1984).

One Art: Selected Letters, edited with an introduction by Robert Giroux (New York: Farrar, Straus and Giroux; London: Chatto & Windus, 1994; London: Pimlico, 1996).

3. RECORDINGS

The Voice of the Poet: Elizabeth Bishop, with companion book introduced by J.D. McClatchy (New York: Random House, 2000).

4. ART

Exchanging Hats: Paintings, ed. William Benton (New York: Farrar, Straus and Giroux, 1996; Manchester: Carcanet, 1997).

5. INTERVIEWS

George Monteiro (ed.): *Conversations with Elizabeth Bishop* (Jackson: University Press of Mississippi, 1996): has all known interviews given by Elizabeth Bishop, including those with Ashley Brown (1966), George Starbuck (1977), Alexandra Johnson (1978), Eileen McMahon (1978), Elizabeth Spires (1978), and Wesley Wehr's class notes (1966). Spires' is the fuller revised text of an interview published elsewhere in two versions. The book also has articles based on other interviews, some from Brazilian publications.

Works on Elizabeth Bishop

1. BIBLIOGRAPHIES

Sandra Barry: *Elizabeth Bishop: An Archival Guide to Her Life in Nova Scotia* (Great Village, Nova Scotia: EBSNS, 1996).
Ronald Baughman (ed.): *Contemporary American Poets,* Contemporary Authors Bibliography Series (1986), 35-69.
Anne Merrill Greenhalgh: *A Concordance to Elizabeth Bishop's Poetry* (New York: Garland, 1985).
Candace W. MacMahon: *Elizabeth Bishop: A Bibliography, 1927-1979* (Charlottesville: University Press of Virginia, 1980).
Diana E. Wyllie: *Elizabeth Bishop and Howard Nemerov: A Reference Guide* (Boston: G.K. Hall, 1983).

2. BIOGRAPHIES

Gary Fountain & Peter Brazeau (eds): *Remembering Elizabeth Bishop: An Oral Biography* (Amherst, MA: University of Massachusetts Press, 1994).
Brett Candlish Millier: *Elizabeth Bishop: Life and the Memory of It* (Berkeley, Los Angeles, Oxford: University of California Press, 1993).
Carmen L. Oliveira: *Rare and Commonplace Flowers: The Story of Elizabeth Bishop and Lota de Macedo Soares* (1985), trs. Neil K. Besner (New Brunswick, NJ: Rutgers University Press, 2002).

3. BOOK-LENGTH STUDIES

Linda Anderson & Jo Shapcott (eds): *Elizabeth Bishop: Poet of the Periphery*, Newcastle / Bloodaxe Poetry Series: 1 (Newcastle: University of Newcastle, and Tarset: Bloodaxe Books, 2002).

Sandra Barry, Gwen Davies & Peter Sanger (eds): *Divisions of the Heart: Elizabeth Bishop and the Art of Memory and Place* (Wolfville, NS: Gaspereau Press, 2001). 25 essays from Acadia University symposium, including Lorrie Goldensohn and Anne Stevenson.

Harold Bloom (ed.): *Elizabeth Bishop: Modern Critical Views* (New York: Chelsea House Publishers, 1985).

———— (ed.): *Elizabeth Bishop: Bloom's Major Poets* (New York: Chelsea House Publishers, 2002).

Anne Colwell: *Inscrutable Houses: Metaphors of the Body in the Poems of Elizabeth Bishop* (Tuscaloosa and London: University of Alabama Press, 1997).

Bonnie Costello: *Elizabeth Bishop: Questions of Mastery* (Cambridge, MA and London: Harvard University Press, 1991).

Carole Kiler Doreski: *Elizabeth Bishop: The Restraints of Language* (New York: Oxford University Press, USA, 1993).

Lorrie Goldensohn: *Elizabeth Bishop: The Biography of a Poetry* (New York: Columbia University Press, 1991).

Victoria Harrison: *Elizabeth Bishop's Poetics of Intimacy* (Cambridge and New York: Cambridge University Press, 1993).

Marilyn May Lombardi: *The Body and the Song: Elizabeth Bishop's Poetics* (Carbondale and Edwardsville: Southern Illinois University Press, 1995).

———— (ed.): *Elizabeth Bishop: The Geography of Gender* (Charlottesville and London: University Press of Virginia, 1993). Includes essays by Joanne Feit Diehl, Lee Edelman, Jacqueline Vaught Grogan, Victoria Harrison, Marilyn May Lombardi, Jeredith Merrin, Brett Candlish Millier, Barbara Page, Thomas Travisano, and book chapters by Bonnie Costello and Lorrie Goldensohn.

Susan McCabe: *Elizabeth Bishop: Her Poetics of Loss* (University Park, PA: Pennsylvania State University Press, 1994).

Laura Jehn Menides & Angela G. Dorenkamp (eds): *'In Worcester, Massachusetts': Essays on Elizabeth Bishop from the 1997 Elizabeth Bishop Conference at WPI* (New York: Peter Lang, 1999).

Robert Dale Parker: *The Unbeliever: The Poetry of Elizabeth Bishop* (Urbana: University of Illinois Press, 1988).

Camille Roman: *Elizabeth Bishop's World War II – Cold War View* (New York and Basingstoke: Palgrave Macmillan, 2001).

Lloyd Schwartz & Sybil P. Estess (eds): *Elizabeth Bishop and Her Art* (Ann Arbor: Michigan University Press, 1983). Includes essays and reviews by Frank Bidart, Bonnie Costello, Sybil Estess, John Hollander, David Kalstone, David Lehman, James Merrill, Marianne Moore, Octavio Paz, Helen Vendler and Alan Williamson, with a foreword by Harold Bloom.

Sally Bishop Shigley: *Dazzling Dialectics: Elizabeth Bishop's Resonating Feminist Reality* (New York: Peter Lang, 1997).

Anne Stevenson: *Elizabeth Bishop*, Twayne's United States Authors Series (New York: Twayne, 1966).

———— : *Five Looks at Elizabeth Bishop*, Agenda/Bellew Poets on Poetry: 1 (London: Bellew/Agenda Editions, 1998).

Thomas J. Travisano: *Elizabeth Bishop: Her Artistic Development* (Charlottesville: University Press of Virginia, 1988).

Zhou Xiaojing: *Elizabeth Bishop: Rebel in Shades and Shadows*, Studies in Modern Poetry, II (New York: Peter Lang, 1999).

4. STUDIES OF ELIZABETH BISHOP AND OTHER POETS

Mutlu Konuk Blasing: *Politics and Form in Postmodern Poetry: O'Hara, Bishop, Ashbery, and Merrill* (Cambridge: Cambridge University Press, 1996).

Eleanor Cook: *Against Coercion: Games Poets Play* (Stanford: Stanford University Press, 1998). Chapters include 'Schemes Against Coercion: Geoffrey Hill, Elizabeth Bishop, and Others', 25-43; 'Fables of War in Elizabeth Bishop', 44-60; 'The Poetics of Modern Punning: Wallace Stevens, Elizabeth Bishop, and Others', 172-86; 'Ghost Rhymes and How They Work', 223-34.

Renée R. Curry: *White Women Writing White: H.D., Elizabeth Bishop, Sylvia Plath, and Whiteness*, Contributions in Women's Studies, 125 (Westport, CN and London: Greenwood Press, 2000).

Margaret Dickie: *Stein, Bishop & Rich: Lyrics of Love, War and Place* (Chapel Hill and London: University of North Carolina Press, 1997).

Joanne Feit Diehl: *Elizabeth Bishop and Marianne Moore: The Psychodynamics of Creativity* (Princeton, NJ: Princeton University Press, 1993). Also available as digital download.

Elizabeth Dodd: *The Veiled Mirror and the Woman Poet: H.D., Louise Bogan, Elizabeth Bishop, and Louise Glück* (Columbia: University of Missouri Press, 1992).

David Kalstone: *Five Temperaments: Elizabeth Bishop, Robert Lowell, James Merrill, Adrienne Rich, John Ashbery* (New York: Oxford University Press, 1977).

———— : *Becoming a Poet: Elizabeth Bishop with Marianne Moore and Robert Lowell* (New York: Farrar, Straus and Giroux; London: Hogarth Press, 1989).

Lynn Keller: *Re-Making It New: Contemporary American Poetry and the Tradition* (Cambridge: Cambridge University Press, 1987).

Lionel Kelly (ed): *Poetry and the Sense of Panic: Critical Essays on Elizabeth Bishop and John Ashbery* (Amsterdam: Rodopi, 2000), including conference papers by Joanne Feit Diehl, Mark Ford, Peter Robinson, Thomas J. Travisano and Cheryl Walker, and an earlier version of Barbara Page's essay in this book.

David Laskin: *A Common Life: Four Generations of American Literary Friendship and Influence* (New York: Simon and Schuster, 1994).

James McCorkle: *The Still Performance: Writing, Self, and Interconnection in Five Postmodern American Poets* (Charlottesville: University Press of Virginia, 1992).

Jeredith Merrin: *An Enabling Humility: Marianne Moore, Elizabeth Bishop and the Uses of Tradition* (New Brunswick, NJ: Rutgers University Press, 1990).

Guy L. Rotella: *Reading and Writing Nature: The Poetry of Robert Frost, Wallace Stevens, Marianne Moore, and Elizabeth Bishop* (Boston: Northeastern University Press, 1991).

Susan Schweik: *A Gulf So Deeply Cut: American Women Poets and the Second World War* (Madison: University of Wisconsin Press, 1991).

Thomas J. Travisano: *Midcentury Quartet: Bishop, Lowell, Jarrell, Berryman, and the Making of a Postmodern Aesthetic* (Charlottesville: University Press of Virginia, 1999).

5. ESSAYS, REVIEWS AND PAPERS ON ELIZABETH BISHOP

Linda Anderson: 'Elizabeth Bishop: The Secret Life of a Poet', in *The Art of Literary Biography*, ed. John Batchelor (Oxford: Oxford University Press, 1995), 173-83.

John Ashbery: 'Throughout is this quality of thingness', review of *Complete Poems*, *New York Times Book Review*, 1 June 1969, 8, 25.

————— : 'Second Presentation of Elizabeth Bishop', *World Literature Today*, 51 no.1 (Winter 1977), 9-11.

Jonathan Ausubel: 'Subjected People: Towards a Grammar for the Underclass in Elizabeth Bishop's Poetry', *Connotations: A Journal for Critical Debate*, 4 no.1/2 (1994-1995), 83-97, with a response by Jacqueline Vaught Brogan, 172-80.

Mary Elizabeth Bailey: 'Elizabeth Bishop: Travel and Connections', *Worcester Review*, 13 no.1/2 (Fall 1992), 79-87.

Ilse Barker: 'The Search for Earthly Paradise', *New Readings* symposium at Vassar College, 22-25 September 1994, http://projects. vassar.edu/bishop/Barker.html.

Sandra Barry: 'The Art of Remembering: The Influence of Great Village, Nova Scotia, on the Life and Works of Elizabeth Bishop',

Nova Scotia Historical Review, 11 no.1 (1991), 137.

————— : 'Shipwrecks of the Soul: Elizabeth Bishop's Reading of Hopkins', *Dalhousie Review*, 5 no.1 (Spring 1994): 25-50.

————— : 'An Artist in the House', *New Readings* symposium at Vassar College, 22-25 September 1994, http://projects.vassar.edu/bishop/Barry.html.

April Bernard: 'Exile's Return', in *The New York Review of Books*, 13 January 1994, 16.

Frank Bidart: 'On Elizabeth Bishop: Introduction to a Reading at Wellesley College, 1976'. In Schwartz & Estess (1983), 214-15.

————— : 'Elizabeth Bishop', *Threepenny Review*, 58 (Summer 1994), 6-7, reprinted in *The Pushcart Prize XX, 1996: The Best of Small Presses* (Wainscott, NY: Pushcart Press, 1995), 296-306.

Sven Bikerts: 'Elizabeth Bishop's Prose: Atmospheres of Identity', *Conjunctions 29 Bi-Annual Volume of New Writing* (1997): 252-59.

Mutlu Konuk Blasing: 'From Gender to Genre and Back: Elizabeth Bishop and "The Moose" ', *American Literary History*, 6 no.2 (Summer 1994), 265-86.

Harold Bloom: '*Geography III* by Elizabeth Bishop', *New Republic*, 176 no.2 (5 February 1977), 29-30.

Eavan Boland: 'An Un-Romantic American', in *Parnassus*, 14 no.2 (1988), 73-92.

Jacqueline Vaught Brogan: 'Elizabeth Bishop: *Perversity* as Voice', *American Poetry* (1990). In Lombardi (1993), 175-95.

————— : 'The Moral of the Story: Naming the Thief of Babylon', *Ellipsis*, 1 no.2 (1991),: 277-86.

————— : 'Planets on the Table: From Wallace Stevens and Elizabeth Bishop to Adrienne Rich and June Jordan', *Wallace Stevens Journal*, 19 no.2 (Fall 1995), 255-78.

Kathleen Brogan: 'Lyric Voice and Sexual Difference in Elizabeth Bishop', in *Writing the Woman Artist: Essays on Poetics, Politics, and Portraiture*, ed. Suzanne Jones (Philadelphia: University of Pennsylvania Press, 1991), 60-71.

David Bromwich: 'Elizabeth Bishop's Dream Houses', *Raritan*, 4 no.1 (Summer 1984), 77-94.

Ronald Christ: 'Elizabeth Bishop's Doctor' (letter), *New York Times Book Review*, 8 May 1994, 27.

Henri Cole (ed.): 'Elizabeth Bishop: Influences', version of a talk given by Elizabeth Bishop on 13 December 1977, Academy of American Poets, 'Conversations', *American Poetry Review*, January–February 1985, 11-16.

Eleanor Cook: 'From Etymology to Paronomasia: Wallace Stevens, Elizabeth Bishop, and Others', *Connotations: A Journal for Critical*

Debate, 2 no.1 (1992), 34-51. See also responses in subsequent issues of *Connotations*: Anthony Hecht, 2 no.2 (1992), 201-04; Jacqueline Vaught Brogan, 2 no.3 (1992), 295-304; Anca Rosu, 2 no.3 (1992), 305-12; Timothy Bahti, 3 no.1 (1993), 90-94; John Hollander, 3 no.1 (1993), 95-98; Eleanor Cook, 3 no.1 (1993), 99-102.

Alfred Corn: review of *Geography III*, *Georgia Review*, 31 (Summer 1977), 533-41.

———— : 'Elizabeth Bishop's Nativities', *Shenandoah*, 36 no.3 (1986), 21-46.

Bonnie Costello: 'Vision and Mastery in Elizabeth Bishop', *Twentieth Century Literature*, 28 (Winter 1982), 351-70.

———— : 'The Impersonal and the Interrogative in the Poetry of Elizabeth Bishop'. In Schwartz & Estess (1983), 109-32.

———— : 'Marianne Moore and Elizabeth Bishop: Friendship and Influence', *Twentieth Century Literature*, 30 (Summer–Fall 1984), 130-49.

———— : 'Attractive Mortality'. In Lombardi (1993), 126-52.

———— : 'Auden and Bishop', *New Readings* symposium at Vassar College, 22-25 September 1994, http://projects.vassar.edu/bishop/Costello.html.

———— : 'Narrative Secrets, Lyric Openings', *Wallace Stevens Journal*, 19 no.2 (Fall 1995), 180-200.

Lois Cucullu: 'Trompe l'œil: Elizabeth Bishop's Radical "I"', *Texas Studies in Literature and Language*, 30 no.2 (1988), 246-71.

———— : " 'Above All I Am Not That Staring Man": Positionality in Elizabeth Bishop's Travel Poetry', MLA Convention (San Francisco, 30 December 1991).

Renée R. Curry: 'Augury and Autobiography: Bishop's "Crusoe in England" ', *Arizona Quarterly*, 47 (Autumn 1991), 70-91.

———— : 'May Sarton and Elizabeth Bishop: A Revisionist Age', *Puckerbrush Review*, 11 no.2 (Winter 1993), 51-57, reprinted in *A Celebration for May Sarton*, ed. Constance Huntington (Orono: Puckerbrush, 1994), 231-44.

Margaret Dickie: 'Elizabeth Bishop: Text and Subtext', *South Atlantic Review*, 59 no.4 (November 1994), 1-19.

———— : 'The Love Poetry of Elizabeth Bishop: Silent and Silenced', in *Semantics of Silences in Linguistics and Literature*, ed. Gudrun M. Grabher & Ulrike Jessner (Heidelberg: Universitätsverlag C. Winter, 1996), 271-89.

———— : 'Introduction: Stevens and Elizabeth Bishop', *Wallace Stevens Journal*, 19 no.2 (Fall 1995), 107-14.

———— : 'Race and Class in Elizabeth Bishop's Poetry', *Yearbook of English Studies*, 24 (1994), 44-58.

————— : 'Seeing and Re-Seeing: Sylvia Plath and Elizabeth Bishop', *American Literature*, 65 no.1 (March 1993): 131-46.

Joanne Feit Diehl: 'At Home with Loss: Elizabeth Bishop and the American Sublime', in *Coming to Light: American Women Poets in the Twentieth Century*, ed. Dianne Wood Middlebrook & Marilyn Yalom (Ann Arbor: University of Michigan Press, 1985), 123-37.

————— : 'Bishop's Sexual Politics', in her *Women Poets and the American Sublime* (Bloomington: Indiana University Press, 1990). In Lombardi (1993), 17-45.

Carole Kiler Doreski: 'Proustian Closure in Wallace Stevens' 'The Rock' and Elizabeth Bishop's *Geography III*', *Twentieth Century Literature*, 44 no.1 (Spring 1998), 34-52.

Lee Edelman: 'The Geography of Gender: Elizabeth Bishop's "In the Waiting Room"', *Contemporary Literature*, 26 (Summer 1985), 179-96. In Lombardi (1993), 91-107.

Betsy Erkkila: 'Differences That Kill: Elizabeth Bishop and Marianne Moore', in *The Wicked Sisters: Women Poets, Literary History and Discord* (New York: Oxford University Press, 1992), 99-151.

————— : 'Elizabeth Bishop, Modernism, and the Left', *American Literary History*, 8 no.2 (Summer 1996): 284-310.

Sybil P. Estess: 'History as Geography', *Southern Review*, 13 (Autumn 1977), 705-27.

————— : 'Description and Imagination in Elizabeth Bishop's "The Map"'. In Schwartz & Estess (1983), 219-22.

Robin Riley Fast: 'Moore, Bishop and Oliver: Thinking Back, Re-Seeing the Sea', *Twentieth Century Literature*, 39 no.3 (Fall 1993), 364-79.

James Fenton: 'The Many Arts of Elizabeth Bishop', in *The Strength of Poetry* (Oxford: Oxford University Press, 2001), 127-44.

Anne Ferry: 'The Naming of Crusoe', *Eighteenth-Century Life*, 16 no.3 (November 1992), 195-207.

Joan L. Fields: 'Uncertainties and Discoveries: Elizabeth Bishop's Dramatized Personae as Little Girls', in *Performance for a Lifetime, A Festschrift Honoring Dorothy Harrell Brown: Essays on Women, Religion, and the Renaissance*, ed. Barbara C. Ewell & Mary A. McCay (New Orleans: Loyola University Press, 1997), 78-94.

Richard Flynn: ' "Home-made! But aren't we all?": Crusoe in the Nursery', *New Readings* symposium at Vassar College, 22-25 September 1994, http://projects.vassar.edu/bishop/Flynn.html.

Gary Fountain: 'Elizabeth Bishop's Lesbianism', in *Queer Representations: Reading Lives, Reading Cultures*, ed. Martin Duberman (New York: New York University Press, 1997).

Lloyd Frankenburg: 'Elizabeth Bishop', in *Pleasure Dome: On Reading Modern Poetry* (Boston: Houghton Mifflin, 1949), 328-31.

Thomas Gardner: 'Elizabeth Bishop and Jorie Graham: Suffering the Limits of Description', *New Readings* symposium at Vassar College, 22-25 September 1994, http://projects.vassar.edu/bishop/Gardner.html.

———— : 'Bishop and Ashbery: Two Ways Out of Stevens', *Wallace Stevens Journal*, 19 no.2 (Fall 1995), 201-18.

Jean Garrigue: 'Elizabeth Bishop's School', review of *Questions of Travel*, *New Leader*, 48 (6 December 1965), 22-23.

Albert Gelpi: 'Wallace Stevens and Elizabeth Bishop', *Wallace Stevens Journal*, 19 no.2 (Fall 1995), 155-65.

Roger Gilbert: 'Framing Water: Historical Knowledge in Elizabeth Bishop and Adrienne Rich', *Twentieth Century Literature*, 43 no.2 (Summer 1997), 144-61.

Dana Gioia: 'Studying with Miss Bishop', *New Yorker*, 15 September 1986, 90-101. In Monteiro (1996), 139-56.

Robert Giroux: 'The Making of "The Moose"', *Princeton University Library Chronicle*, 55 no.3 (Spring 1994), 400-10.

Lorrie Goldensohn: 'Elizabeth Bishop's Originality', *American Poetry Review*, 7 no.2 (March/April 1978), 18-22.

———— : 'Elizabeth Bishop: An Unpublished, Untitled Poem', *American Poetry Review*, 17 (January–February 1988), 35-46.

———— : 'The Body's Roses: Race, Sex, and Gender in Elizabeth Bishop's Representation of the Self'. Chapter from *Elizabeth Bishop: The Biography of a Poetry* (1992); repr. in Lombardi (1993), 70-90.

Celeste Goodridge: 'Elizabeth Bishop and Wallace Stevens: Sustaining the Eye/I', *Wallace Stevens Journal*, 19 no.2 (Fall 1995), 133-54.

Jan B. Gordon: 'Days and Distances: The Cartographic Imagination of Elizabeth Bishop', *Salmagundi*, 22-3 (1973), 294-305. In Bloom (1985), 9-19.

Jean Gould: 'Elizabeth Bishop', in her *Modern American Women Poets* (New York: Dodd, Mead, 1984), 51-74.

Vicki Graham: 'Bishop's "At the Fishhouses"', *Explicator*, 53 no.2 (Winter 1995): 114-17.

Jeffrey Gray: 'Bishop's "Brazil, January 1, 1502"', *Explicator*, 54 no.1 (Fall 1995), 36.

Thom Gunn: review of *Becoming a Poet: Elizabeth Bishop with Marianne Moore and Robert Lowell* by David Kalstone, *Times Literary Supplement*, 27 July–2 August 1990, 791-92.

Steven Hamelman: 'Bishop's "Crusoe in England"', *Explicator*, 51 no.1 (Fall 1992), 50-53.

Langdon Hammer: 'Useless Concentration: Life and Work in Elizabeth Bishop's Letters and Poems', *American Literary History*, 9 no.1 (Spring 1997), 162-80.

184 ELIZABETH BISHOP: A BIBLIOGRAPHY

Carolyn Handa: 'Vision and Change: The Poetry of Elizabeth Bishop',
American Poetry, 3 (Winter 1986), 18-34.

Victoria Harrison: 'Recording a Life: Elizabeth Bishop's Letters to
Ilse and Kit Barker', *Contemporary Literature*, 29 no.4 (Winter
1988), 498-517. In Lombardi (1993), 215-32.

Seamus Heaney: discussion of 'At the Fisheries' in 'The Govern-
ment of the Tongue', in *The Government of the Tongue: The 1986
T.S. Eliot Memorial Lectures and Other Critical Writings* (London:
Faber & Faber, 1988), 101-07; slightly revised for *Finders Keepers:
Selected Prose 1971-2001* (London: Faber & Faber, 2002), 189-90.

————— : 'Counting to a Hundred: On Elizabeth Bishop', in *The
Redress of Poetry: Oxford Lectures* (London: Faber and Faber, 1995),
164-85; reprinted in *Finders Keepers: Selected Prose 1971-2001*
(London: Faber & Faber, 2002), 332-46.

John Hollander: 'Questions of Geography', *Parnassus*, 5 (Spring–
Summer), 360-66.

————— : 'Elizabeth Bishop's Mappings of Life'. In Schwartz &
Estess (1983).

Gillian C. Huang-Tiller: 'Elizabeth Bishop's Feminist Poetic Travel
from "Sonnet" (1928) to "Sonnet" (1979)', *New Readings* sym-
posium at Vassar College, 22-25 September 1994, http://projects.
vassar.edu/bishop/Huang_Tiller.html.

Mihaela Irimia: 'The Art of Losing: W.H. Auden and Elizabeth
Bishop', *Critical Survey*, 6 no.3 (1994), 361-65.

David R. Jarraway: ' "O Canada!": The Spectral Lesbian Poetics
of Elizabeth Bishop', *PMLA*, 113 no.2 (March 1998), 243-57.

Randall Jarrell: review of *North & South* (1947), reprinted in *Poetry
and the Age* (New York: Knopf, 1953), 209-11.

————— : review of *Poems* (1955) in 'The Year in Poetry', *Harper's*,
October 1955, reprinted in *Kipling, Auden & Co.* (New York:
Farrar, Straus & Giroux, 1980), 245; rewritten as part of 'Fifty
Years of American Poetry', for a 1962 lecture published in *Prairie
Schooner* (1963) reprinted in *The Third Book of Criticism* (New
York: Farrar, Straus and Giroux, 1969), 325. In Schwartz &
Estess (1983), 198.

David Kalstone: 'All Eye', review of *Complete Poems* (1969),
Partisan Review, 37 (Spring 1970), 310-15.

————— : 'Elizabeth Bishop: Questions of Memory, Questions of
Travel'. In Schwartz & Estess (1983), first published in his *Five
Temperaments* (New York: Oxford University Press, 1977), 12-41.

————— : 'Trial Balances: Elizabeth Bishop and Marianne Moore',
Grand Street, 3 (Autumn 1983), 115-35, in *Coming to Light:
American Women Poets in the Twentieth Century*, ed. Dianne

Wood Middlebrook & Marilyn Yalom (Ann Arbor: University of Michigan Press, 1985), 105-23.

————— : 'Prodigal Years: Elizabeth Bishop and Robert Lowell 1947-49', *Grand Street* (Summer 1985), 170-93.

Weldon Kees: letter to Norris Gerry, 18 March 1950, quoted in 'The New York Intellectuals, 1941-50: Some Letters by Weldon Kees', *Hudson Review*, 38 no.1 (Spring 1985), 15-55.

Lynn Keller: 'Words Worth a Thousand Postcards: The Bishop/Moore Correspondence', *American Literature*, 55 no.3 (October 1983), 405-29.

Lynn Keller & Christianne Miller: 'Emily Dickinson, Elizabeth Bishop, and the Rewards of Indirection', *New England Quarterly*, 57 (December 1984), 533-53.

Ann Keniston: 'Efforts of Influence: Moore and Bishop', *Contemporary Literature*, 36 no.2 (Summer 1995), 384-91.

Ryan Lankford: 'Bishop's "Sestina" ', *Explicator*, 52 no.1 (Fall 1993), 57-59.

Penelope Laurens: 'Old Correspondence: Prosodic Transformations in Elizabeth Bishop'. In Schwartz & Estess (1983), 75-95.

David Lehman: ' "In Prison": A Paradox'. In Schwartz & Estess (1983), 61-74.

George Lensing: 'The Subtraction of Emotion in the Poetry of Elizabeth Bishop', *Gettysburg Review*, 5 no.1 (Winter 1992), 48-61.

————— : 'Wallace Stevens and Elizabeth Bishop: The Way a Poet Should See, the Way a Poet Should Think', *Wallace Stevens Journal*, 19 no.2 (Fall 1995), 115-32.

William Logan: 'The Unbearable Lightness of Elizabeth Bishop', *Southwest Review*, 79 no.1 (Winter 1994), 120-46.

James Logenbach: 'Elizabeth Bishop's Social Conscience', *ELH*, 62 no.2 (Summer 1995), 467-86.

Marilyn May Lombardi: 'The Closet of Breath: Elizabeth Bishop, Her Body and Her Art', *Twentieth Century Literature* (Summer 1992). In Lombardi (1993), 46-69.

Robert Lowell: 'Thomas, Bishop, and Williams', *Sewanee Review*, 55 (July–September 1947), 498. In Schwartz & Estess (1983), 186-99.

————— : 'On Skunk Hour'. In Schwartz & Estess (1983), 199.

Susan Lurie: ' "Caught in a Skein of Voices": Feminism and Colonialism in Elizabeth Bishop', in her *Unsettled Subjects: Restoring Feminist Politics to Poststructuralist Critique* (Durham, NC: Duke University Press, 1997), 119-54.

Susan McCabe: 'Writing Loss', *AI*, 50 no.1 (Spring 1993), 69-110.

J.D. McClatchy: 'Some Notes on "One Art" ', *Field*, 31 (Fall 1984), 34-39.

——————— : 'The Other Bishop', review of *Geography III, Canto*, 1 (Winter 1977), 165-74.

James McCorkle: 'Colonialism, Gender, and Lyric Identity: Refigurations of Crusoe in the Poetry of Elizabeth Bishop and Derek Walcott', *New Readings* symposium at Vassar College, 22-25 September 1994, http://projects.vassar.edu/bishop/McCorkle.html.

Heather McHugh: 'Moving Means, Meaning Moves: Notes on Lyric Destination', in *Poets Teaching Poets: Self and the World*, ed. Gregory Orr & Ellen Bryant Voigt (Ann Arbor: University of Michigan Press, 1996), 207-20.

Helen McNeil: 'Elizabeth Bishop', in *Voices & Visions: The Poet in America*, ed. Helen Vendler (New York: Random House, 1987), 394-425.

Sandra McPherson: ' "The Armadillo: A Commentary', *Field*, 31 (Fall 1984), 10-12.

Charles Edward Mann: 'Elizabeth Bishop and Revision: A Spiritual Act', *American Poetry Review*, 25 no.2 (March/April 1996), 43-50.

Klaus Martens: 'The Moose of It: Ein Gedicht von Elizabeth Bishop in seinen angloamerikanischen Traditionen', in *Transatlantic Encounters: Studies in European-American Relations, Presented to Winfried Herget*, ed. Udo J. Hebel & Karl Ortseifen (Trier, Germany: Wissenschaftlicher Verlag Trier, 1995). 279-94.

Jerome Mazzaro: 'Elizabeth Bishop's Poems', *Shenandoah*, 20 no.4 (Summer 1969), 99-101.

——————— : 'The Poetics of Impediment: Elizabeth Bishop', first published as ch. 7 of his *Postmodern American Poetry* (Urbana: University of Illinois Press, 1980). In Bloom (1985), 23-50.

James Merrill: 'Elizabeth Bishop, 1911-1979', *New York Review of Books*, 6 December 1979, 6. In Schwartz & Estess (1983), 259-62.

Jeredith Merrin: 'Elizabeth Bishop: Gaiety, Gayness, and Change'. In Lombardi (1993), 153-72.

——————— : 'Marianne Moore and Elizabeth Bishop', in *The Columbia History of American Poetry*, ed. Jay Parini & Brett C. Millier (New York: Columbia University Press, 1993), 343-69.

Cynthia Messenger: ' "But How Do You Children Write Chagall?" Ekphrasis and the Brazilian Poetry of P.K. Page and Elizabeth Bishop', *Canadian Literature*, 142/143 (Fall/Winter 1994).

Cristanne Miller, 'Bishop Studies: Questions of Biography', *New England Quarterly*, 67 no.3 (September 1994), 487-99.

Brett Candlish Millier: 'Modesty and Morality: George Herbert, Gerard Manley Hopkins, and Elizabeth Bishop', *Kenyon Review*, 11 (Spring 1989), 47-56.

——————— : 'Elusive Mastery: The Drafts of Elizabeth Bishop's

"One Art" ', *New England Review* (Winter 1990). In Lombardi (1993), 233-43.

———— : 'The Prodigal: Elizabeth Bishop and Alcohol', *Contemporary Literature*, 39 no.1 (Spring 1998): 54-76.

Mena Mitrano: 'Bishop's "Pink Dog" ', *Explicator*, 54 no.1 (Fall 1995), 33-36.

Marianne Moore: 'A Modest Expert: *North & South*', *The Nation*, 28 September 1946, 354, reprinted in her *Complete Prose* (New York: Sifton-Penguin, 1987), 524-26. In Schwartz & Estess (1983), 177-79.

Andrew Motion: 'Elizabeth Bishop', Chatterton Lecture on Poetry, 1984, *Proceedings of the British Academy*, 70 (Oxford: Oxford University Press, 1984).

Howard Moss: 'The Canada-Brazil Connection', *World Literature Today*, 51 (Winter 1977), 29-33.

———— : 'A Long Voyage Home', review of *The Complete Prose*, *New Yorker*, 1 April 1985, 104.

Richard Mullen: 'Elizabeth Bishop's Surrealist Inheritance', *American Literature*, 54 no.1 (March 1982), 63-80.

Howard Nemerov: 'The Poems of Elizabeth Bishop', *Poetry*, 87 no.3 (December 1955), 179-82.

Elisa New: 'Awe, Wonder, and Wit: Elizabeth Bishop and the Modernization of Calvinist Mood', in *The Calvinist Roots of the Modern Era*, ed. Aliki Barnstone, Michael Tomasek Manson & Carol J. Single (Hanover, NH: University Press of New England, 1997), 107-24.

Anne R. Newman: 'Elizabeth Bishop's "Roosters" ', in *Pebble: A Book of Rereadings in Recent American Poetry*, 18-20 (1980), 171-83. In Bloom (1985), 111-20.

Alicia Ostriker: 'I Am (Not) This: Erotic Discourse in Bishop, Olds, and Stevens', *Wallace Stevens Journal*, 19 no.2 (Fall 1995), 234-54.

Barbara Page: 'Shifting Islands: Elizabeth Bishop's Manuscripts', *Shenandoah*, 33 no.1 (1982), 51-62.

———— : 'Nature, History, and Art in Elizabeth Bishop's "Brazil, January 1, 1502" ', *Perspectives on Contemporary Literature*, 14 (1988), 39-46.

———— : 'Off-Beat Claves, Oblique Realities: The Key West Notebooks of Elizabeth Bishop'. In Lombardi (1993), 196-211.

———— : 'Elizabeth Bishop and Postmodernism', *Wallace Stevens Journal*, 19 no.2 (Fall 1995): 166-79.

———— : 'The Rising Figure of the Poet: Elizabeth Bishop in Letters and Biography', *Contemporary Literature*, 37 no.1 (Spring 1996), 119-31.

John Palatella: ' "That Sense of Constant Re-adjustment": The Great

Depression and the Provisional Politics of Elizabeth Bishop's *North & South*', *Contemporary Literature*, 34 no.1 (Spring 1993), 18-43.

Priscilla M. Paton: 'Landscape and Female Desire: Elizabeth Bishop's "Closet" Tactics', *Mosaic: A Journal for the Interdisciplinary Study of Literature*, 31 no.3 (September 1998), 133-51.

Tom Paulin: 'Writing to the Moment: Elizabeth Bishop', in *Writing to the Moment* (London: Faber & Faber, 1996).

Octavio Paz: 'Elizabeth Bishop, or the Power of Reticence'. In Schwartz & Estess (1983), 211-13.

Marjorie Perloff: 'Elizabeth Bishop: The Course of a Particular', *Modern Poetry Studies*, 8 (Winter 1977), 177-92.

Robert Pinsky: 'Elizabeth Bishop, 1911-1979', *New Republic*, 181 (10 November 1983), 32-33. In Schwartz & Estess (1983), 255-58.

————— : 'The Idiom of a Self: Elizabeth Bishop and William Wordsworth'. In Schwartz & Estess (1983), 133-53.

Jeffrey Powers-Beck: ' "Time to Plant Tears": Elizabeth Bishop's Seminary of Tears', *South Atlantic Review*, 60 no.4 (November 1995): 69-87.

Norma Procopiow: 'Survival Kit: The Poetry of Elizabeth Bishop', *Centennial Review*, 25 (Winter 1981), 1-19.

Josef Raab: 'The Political Dimension of Elizabeth Bishop', *New Readings* symposium at Vassar College, 22-25 September 1994, http://projects.vassar.edu/bishop/Raab.html.

————— : 'Elizabeth Bishop's Autobiographical Silences', in *Semantics of Silences in Linguistics and Literature*, ed. Gudrun M. Grabher & Ulrike Jessner (Heidelberg: Universitaetsverlag C., 1996), 291-308.

————— : 'The Poetics of Life: Robert Lowell and Elizabeth Bishop', in *Poetics in the Poem: Critical Essays on American Self-Reflexive Poetry*, ed. Dorothy Z. Baker (New York: Peter Lang, 1997), 195-219.

Deryn Rees-Jones: 'Objecting to the Subject: Science, Creativity and Poetic Process in the work of Lavinia Greenlaw and Elizabeth Bishop' in *Kicking Daffodils*, ed. Vicki Bertram (Edinburgh: Edinburgh University Press, 1997), 267-76.

Christopher Reid: 'Elizabeth Bishop', in *The Oxford Companion to Twentieth-century Poetry*, ed. Ian Hamilton (Oxford and New York: Oxford University Press, 1994).

Adrienne Rich: 'The Eye of the Outsider: The Poetry of Elizabeth Bishop', *Boston Review*, 8 (April 1983), 15-17. In her *Blood, Bread and Poetry* (New York: Norton, 1986), 124-35.

Susan Rosenbaum: 'Re-Reading Confessional Poetry: Elizabeth Bishop and the Confessional Moment in American Poetry',

New Readings symposium at Vassar College, 22-25 September 1994, http://projects.vassar.edu/bishop/Rosenbaum.html.

Charles Sanders: 'Bishop's "Sonnet" ', *Explicator*, 40 (Spring 1982), 63-64.

Sherod Santos: 'The End of March', *Field*, 31 (Fall 1984), 29-32.

Judith P. Saunders: ' "Large Bad Picture" and "The Rime of the Ancient Mariner": A Note on Elizabeth Bishop's Modernist Aesthetics', *ANQ*, 8 no.3 (Summer 1995): 17-22.

Lloyd Schwartz: 'Annals of Poetry: Elizabeth Bishop and Brazil', *New Yorker*, 67 no.32 (30 September 1991), 85-97.

Nathan A. Scott, Jr: 'Elizabeth Bishop: Poet Without Myth', *Virginia Quarterly Review*, 60 (Spring 1984), 255-75.

Anne Shifrer: 'Elizabeth Bishop as Delicate Ethnographer', *New Readings* symposium at Vassar College, 22-25 September 1994, http://projects.vassar.edu/bishop/Shifrer.html.

Jane Shore: 'Elizabeth Bishop: The Art of Changing Your Mind', *Ploughshares*, 5 (1979), 178-91.

Manfred Siebald: ' "Questions of Travel": Die Dekonstruktion des touristischen Blicks in der Reiselyrik Elizabeth Bishop', *Amerikastudien/American Studies*, 41 no.4 (1996), 623-35.

Willard Spiegelman: 'Landscape and Knowledge: The Poetry of Elizabeth Bishop', *Modern Poetry Studies*, 6 (1975), 203-24.

————— : 'Elizabeth Bishop's "Natural Heroism" ', *Centennial Review*, 22 (Winter 1978), 28-44. In Bloom (1985), 97-110.

Elizabeth Spires: 'One life, one art: Elizabeth Bishop in her Letters', *The New Criterion*, 12 no.9 (1994), 18-23.

Donald Stanford: 'From the Letters of Elizabeth Bishop, 1933-34', *Verse*, 4 no.3 (November 1987), 19-27.

Anne Stevenson: 'Letters from Elizabeth Bishop', *Times Literary Supplement*, 7 March 1980, 261.

————— : 'The Iceberg and the Ship: The Poetry of Elizabeth Bishop', *Michigan Quarterly Review*, 35 no.4 (Fall 1996), 704-19.

Ernesto Suarez-Toste: ' "Straight from Chirico": Pictorial Surrealism and Early Elizabeth Bishop', *Studies in the Humanities*, 23 no.2 (December 1996), 185-201.

Joseph H. Summers: 'George Herbert and Elizabeth Bishop', *George Herbert Journal*, 18 no.1/2 (Fall 1994–Spring 1995), 48-58.

Eleanor Ross Taylor: 'Interview with Eleanor Ross Taylor' by Jean Valentine, *Southern Review*, 33:4 (Autumn 1997): 790-814.

Colm Tóibín: 'Elizabeth Bishop: The Casual Perfect', in *Love in a Dark Time: Gay Lives from Wilde to Almodóvar* (London: Picador, 2001), 172-94.

Thomas J. Travisano: 'Heavenly Dragons: A Newly Discovered

Poem by Elizabeth Bishop', *Western Humanities Review*, 45 (Winter 1991), 28-33.

————— : 'Emerging Genius: Elizabeth Bishop and *The Blue Pencil*, 1927-1930', *Gettysburg Review*, 5 no.1 (Winter 1992), 32-47.

————— : 'The Flicker of Impudence: Delicacy and Indelicacy in the Art of Elizabeth Bishop'. In Lombardi (1993), 111-25.

————— : *Expulsion From Paradise: Elizabeth Bishop, 1927-1957* (Jolicure, New Brunswick: Anchorage Press, 1995), the first EBSNS Elizabeth Bishop Memorial Lecture, presented in Great Village on 9 June 1995.

————— : 'Bishop's Influence on Stevens', *Wallace Stevens Journal*, 19 no.2 (Fall 1995), 279-86.

————— : 'The Elizabeth Bishop Phenomenon', *New Literary History*, 26 no.4 (Fall 1995), 903-30, reprinted in *Gendered Modernisms: American Women Poets and the Readers*, ed. Margaret Dickie & Thomas J. Travisano (Philadelphia: University of Pennsylvania Press, 1996), 217-44.

Chase Twichell: 'Everything Only Connected by "And" and "And": The Skewed Narrative of Elizabeth Bishop', *NER/BLQ*, 8 no.1 (1985), 130-37.

Lee Upton: 'Through the Lens of Edward Lear: Contesting Sense in the Poetry of Elizabeth Bishop', *Studies in Humanities*, 19 no.1 (June 1992), 68-79.

Kathrine Varnes: 'Is It a Boy or a Girl: Gender as the Ever-Present Authority and Anxiety in Bishop Studies', *Connotations: A Journal for Critical Debate*, 4 no.3 (1994-95), 313-18 (response to interchange between Jonathan Ausubel and Jacqueline Vaught Brogan in *Connotations*, 4 no.1/2 (1994-1995), 83-97, 172-80).

Helen Vendler: 'Recent Poetry: Eight Poets', *Yale Review*, 66 (Spring 1977), 407-24.

————— : 'Elizabeth Bishop', in her *Part of Nature, Part of Us* (Cambridge, MA and London: Harvard University Press, 1980), 97-110.

————— : 'Domestication, Domesticity, and the Otherworldly'. In Schwartz & Estess (1983), 32-60.

Cheryl Walker: 'Reading Elizabeth Bishop as a Religious Poet', *New Readings* symposium at Vassar College, 22-25 September 1994, http://projects.vassar.edu/bishop/Walker.html.

Patricia Walker: 'Erasing the Maternal: Rereading Elizabeth Bishop', *Iowa Review*, 22 no.2 (Spring 1992), 82-103.

Wesley Wehr: 'Elizabeth Bishop: Conversations and Class Notes', *Antioch Review*, 39 no.3 (Summer 1981), 319-28. In Monteiro (1996), 38-46.

David G. Williams: 'Elizabeth Bishop and the "Martian" Poetry of Craig Raine and Christopher Reid', *English Studies*, 78 no.5 (September 1997), 451-58.

————— : 'Responses to Elizabeth Bishop: Anne Stevenson, Eavan Boland, and Jo Shapcott', *English*, 44 (1995): 229-45.

Oscar Williams: 'North but South', *New Republic* (21 October 1946), 525. In Schwartz & Estess (1983), 184-85.

Alan Williamson: '*A Cold Spring*: The Poet of Feeling'. In Schwartz & Estess (1983), 96-108.

Shira Wolosky: 'Representing Other Voices: Rhetorical Perspectives in Elizabeth Bishop', *Style*, 29 no.1 (1995), 1-17.

Patricia Yaeger: 'Toward a Female Sublime' (includes discussion of 'The Fish' and 'The Moose'), in *Gender & Theory*, ed. Linda Kauffman (Oxford: Blackwell, 1989).

Zhou Xiaojing: 'Bishop's "Casabianca"', *Explicator* 52 no.2 (Winter 1994), 109-11.

————— : 'Bishop's "Trouvée"', *Explicator*, 54 no.2 (Winter 1996), 102.

————— : '"My Real Hopes and Ambitions": Re-Reading Elizabeth Bishop's "In Prison"', *Texas Studies in Literature and Language*, 39 no.1 (Spring 1997), 65-79.

————— : '"The Oblique, the Indirect Approach": Elizabeth Bishop's "Rainy Season; Sub-Tropics"', *Chicago Review*, 40 no.4 (1994): 75-92.

Lee Zimmerman: 'Against Vanishing: Winicott and the Modern Poetry of Nothing', *American Image*, 54 no.1 (Spring 1997), 81-102.

6. SPECIAL ELIZABETH BISHOP ISSUES OF JOURNALS

Connotations: A Journal for Critical Debate, 2 no.1 (1992), 34-51, 90-102, 295-312.

Gettysburg Review, 'A Special Feature on Elizabeth Bishop', 5 no.1 (Winter 1992), 11-72.

Harvard Review, 'Elizabeth Bishop Lives', 16 (Spring 1999), 1-84.

Wallace Stevens Journal, 'Special Issue: Stevens and Elizabeth Bishop', 19 no.2 (Fall 1995).

War Literature and the Arts: An International Journal of the Humanities, 2 no.1 (Spring/Summer 1999), 1-42, 93-148.

The Worcester Review, 'Elizabeth Bishop (1911-1979)', 18 no.1/2 (1997).

World Literature Today, ed. Ivan Ivask, 'Homage to Elizabeth Bishop, Our 1976 Laureate', 51 no.1 (1977), 4-52.

7. ELIZABETH BISHOP SOCIETIES AND JOURNALS

The Elizabeth Bishop Society publishes *The Elizabeth Bishop Bulletin*, edited by Barbara Page, published twice yearly since 1992 (annual membership US$5.00 or $20.00 for five years). For more information, write to: Gary Fountain, English Department, 350 Muller Center, Ithaca, NY 14850-7281, USA.

The Elizabeth Bishop Society of Nova Scotia publishes *The EBSNS Newsletter*, edited by Sandra Barry and Brian Bartlett, published twice yearly since 1994 (annual membership Canadian $8.00 or $20.00 for three years). For more information, write to: EBSNS, P.O. Box 138, Great Village, Nova Scotia, Canada B0M 1L0.

The EBSNS's publications include Sandra Barry's *Elizabeth Bishop: An Archival Guide to Her Life in Nova Scotia*, Thomas Travisano's *Expulsion From Paradise* (see above) and *Elizabeth Bishop and Nova Scotia* (pamphlet prepared by EBSNS, 2000).

8. ELIZABETH BISHOP WEBSITES

The most comprehensive Elizabeth Bishop website is that set up by Vassar College, where the Elizabeth Bishop Papers are held: http://projects.vassar.edu/bishop/

Vassar's Bishop website, managed by Barbara Page, includes the papers presented at the *New Readings* symposium at Vassar College, 22-25 September 1994, as well as other information and an extensive bibliography.

The Elizabeth Bishop Society of Nova Scotia has a section at: http://nexusmedia.ca/develop/bishop

The above bibliography draws on Vassar's current website bibliography as well as on the bibliographies in many of the books on Elizabeth Bishop. The Vassar bibliography provides much more comprehensive information about Elizabeth Bishop's own publishing and recording history, but only covers articles about Bishop published between 1990 and 2001. This bibliography, compiled in February 2002, provides fuller information about Bishop criticism published over a longer period. However, the Vassar bibliography is updated regularly, and should be consulted for details of material published from 2002 onwards.

Elizabeth Bishop: Chronology

1911   Elizabeth Bishop born 8 February, at 875 Main Street, Worcester, Massachusetts, daughter of William T. Bishop and Gertrude Bulmer [Boomer] Bishop. Her father dies on 13 October, aged 39, of Bright's disease. Her mother moves to live with her sisters in Boston, but spends much of the next five years in mental asylums and rest homes.

1915   EB moves with her mother to live with her maternal grandparents in Great Village, Nova Scotia, Canada (see EB's autobiographical short story 'In the Village').

1916   Following a mental breakdown, her mother is admitted to a state sanatorium, leaving EB with her family in Great Village. EB never sees her again (she did not die until 1934).

1917   EB is 'kidnapped' by her paternal grandparents and taken back to the States. She lives with them for nine months in Worcester, Massachusetts, developing asthma and eczema.

1918   EB taken to live with her mother's married sister, Aunt Maud Shepherdson, and Uncle George, in Revere, Boston, spending summers in Great Village until 1923.

1923   Deaths of EB's maternal grandparents in Nova Scotia.

1924   EB spends the first of five summers at Camp Chequesset in Wellfleet, Massachusetts, where she learns to sail and swim and makes friends with girls of her own age.

1927   After repeating a year at a private school in Swampscott (because of illness), EB enters Walnut Hill boarding school in Natick, Massachusetts, aged 16, making close, lifelong friendships with some girls, and publishing her first poems and stories in the school magazine, *The Blue Pencil*.

1930   EB enters Vassar College, the exclusive women's college at Poughkeepsie, New York. Her friends include Frani Blough (from Walnut Hill), Margaret Miller and Louise Crane (Mary McCarthy, a year ahead of her, later wrote *The Group*, based on her Vassar classmates). Her poems appear in *Con Spirito*, a radical literary magazine launched with her contemporaries. She edits the College Yearbook with Margaret Miller in her final (fourth) year.

1934   March: EB's first meeting with Marianne Moore. May:
       EB's mother dies in the sanatorium at Dartmouth. June:
       EB graduates with a B.A. from Vassar, finds a small apart-
       ment on the edge of Greenwich Village, NYC, and spends
       part of the summer on the Massachusetts coast. She sees
       Moore often in Brooklyn. Her first, short-lived job is as a
       writing instructor at the U.S.A. School of Writing, where
       she steps into the shoes of 'Mr Margolies'. Alone with 'flu
       on New Year's Eve, she studies a framed map of the North
       Atlantic, and begins 'The Map' (published in an anthology,
       Trial Balances, in October 1935).

1935   July: EB sails for Europe aboard with college friend Hallie
       Tompkins. Her travels, later recounted in 'Over 2000 Illus-
       trations and a Complete Concordance', take her to France,
       England, Morocco, Spain and Mallorca; in Paris she lives
       in some luxury with Louise Crane at her wealthy parents'
       expense, studying French, writing and drinking, but becomes
       seriously ill with mastoiditis. Poems from this European
       period include 'Paris 7 A.M.' and 'The Man-Moth'.

1936   June: EB returns to New York, spending the summer at
       West Falmouth, Massachusetts. Marianne Moore begins to
       manage EB's literary career (until their disagreement in
       1940). November: suicide of EB's college "boyfriend", Bob
       Seaver, who had hoped to marry her; his only note, a post-
       card received a few days later: 'Go to hell, Elizabeth.' EB
       departs for Florida with Louise Crane, visiting Key West
       for the first time.

1937   After wintering in Florida, EB spends several months in
       Europe with Louise Crane and Margaret Miller, who loses
       her arm in an accident when Louise's car is forced off the
       road. EB declines an offer of a book from New Directions.

1938   EB moves to Key West, living first in a boarding-house (see
       'Sunday at Key West' and 'Cootchie') near her Aunt Maud
       and Uncle George; then buys 624 White Street, the first of her
       three loved houses, with Louise Crane. She meets painters
       Gregorio Valdes and Loren MacIver, philosopher John Dewey
       and daughter Jane, and Pauline Pfeiffer Hemingway. 'Cirque
       d'Hiver', written in her beach shack, is the first of many
       poems published in *The New Yorker*; other Key West poems
       from 1938-40 include 'The Fish' and 'Roosters'.

1939   EB submits a first collection to Random House, which is
       rejected without encouragement, later refusing offers of pub-
       lication as token woman in a five-poet introduction volume

including John Berryman and Randall Jarrell as well as a pamphlet from New Directions. Louise Crane leaves Key West and EB spends the summer and autumn in New York, apparently drinking heavily. Her manuscript is rejected by Viking, then by Simon and Schuster.

1940   *Partisan Review* publishes 'The Fish', promoting interest from Harcourt Brace, who think the collection incomplete, the poems not yet strong enough. By the end of 1940 she has written most of *North & South*, but the next five years see an impasse as EB awaits further interest from Harcourt Brace and they await further poems. August: death of Aunt Maud Shepherdson. October: disagreement between EB and Marianne Moore over her re-write of 'Roosters'.

1941   EB moves in with Marjorie Stevens as Key West becomes militarised. December: Pearl Harbor, the US enters the war.

1942   EB and Marjorie Stevens spend several months in Mexico, where they meet Neruda, who finds them an apartment. EB returns to New York for the autumn, where she sits for a portrait by Loren MacIver, and is introduced at her studio to Brazilian aristocrat Lota de Macedo Soares with her then companion Mary Stearns Morse. November: EB returns to Marjorie Stevens in Key West, where she stays until 1944. She writes few letters and publishes no poems in 1942-43.

1943   EB briefly employed, grinding binocular lenses at a US Navy optical shop, but gives up after five days due to eye-strain, sickness and eczema. Writing again by November: drafting 'Large Bad Picture', 'Songs for a Colored Singer'; then notes towards 'Faustina, or Rock Roses' (published three years later).

1944   EB suffering from asthma, finally leaving Florida for New York in August, where she takes a garret at 46 King Street. December: EB jarred out of alcoholic misery by invitation to submit a collection for Houghton Mifflin's first annual Poetry Prize Fellowship ($1000 and publication of a book).

1945   EB back in Key West. Wins the Houghton Mifflin Prize for *North & South*, but quarrels over publication details.

1946   End of EB's relationship with Marjorie Stevens. Treatment by psychiatrist Dr Ruth Foster fails to cure her alcoholism. August: *North & South* finally published when EB is in Nova Scotia, a trip inspiring both 'At the Fishhouses' and 'The Moose', the latter on the return bus journey (the poem not begun until 1956 and not completed until 1972). EB given "first-read" contract with *New Yorker*.

1947   Lukewarm initial response to *North & South*, until reviews by Marianne Moore and Randall Jarrell (amongst others); January: Jarrell introduces EB to Robert Lowell, whose review reaches her that summer when she is again in Nova Scotia, this time with Marjorie Stevens. April: EB wins $2500 Guggenheim Fellowship. Start of EB's treatment by Dr Anny Baumann as well as her friendship with Lowell.

1948   After wintering in Key West, EB taken to see Ezra Pound by Robert Lowell, who believed 'it would be just a matter of time before I proposed, and I half believed that you would accept'. June: EB in Maine with Tom Wanning (drinking and drafting 'The Bight'), her last attempt at a heterosexual relationship (which ended in 1949).

1949   EB in Key West, Haiti, Blythwood (for alcholism), Yaddo (affected by Lowell's impending marriage to Elizabeth Hardwick), then Washington, beginning her year as Consultant in Poetry at the Library of Congress (see 'View of the Capitol from the Library of Congress'), when she organised recordings of Dylan Thomas and many others; visiting Pound went with the job (see 'Visits to St Elizabeths', written in 1956).

1950   Autumn: writing at Yaddo, including ' "O Breath" ' (from her asthma) and 'The Prodigal' (alcoholism). Death of Dr Ruth Foster. Start of friendship with Kit and Ilse Barker.

1951   After Yaddo, EB in New York, Maryland ('A Cold Spring') with Jane Dewey, and Sable Island, Nova Scotia; helped by a Bryn Mawr College fellowship, then an American Academy of Arts and Letters Award. After death of Pauline Pfeiffer, EB sails in November on a world trip ('Questions of Travel'), stopping off ('Arrival at Santos') then staying in Brazil after suffering a violent allergic reaction to cashew fruit.

1952   After recuperation, EB lives with Lota de Macedo Soares in the house she is building at Petrópolis on her family's Samambaia estate, 60 miles inland from Rio, while Mary Morse stays mostly at their city flat. She is given a toucan, which she calls Uncle Sam or Sammy. August: EB sends Marianne Moore 'The Shampoo', but this celebratory love poem is unpublished for three years; otherwise she is writing or finishing autobiographical prose, including 'In the Village'.

1953   Lota builds EB's studio. April: first visit to the 18th-century town of Ouro Prêto. EB begins translating Alice Brant's *Minha Vida de Menina*. She now has an MG two-seater ('very adolescent taste') and a cat, Tobias ('black with white feet and vest – perfect evening wear... handsome, and a brilliant cat intellectually, of course').

1954   EB's life is less stressed in Brazil than in New York; she's able to live off income from her father's estate and by living with Lota without career money pressures, her asthma relieved by new cortisone treatments, her drinking less frequent.

1955   After much wrangling with Houghton Mifflin, EB's second collection *A Cold Spring* is combined with *North & South* as *Poems* with a cover by Loren MacIver. She writes to Randall Jarrell that 'Exile seems to work for me'; and she is 'doing a hideous rush job of translation' (Henrique Mindlin's *Modern Architecture in Brazil*).

1956   *Poems* wins the Pulitzer Prize ($500) and the *Partisan Review* fellowship ($2700), and is published by Chatto & Windus, her first British volume. *New Yorker* publishes 'Questions of Travel' and 'Manuelzinho', her 'first attempt to say anything much about Brazil' ('It's supposed to be Lota talking'). EB's translation of *Minha Vida de Menina*, the work of two years, is turned down by Houghton Mifflin. 'I've written a long poem about Nova Scotia,' she writes to her Aunt Grace of 'The Moose', then in its first drafts.

1957   EB and Lota stay in New York from April to October, seeing numerous friends, including Lowell, amorous, manically depressed and writing *Life Studies*. She works on arrangements for the Brant translation, published by Farrar, Straus and Cudahy as *The Diary of "Helena Morley"*.

1958   EB accidentally poisons her toucan Sammy. EB anxious for Margaret Miller, mentally ill and hostile, a recurrent pattern amongst those she loved. She visits the new capital of Brasilia with Aldous Huxley, as well as Indian tribes of the Mato Grosso, and works on further Brazilian poems.

1959   EB continues work on Brazilian poems for her third collection, then to be called *January River*, but she and Lota cancel an American trip, due to financial restraints caused by soaring inflation in Brazil.

1960   EB travels down the Amazon from Manaus to Belém with Lota's friend Rosinha Leão and her nephew, a trip which prompts 'On the Amazon' and 'Santarém' as well as the prose account (posthumously published) 'A Trip to Vigia'. EB given a $7000 travel grant by the Chapelbrook Foundation. October: EB uprooted to Rio for Lota's work, where they live with Mary Morse and her adopted daughter Monica, only spending weekends in Petrópolis.

1961   EB accepts a $10,000 commission from Time, Inc. Books to write a guide to Brazil for their Life World Library, but disagrees with them over content and balance, finishing it in New York during a five-week stay with Lota.

1962 EB adding Nova Scotian poems ('First Death in Nova Scotia') to a manuscript now titled *Questions of Travel*, and translating stories by Clarice Lispector and poems by João Cabral de Melo Neto and Carlos Drummond de Andrade. The Lowells visit EB in Brazil, Elizabeth Hardwick leaving Robert Lowell behind as he grows more manic, and is returned to Boston from Buenos Aires in a straitjacket.

1963 EB feeling increasingly isolated, with Lota stressed and then seriously ill, estranged from the confessional and Beat poets she reads in the journals (and ending her *New Yorker* publication contract), affected by deaths of several writers and later by Kennedy's assassination, drinking heavily and finally signing herself into a clinic. At the same time she begins a revealing three-year correspondence with Anne Stevenson, who is writing her Twayne monograph.

1964 After the April coup, which sees Lota barricaded with her friend and backer Carlos Lacerda in his Governor's Palace, EB travels with her to Italy for a month, going on alone to England in June (her first visit since 1937), where she stays mostly with the Barkers, sailing back to Brazil in July. She begins a friendship with Ashley Brown, taking him on one of many trips to Lilli Correia's in Ouro Prêto.

1965 EB's *New York Times* article on Rio is misrepresented in the Brazilian press, causing local friction. Leaving Lota ill and exhausted in Rio, EB spends several weeks with Lilli ('Under the Window: Ouro Prêto'); she receives a $5000 award from the Academy of American Poets, and buys and starts restoring her own house in Ouro Prêto, 'Casa Mariana'. *Questions of Travel* is published by Farrar, Straus and Giroux in November, mostly to highly appreciative reviews.

1966 Against Lota's wishes, EB takes up a six-month residency at the University of Washington in Seattle, drinking with Henry Reed, suffering from asthma and Asian 'flu, and falling in love with 'Suzanne Bowen' [pseudonym], 26, married and pregnant. She returns to a distraught Lota, whose health is deteriorating. They cut short a visit to Amsterdam and London meant to ease Lota's mental state.

1967 After a disastrous Christmas at Petrópolis, EB leaves Lota at new year, staying in a Rio hotel before checking herself into a clinic. Reunited briefly with Lota in Petrópolis, she begins writing again after a two-year block, completing the prose poems of 'Rainy Season; Sub-Tropics'. In May she travels alone in a boat-party on the Rio São Francisco, and in July stays in New York and then Long Island, where she completes 'Going to the Bakery' and starts 'In the Waiting Room'. Against medical advice, Lota joins her on 19 September; with a heart condition, she overdoses, dying in a coma after five days. EB is too ill for the funeral in Rio, returning in November with a broken arm and shoulder, having inherited the flat and wanting to move to Ouro Prêto.

1968 Instead, EB moves into a San Francisco apartment with Suzanne Bowen and her 18-month-old son, where she works on an anthology of modern Brazilian poetry, as the 1960s counterculture reaches its apotheosis. Drinking heavily, she gives several readings; falls and breaks her wrist, then has a wisdom tooth removal; travels by train with Suzanne to Canada, but gets osteomyelitis of the jaw, an abscess, and has more teeth removed. Back home, she buys a mynah bird, Jacob, writes about a rock band, and interviews Black Panther Kathleen Cleaver while her car is vandalised outside.

1969 EB's first *Complete Poems* is published by Farrar, Straus and Giroux in April. Assisted by a $5000 Ingram-Merrill award, she takes Suzanne to Ouro Prêto, where she quarrels with Lilli and Suzanne; work on the house moves slowly because of legal problems and local antagonism. After the death of her cat Tobias, EB suffering from acute alcholism, emotional collapse and asthma, feeling herself lost in 'a totally wasted stretch' while Brazil is engulfed by anarchic repression.

1970 EB given a National Book Award. Suzanne has a breakdown and returns to America; EB begins a new relationship with Ouro Prêto friend Linda Nemer, and is writing again, working on poems including 'Poem' and 'Crusoe in England'. She teaches a semester at Harvard in the autumn, memorably described by Dana Gioia in Monteiro (1996), and meets Alice Methfessel, her 'saving grace'.

1971 EB returns to Ouro Prêto, soon learning of the suicide of Lota's nephew Flavio; by April she is packing everything to leave Brazil; May, she returns to America suffering from typhoid or dysentery. After another return to Ouro Prêto, she travels to the Galápagos Islands and to Machu Picchu with Alice. 'In the Waiting Room' and 'Crusoe in England' published in *The New Yorker*; she teaches another semester at Harvard until hospitalised for acute asthma.

1972   After Berryman's suicide and Moore's death, EB embroiled
       in a profound disagreement with Lowell over his manuscript
       of poems for *The Dolphin* which reworks letters from Eliza-
       beth Hardwick. She translates poems by Octavio Paz, then
       at Harvard; sees the Brazilian anthology published; works all
       spring on 'The Moose', reading an almost final version at the
       Harvard-Radcliffe Phi Beta Kappa ceremony on 13 June.
1973   EB teaching in Seattle, before returning to Boston, where
       she buys an apartment under conversion on Lewis Wharf,
       visiting Nova Scotia with Alice and spending the autumn
       in Cambridge.
1974   EB returns to teach at Harvard; she writes her memoir of
       Marianne Moore and 'The End of March', and spends her
       first summer writing at Sabine Farm on North Haven, off
       the coast of Maine, where she later keeps a journal.
1975   Continuing at Harvard, EB visits Mexico, and works at
       North Haven on 'Memories of Uncle Neddy', a story she
       had begun 20 years earlier. In the autumn, she falls apart,
       drinking, depressed and wracked with guilt and insecurity,
       but writes her villanelle 'One Art', fearing she may lose Alice
       on top of all the other losses recalled in the poem; and spends
       Christmas at Ft Myers, Florida ('Florida Revisited').
1976   At a time of personal crisis, EB is awarded the $10,000
       Neustadt International Prize for Literature, marked with a
       special issue of *World Literature Today*. She visits England,
       Rotterdam for the International Poetry Conference, and tours
       Portugal with Alice, but becomes ill on their return, and is
       rushed to hospital in Boston. She completes *Geography III*,
       published in December, which wins the 1977 Book Critics'
       Circle Award.
1977   Retiring from Harvard, EB seriously ill with hiatal hernia
       and anaemia. Shocked at Lowell's sudden death, she begins
       'North Haven' on the island. She teaches a semester at New
       York University, but falls ill again.
1978   EB finishes 'Santarém', recalling her 1960 Amazon River
       trip. She is awarded a $21,000 Guggenheim Fellowship.
1979   After visiting England, EB and Alice take a Greek cruise
       from Venice, spending the rest of the summer at North
       Haven. EB is too ill to begin her autumn semester teaching
       at MIT. She dies of a cerebral aneurism at Lewis Wharf
       on 6 October. She had asked that 'Awful, but cheerful' be
       inscribed on her tombstone in the Bishop family plot at
       Worcester (completed in 1997).

INDEX

Bold face figures indicate writings by the author concerned

Anderson, Linda **7-11**, **159-74**, 179, 207
Appelbaum, David 12-14, 15, 16, 21, 24
Astley, Neil **175-200**, 207
Auden, W.H. 9, 119-20, 149, 159
Austen, Jane 145
Austin, J.L. 110

Barker, Ilse 49, 179, 196, 198
Barker, Kit 49, 196, 198
Baudelaire, Charles 33, 123-25, 128-32, 134, 141
Baumann, Anny 111, 117, 196
Beckett, Samuel 14
Benton, William 86*n*, 174*n*
Berger, John 139
Bernard, April 64
Berryman, John 179, 195, 200
Bidart, Frank 50, 160, 178, 180
Bishop, Elizabeth
POETRY:
'Arrival at Santos' 40, 113, 196
'At the Fishhouses' 22, 26, 33-37, 39, 86*n*, 195
'The Baptism' 81
'The Bight' 124-26, 128, 137, 171, 196
'Brazil' 116
'Cape Breton' 39, 84
'Casabianca' 123
'Chemin de Fer' 106
'Cirque d'Hiver' 77-79, 164-65
'A Cold Spring' 196
A Cold Spring 12, 31, 33, 110, 111, 116, 197
'Cootchie' 138, 194
Complete Poems 43, 50, 110, 116, 199

'Crusoe in England' 20, 56-57, 117, 123, 151, 155, 168, 197
'Dead' 81
'Electrical Storm' 84
'Elsewhere' 116
'The End of March' 17, 84, 200
'Exchanging Hats' 50
'The Farmer's Children' 81
'Faustina, or Rock Roses' 21-22, 54, 195
'Filling Station' 87, 94-96, 100
'First Death in Nova Scotia' 80, 81-84, 87, 198
'The Fish' 22, 48, 87, 89-93, 96, 100, 165, 194
'Five Flights Up' 76
'Florida Revisited' 200
'For C.W.B.' 67-68, 83
'From the Country to the City' 32
Geography III 24, 32, 39, 43, 53, 200
'The Gentleman of Shalott' 32, 82, 123
'Going to the Bakery' 199
'The Imaginary Iceberg' 69-71, 82
'In the Waiting Room' 24-25, 27-28, 48-49, 57, 79-80, 142, 155, 166, 199
'Large Bad Picture' 170, 171, 195
'Love Lies Sleeping' 16, 32-33, 161
'The Man-Moth' 45-46, 151, 161, 165, 194
'Manuelzinho' 197

'The Map' 116, 135, 139-40, 194
'The Moose' 13, 25-28, 31, 48-49, 76, 86n, 87, 96-101, 155-56, 165-66, 195, 197, 200
North & South 12, 31, 33, 116, 195, 197
'North Haven' 43, 136
'O Breath' 196
'On the Amazon' 197
'One Art' 22-24, 65, 76, 106, 200
'Over 2,000 Illustrations and a Complete Concordance' 37-39, 194
'Paris, 7 A.M.' 12, 33, 74-77, 80, 194
'Poem' 14-15, 20, 73, 140, 170, 199
'The Prodigal' 196
'Quai d'Orléans' 33
Questions of Travel 31, 39, 110
'Questions of Travel' 19, 25, 40, 82, 196, 197, 198
'Rainy Season: Sub-Tropics' 87, 160, 199
'Roosters' 194
'Sandpiper' 37, 87, 102n, 123, 126-31, 134-35, 137
'Santarém' 19, 27, 54, 123, 197, 200
'Sestina' 88
'The Shampoo' 103, 107, 109-112, 196
'Sleeping on the Ceiling' 33
'Sleeping Standing Up' 164
'Songs for a Colored Singer' 195
'Sonnet' 172-73
'Sunday, 4 A.M.' 135-36, 140-41

'Sunday at Key West' 194
'Trouvée' 171
'12 O'Clock News' 125
'Under the Window: Ouro Prêto' 137-39
'Varrick Street' 84
'Visits to St Elizabeths' 123, 196
'The Weed' 17, 33, 37, 80, 161
PROSE:
Brazil 53, 175, 197-98
'The Country Mouse' 24-25, 72, 79, 115-16, 167
Diary of "Helena Morley" 141, 196, 197
'Efforts of Affection: A Memoir of Marianne Moore', 128, 147
'Gregorio Valdes' 160
'Gwendolyn' 31
'In Prison' 17
'In the Village' 17-19, 31, 72, 88, 169, 194, 196
Letters 66, 101n
'Memories of Uncle Neddy' 64, 66, 200
'The Sea & Its Shore' 151
'A Trip to Vigia' 197
'U.S.A. School of Writing' 151
UNPUBLISHED WRITING:
'Dimensions for a Novel' 172
Drafts of poems 15, 18, 23
'Grandmother's Glass Eye: An Essay on Style' 167
'Memoir of Great Village' 73-74, 80
Notebooks 16, 33, 55, 65-66, 71, 159, 162-64, 167-79
'Vaguely Love Poem' 21-22
Bishop, Gertrude Boomer [Bulmer] 193, 194
Bishop, William T. 193

Blake, William 123, 127
Blough, Frani 152, 154, 193
Boland, Eavan 13, 14, 180, 191
'Bowen, Suzanne' 198, 199
Brant, Alice ('Helena Morley')
 141, 175, 196, 197
Brazeau, Peter 109, 176
Brown, Ashley 176, 198
Bulmer, Grace (Aunt Grace) 67,
 150, 197
Breton, André 163, 165
Brasil, Emanuel 175
Bridges, Robert 141, 146
Brueghel, Pieter 159-60, 162
Burns, Robert 73-4
Byron, Lord 144

Calder, Alexander 160
Chartier, Roger 150
Chekhov, Anton 150
Cleaver, Kathleen 199
Coleridge, Samuel Taylor 144,
 145, 146
Colwell, Anne, 68-69, 177
Cornell, Joseph, 49
Correia, Lilli 198, 199
Costello, Bonnie 15, 16, 76, 119,
 124, 126, 170, 177, 178, 181
Crane, Hart 145
Crane, Louise 154, 159, 193,
 194, 195
Crashaw, Richard 69
Croll, M.W. 19, 139

Dana, Richard Henry Jr. 141
Darwin, Charles 10, 37, 39, 92,
 133, 141
de Andrade, Carlos Drummond
 198
Deane, Nichola 8, 143-58, 207
de Chirico, Giorgio 160
Defoe, Daniel 56
de Melo Neto, João Cabral 198

de Nerval, Gérard 133
Derrida, Jacques 169, 172
Descartes 13-14, 15, 16, 17, 20,
 25
Dewey, Jane 194, 196
Dewey, John 194
Dickinson, Emily 82
Diehl, Joanne Feit, 29n, 111,
 177, 178, 179, 182
Dolittle, Hilda (H.D.) 43
Donaghy, Michael 9, 119-22,
 151, 207
Dürer, Albrecht 139

Eliot, George 41
Eliot, T.S. 17
Ellis, Jonathan 8, 61n, 63-86,
 207
Ernst, Max 49, 160

Farmer, Fannie 50-52, 55
Feaver, Vicki 10, 87-102, 207
Fenton, James 8, 182
Fizdale, Robert 149
Foster, Ruth 195
Fountain, Gary 109, 176, 182,
 192
Foster, Hal 163
Freud, Sigmund 58, 98, 102n
Frost, Robert 132-34

Ginsberg, Allen 63
Giroux, Robert 8, 144, 145
Goethe, Johann Wolfgang von
 131
Gioia, Dana 176, 183, 199
Gold, Arthur, 149
Goldensohn, Lorrie 65, 68-69,
 77, 160, 177, 183
Greenlaw, Lavinia 8, 43
Griggs, Earl Leslie 144, 145

Hardwick, Elizabeth 146, 196,
 198

Hardy, Thomas 146, 147
Harrison, Victoria 23, 28n, 29n, 177, 184
Heaney, Seamus 7-8, 46, 47-48, 58, 113-14, 128, 184
Herbert, George 33, 106, 112, 131, 134, 145
Hemans, Felicia 12
Hemingway, Ernest 89, 101n, 194
Hemingway, Pauline: see Pfeiffer, Pauline
Hockney, David 15, 17
Holbein, Hans 125
Hopkins, Gerard Manley 34, 69-70, 141, 145, 147, 163
Hopper, Edward 96
Hutchinson, George 14
Huxley, Aldous 197

Ibsen, Henrik 15
Irigaray, Luce 102

James, Henry 145, 146
Jarrell, Randall 50, 138, 145, 160, 179, 184, 195, 196, 197
Johnson, Samuel 147
Joyce, James 138
Jung, Carl 98

Kafka, Franz 68
Kalstone, David 81, 124, 127, 129, 142, 160, 178, 183, 184
Kazin, Pearl 103, 112
Keats, John 18, 24, 84, 143, 144, 145, 150, 152, 157n
Kerouac, Jack 96
Klee, Paul 160, 172, 174n
Kristeva, Julia 87, 115

Lacerda, Carlos 198
Laurens, Penelope 65
Leach, Edmund 53

Leão, Rosinha 197
Lessing, G.E. 139, 141
Lispector, Clarice 175, 198
Lévi-Strauss 52-3, 55, 56-8, 61n
Lowell, Robert 10, 37, 43, 46, 47, 50, 55, 58, 64-65, 115, 124, 131, 136, 144, 146, 147-48, 152, 178, 179, 183, 185, 188, 196, 197, 198, 200

McCarthy, Mary 193
MacIver, Loren 160, 194, 195, 197
McKendrick, Jamie 9, 123-42, 207
MacNeice, Louis 108
Mazzaro, Jerome 123, 134, 137, 139, 141, 186
Merrill, James 10, 37, 63, 97, 120, 178, 186
Methfessel, Alice 6, 23, 199
Miller, Margaret 193, 194, 197
Millay, Edna St Vincent 145
Millier, Brett Candlish 23, 25-26, 29n, 109, 146, 176, 177, 186
Mindlin, Henrique 197
Montagu, Lady Mary Wortley 145
Moore, Marianne 12, 16, 44, 66, 76, 78, 89-91, 93, 119, 123, 128, 147, 149, 153-54, 155, 167, 178, 179, 181, 182, 183, 184, 185, 186, 187, 194, 195, 196, 200
Morse, Mary Stearns 195, 196, 197
Motion, Andrew 7, 187
Moucha, J. 138
Muldoon, Paul 132

Nemer, Linda 199
Neruda, Pablo 195
Newton, Isaac 16

O'Connor, Flannery 145
Olds, Sharon 93-94, 187
O'Shea, Jimmy ['James Shea']
    151-52
Ostriker, Alicia 79, 187

Page, Barbara 6, 8, **12-30**, 104,
    177, 187, 192, 207-08
Pascal, Blaise 19, 25
Paulin, Tom 8, 137, 188
Paz, Octavio 200
Pfeiffer (Hemingway), Pauline
    194, 196
Pierson, Miss 149, 152
Plath, Sylvia 43, 44-45, 59n,
    63-64, 178, 182
Poirier, Richard 133
Pound, Ezra 123, 196

Reed, Henry 198
Rees-Jones, Deryn 10, **42-62**,
    188, 208
Rimbaud, Arthur 135
Robinson, Peter 9-10, **103-12**,
    179, 208
Rousseau, Jean Jacques 56
Ruskin, John 52

Searle, John R. 9, 103, 107-08
Seaver, Bob 194
Sedgwick, Eve 166
Shapcott, Jo 7, 43, **113-18**, 191,
    208
Shapiro, Meyer 160
Shepherdson, Maud and George
    193, 194
Shifrer, Anne 117, 189
Soares, Lota de Macedo 31, 80,
    103, 110, 110, 112, 120, 195,
    196, 197, 198, 199
Smith, Sydney 145
Smith, Stevie 94
Stanford, Donald 33, 189

Stevens, Marjorie 195
Stevens, Wallace 22, 119, 149,
    163, 178, 179, 180, 181, 182,
    183, 185, 187, 190, 191
Stevenson, Anne 9, 10, 12, 16,
    31-41, 44, 61n, 81, 92, 127,
    163, 177, 178, 189, 191,
    198, 208

Thomas, Dylan 196
Tompkins, Hallie 194
Tompkins, Silvan 165-66
Traherne, Thomas 69
Travisano, Thomas 74, 177,
    178, 179, 189, 190, 192
Tsvetaeva, Marina 116

Unterecker, John 47

Valdes, Gregorio 160, 194
Van Gogh, Vincent 153
Vendler, Helen 24, 110, 178,
    186,
Vermeer, Jan 138-39, 160
Vuillard, Edouard 160

Wehr, Wesley 160, 176, 190
Wilde, Oscar 145
Williams, William Carlos 120
Wittgenstein, Ludwig 12, 19, 20,
    22, 24, 29n, 108, 151
Wodehouse, P.G. 78
Wollheim, Richard 150-51
Woolf, Virginia 117, 145
Wordsworth, William 20, 152

Yaeger, Patricia 102n, 191
Yeats, W.B. 47, 58, 109

NOTES ON CONTRIBUTORS

Linda Anderson is Professor of Modern English and American Literature at the University of Newcastle upon Tyne and head of department. She has published *Women and Autobiography in the Twentieth Century* (Prentice Hall, 1997), *Autobiography* (Routledge, 2001), and *Territories of Desire in Queer Culture*, edited with David Alderson (Manchester University Press, 2000). She is currently writing a monograph on Elizabeth Bishop.

Neil Astley is Editor of Bloodaxe Books. His books include a critical anthology on Tony Harrison, several poetry anthologies, three collections, and a novel, *The End of My Tether* (Flambard, 2002). He was given an honorary D.Litt by Newcastle University in 1996.

Nichola Deane is writing a PhD on correspondence of the Romantic period at Manchester University.

Michael Donaghy was born in New York and moved to Britain in 1985. He has published three collections of poetry, *Shibboleth* (Oxford University Press, 1988), winner of the Whitbread Poetry Award, *Errata* (Oxford University Press, 1993), and *Conjure* (Picador, 2000), which won the Forward Prize. *Dances Learned Last Night: Poems 1975-1995* (Picador, 2000) gathers together two decades of his poetry.

Jonathan Ellis has just been awarded a PhD at the University of Hull for a thesis on 'Art and Memory in the Work of Elizabeth Bishop'. He is now a teaching fellow at the University of Hull.

Vicki Feaver is Professor of Poetry at University College Chichester. She has published two collections of poetry, *Close Relatives* (Secker, 1981), and *The Handless Maiden* (Cape, 1994), which won a Royal Society of Literature Award under the W.H. Heineman Bequest and was shortlisted for the Forward Prize.

Jamie McKendrick is poet in residence at Hertford College, Oxford. He has published three collections of poetry, *The Sirocco Room* (Oxford University Press, 1991), *The Kiosk on the Brink* (Oxford University Press, 1993), and *The Marble Fly* (Oxford University Press, 1997), which won the Forward Prize. His selected poems, *Sky Nails*, was published by Faber in 2000.

Barbara Page is Professor of English and Associate Dean of the Faculty at Vassar College. Her essays about Bishop include: 'Shifting Islands: Bishop's Manuscripts' (*Shenandoah*), ' "Off-Beat Claves,

Oblique Realities: The Key West Notebooks of Elizabeth Bishop'
(in *Elizabeth Bishop: The Geography of Gender*), 'Elizabeth Bishop
and Postmodernism' (*Wallace Stevens Journal*) and 'Bishop as a Poet
of Childhood Recollected' (in *'In Worcester, Massachusetts': Essays
on Elizabeth Bishop*).

Deryn Rees-Jones is Reader in Poetry at Liverpool Hope University.
Her debut collection, *The Memory Tray* (Seren), was shortlisted
for the Forward Prize for best first collection in 1995; her second
collection, *Signs Around a Dead Body* (Seren), was published in
1998. Her monograph, *Carol Ann Duffy* (Manchester University
Press) was published in 1999, and *Consorting with Angels: Modern
Women Poets* is forthcoming from Bloodaxe.

Peter Robinson is visiting Professor of English at Tohoku Univer-
sity, Sendai, Japan. He has written five books of poetry, the most
recent of which is *About Time Too* (Carcanet, 2001). He has edited
the poems of Adrian Stokes, a collection of essays on Geoffrey Hill,
and a volume of critical writings, *In the Circumstances: About Poems
and Poets* (Clarendon Press, 1992). He has recently co-edited *The
Thing About Roy Fisher: Critical Studies* (Liverpool University Press,
2000) and *News for the Ear: A Homage to Roy Fisher* (Stride Pub-
lications, 2000).

Jo Shapcott is currently visiting Professor at the University of
Newcastle upon Tyne and poet in residence at the Royal Society,
and gave the first Newcastle/Bloodaxe Poetry Lectures in 2001.
She has won the National Poetry Competition twice, and has pub-
lished five books of poetry, including *Electroplating the Baby* (Blood-
axe Books, 1988), *Phrase Book* (Oxford University Press, 1992), *My
Life Asleep* (Oxford University Press 1998), which won the Forward
Prize, and a selected poems, *Her Book* (Faber, 2000). *Tender Taxes*,
based on the French poems of Rainer Maria Rilke, was published
by Faber in 2001.

Anne Stevenson has written ten books of poetry, including *Collected
Poems 1955-1995* (Oxford University Press, 1996; Bloodaxe Books,
2000) and *Granny Scarecrow* (Bloodaxe Books, 2000). She is the
author of *Elizabeth Bishop* (Twayne, 1966), *Bitter Fame: A Life of
Sylvia Plath* (Viking, 1989; revised 1998), a recently published
book of essays, *Between the Iceberg and the Ship* (University of
Michigan Press), and *Five Looks at Elizabeth Bishop* (Agenda/Bellew,
1998). She lives in Durham and North Wales, and won the first
Northern Rock Foundation Writer Award in 2002.